Religion in America

ADVISORY EDITOR

Edwin S. Gaustad

AMERICA

AND THE

AMERICAN CHURCH

Henry Caswall

ARNO PRESS & THE NEW YORK TIMES

New York 1969

Reprint edition 1969 by Arno Press, Inc.

*

Library of Congress Catalog Card No. 77-83413

*

Reprinted from a copy in
The New York State Library

*

Manufactured in the United States of America

AMERICA,

AND THE

AMERICAN CHURCH.

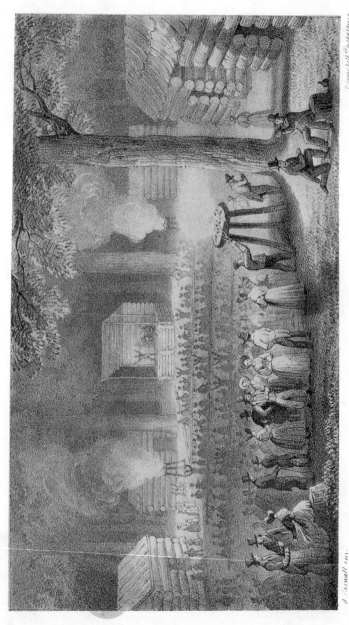

R. Caswall inv.

Engrav'd with Flash & Quiver

MÉTHODIST CAMP-MEETING in KÉNTUCKY at NIGHT

Published by J. G & F. Rivington. London Nov 1819.

AMERICA,

AND THE

AMERICAN CHURCH.

BY THE

REV. HENRY CASWALL, M.A.

RECTOR OF CHRIST CHURCH, MADISON, INDIANA,

AND LATE PROFESSOR IN THE THEOLOGICAL SEMINARY OF THE

DIOCESE OF KENTUCKY.

TEN YEARS RESIDENT IN THE UNITED STATES.

LONDON:

PRINTED FOR J. G. & F. RIVINGTON,

ST. PAUL'S CHURCH YARD,

AND WATERLOO PLACE, PALL MALL.

1839.

LONDON:
GILBERT AND RIVINGTON, PRINTERS,
ST. JOHN'S SQUARE.

TO THE

RIGHT HONOURABLE LORD KENYON,

THE ABLE DEFENDER

OF THE CHURCH OF ENGLAND,

AND THE

WARM FRIEND OF THE CHURCH IN AMERICA,

THIS VOLUME

IS, WITH PERMISSION, INSCRIBED,

AS A TOKEN OF SINCERE RESPECT,

BY THE

FIRST-ORDAINED GRADUATE OF KENYON COLLEGE.

A 2

PREFACE.

————

AT a period when the opponents of the Church of England are actively engaged in attempts to undermine her influence and destroy her reputation, it appears to the author that no work can better exhibit to the British public the vital energy of the Episcopal system, and the real benefits of an adherence to its essential principles, than a circumstantial account of the American Church.

The contemplation of a remote branch of the English establishment rising from its ruins, and not merely sustaining itself, but increasing with unprecedented rapidity, will induce Englishmen, it is hoped, to prize more highly those blessings which they now enjoy, and which so many in America are labouring to extend. The view of a thousand republican clergymen, and five hundred thousand republican laymen, contending for a liturgy and for the " sacred regimen" of bishops, will be sufficient to prove that

the system which has flourished under the tyranny
of the Roman empire, and the constitutional
monarchy of England, contains in itself nothing
repugnant to the principles of political self-govern-
ment.   At the same time the wonderful progress
and improvement of the American Church serve to
confute the Romanist, who asserts that the Church
of England is sustained merely by the secular arm,
and that in the event of her losing that support,
she must of necessity become extinct.

The author has carefully avoided political discus-
sions.   Yet, as he may appear to speak occasionally like a republican, he deems it incumbent on
him to state, that he regards the American form of
government as being, on the whole, well adapted to
the present condition of the people, and to the
independence which naturally belongs to the pos-
sessors of a territory more than sufficiently ample
for the population.   But, though he may be a
republican in America, he is satisfied that he never
could become a republican in England.   In like
manner, he admires the popular constitution of the
American Church, chiefly on account of its fitness
to the peculiar habits and feelings of the nation.   It
is a beautiful scheme, by which, on the one hand,
the proper influence of the three orders in the
ministry is maintained ; while, on the other hand,
the voice of the people not only receives due

respect, but exerts as much authority as the most democratic Christian could desire. Although the author considers that many regulations similar to those of the American Church might be adopted in England with safety and advantage, he believes it must be plain, that a large portion of the peculiarities of the system are exclusively American, and would be exotics in any other portion of Christendom.

The reader is supposed to be acquainted with the general features of the political government of the United States, since they have been often and well explained by travellers and other writers. For instance, it is taken for granted, that he is aware of the fact that every State is a distinct sovereignty, possessing its own legislative, executive, and judicial departments, while Congress provides for the general welfare of all, and their necessary intercourse with foreign powers. The present object of the author is merely to give such a description of America as will add interest to his work, and afford a sufficient ground-work for his more particular account of the Church and its institutions.

It may be said, that the author has given too favourable a character of the American people. In reply to this he can only aver that he has stated all those facts which he considered necessary to the illustration of his subject; and that he has not

intentionally concealed what he believes to be wrong,
nor unduly extolled that which he considers to be
praiseworthy. He is persuaded that many writers
on the United States have attacked human nature
in general, while they intended to be severe on the
Americans in particular, and he has endeavoured to
avoid the error into which they have fallen. He
believes that the circumstances in which he has
been placed, have qualified him to judge impartially,
though not infallibly. On the one hand, as a
British subject, he is attached to his country and
his sovereign by a thousand early associations ;
on the other hand, he loves America as the birth-
place of his wife and children, and as the residence
of some of the purest characters which the world
has produced. He believes, also, that he has seen
enough of America to correct the first vague
impressions, whether painful or agreeable, experienced by every one on his first arrival in a foreign
country. He has resided nearly ten years in the
United States, and has travelled no less than eight
thousand miles within their spacious boundaries.
As a student, he has mingled with students, as a
teacher with teachers, and as a clergyman with
clergymen. He has seen society in the log-cabin
as well as in the drawing-room, while in his pastoral
capacity he has been called to study the foibles of
his parishioners, no less than their excellencies.

Regarding his subject more as a traveller and a spectator, than as an essayist, he has been constrained to give more prominence to himself and to his own experience than he would otherwise have desired. Yet he has endeavoured to avoid a wearisome uniformity; and he hopes that by presenting his description in the varied form of letters, journals, narratives, and biographies, the interest of the work to the general reader will be materially enhanced. If it should throw any light on the fundamental principles of ecclesiastical polity; if it should in any degree promote charity between two great nations, and a spirit of Catholic union between two important portions of the One Apostolic Church, the author will consider himself amply rewarded for his novel and laborious undertaking.

MADISON, INDIANA,
UNITED STATES, 1838.

A 5

CONTENTS.

CHAPTER I.

LETTER TO A FRIEND——VOYAGE AND JOURNEY FROM ENGLAND TO OHIO.

CHAPTER II.

LETTER TO A FRIEND.——GAMBIER AND ITS VICINITY.

CHAPTER III.

LETTER TO A FRIEND.—OHIO.

CHAPTER IV.

RELIGION AND THE CHURCH.

CHAPTER V.

THE SAME SUBJECT CONTINUED.

CHAPTER VI.

THE LAY-READER.

CHAPTER VII.

JOURNEY FROM PORTSMOUTH TO ANDOVER.

CHAPTER VIII.

NEW ENGLAND.

CHAPTER IX.

THE CHURCH IN HARTFORD, NEW YORK, PHILADELPHIA, &c.

PAGE

CHAPTER X.

HISTORY OF THE AMERICAN CHURCH.

1

CHAPTER XI.

THE SAME SUBJECT CONTINUED.

CHAPTER XII.

EDUCATION.

CHAPTER XIII.

LEXINGTON, &c.

CHAPTER XIV.

PRAYER BOOK OF THE AMERICAN CHURCH.

CHAPTER XV.

MISSIONARY OPERATIONS OF THE CHURCH.

CHAPTER XVI.

CHURCH BUILDINGS IN AMERICA.

CHAPTER XVII.

CLERICAL DUTY AND COMPENSATION.

CHAPTER XVIII.

NON-EPISCOPALIANS AND ROMAN CATHOLICS.

CHAPTER XIX.

EXTRANEOUS INFLUENCES ON THE CHURCH.

CHAPTER XX.

LETTER TO A CLERGYMAN PROPOSING TO EMIGRATE.

LIST OF ILLUSTRATIONS.

N.B. These Sketches were taken by the Author.

AMERICA

AND

THE AMERICAN CHURCH.

CHAPTER I.

LETTER TO A FRIEND—VOYAGE AND JOURNEY FROM ENGLAND TO OHIO.

Packet-ship.—First night at sea.—Calm.—Banks of Newfoundland.—Storm.—First sight of land.—New York harbour.—First view of New York.—Sunday in New York.—Episcopal service.—Methodists.—Voyage to Albany.—Stage-coach.—Canal-boat.—Little Falls.—Indians.—Auburn, Geneva, &c.—Falls of Niagara.—Island at the Falls.—Sandusky.—Arrival at Gambier.

KENYON COLLEGE, Gambier, Ohio;
October 1828.

MY DEAR EDWARD,

Having promised you a circumstantial account of my voyage and journey from England to this place, I hasten to fulfil my engagement: premising, however, that you must expect nothing of an adventurous character, or materially differing from a hundred narratives of the same kind already before the public.

B

After leaving you, I passed through a beautiful and romantic portion of our native island; and on the evening of the second day arrived at Liverpool. Here I ascertained that the line of New York packets had been so arranged, that two of those vessels regularly sailed every week. Accordingly, I took a berth on board the Canada of New York, a fine ship of five hundred and seventy tons burden, under the command of Captain Hugh Graham, and, proceeding to the packet office, paid thirty-eight guineas for my passage across the Atlantic. The whole of the following day was occupied in preparing for the voyage, by procuring a variety of articles of clothing. I have great reason to regret that my purchases were not much more extensive, since I have found that clothing of all kinds is more expensive in America than in England. At twelve o'clock on the next day, August 16th, I embarked; not without some painful feelings, as you may imagine. In a few minutes afterwards, the Canada unmoored, left the docks, and entered the river. Then her white sails were unfurled, and in a short time Liverpool disappeared.

I must now describe the vessel and her inmates; and I beg you to recollect this description will apply to the New York packets in general, equally with the Canada. Figure to yourself a number of genteel looking persons, of both sexes, occupying

the after part of the well-washed deck. Some are
leaning over the stern, overcome with emotion, and
some are casting a melancholy and lingering look
upon the receding shore. Others are seated on the
green painted hen-coops, apparently absorbed in
meditation ; while not a few are pacing the deck
with the coolness and indifference of those to whom
scenes of this kind are familiar. The dingy looking
steerage passengers, restricted to the forward part
of the ship, are lounging over the bows, and watch-
ing each approaching wave : the sailors are busily
engaged above in spreading the sails; while the
steersman is holding with his muscular grasp the
polished wheel, and alternately casting his eyes on
the swelling canvas aloft, and on the compass before
him, which already fluctuates with the increasing
motion. You must now accompany me into the
cabin. It is an elegant room, about fifty feet in
length, and twenty in breadth. Four small windows
at one end give you an alternate glimpse of the sea
and of the sky, as the stern sinks or rises with the
swell. Two doors at the other extremity give you
an occasional view of the interior of the ladies'
cabin, where a handsome pier-glass and an elegant
sideboard allow you to form some idea of the conveniences provided for the occupants. Two spacious
sky-lights in the ceiling of the main cabin admit
light upon a long table, on which the cloth is

already laid, while four black servants are arranging the materials of a comfortable hot dinner. A barometer, a glass lamp, and two inverted compasses, are suspended above. Ten doors on each side of the cabin, open into as many state cabins, each ornamented with fluted and gilded pilasters. The mizen-mast, encased with carved mahogany, passes through the dinner-table; and a large gilt eagle spreads his wings over the seat appropriated to the captain. You may now form a tolerably correct idea of the home provided for myself and about twenty-eight others, during a sojourn of nearly five weeks.

As the evening came on, many of the passengers began to suffer from the first attacks of sea-sickness; but, happily, I was little affected by it. We were now fairly out among the broken waves of the Irish Sea, and the motion of the vessel became excessively unpleasant. There was, however, no alternative but to bear it; as escape was, of course, entirely out of the question. I lay down in my berth, in one of the state cabins, and sought for rest, but in vain. The seamen on deck were running backwards and forwards, and throwing down huge coils of cordage; while the timbers of the ship were creaking, and the cabin doors banging violently at every roll. The sick were groaning with lamentable tones, the black servants were

running from door to door,—children were crying,
—pigs grunting,—poultry cackling,—and in short,
every variety of acoustic torment was inflicted upon
the distracted landsman. In the morning, the
return of which was joyfully greeted, the high hills
of Holyhead were full in sight, at the distance of
fifteen miles, together with the adjoining coast of
Anglesea. We then stood for the Irish coast, and
having obtained a view of the hills in Dublin Bay,
on the afternoon of the 18th, we went on the other
tack, and came in sight of Small's lighthouse on the
Welsh coast, at ten o'clock at night, on the 19th.
We then stood for the south west, and the next
morning I beheld the last mountain of Wales slowly
sinking behind the horizon. I watched it with
melancholy interest until the evening, when it was
at length hidden by the interposing waters. On the
afternoon of the 21st we passed Cape Clear, the
south-western extremity of Ireland, and immediately
experienced the long and regular swell of the
Atlantic. The wind now blew fresh from the west-
north-west, so that we made but slow progress
towards our destination, being obliged to steer to
the south-south-west. Continuing this course we
found the climate daily becoming warmer; and on
the 30th of August, a fortnight after our embarka-
tion, we passed within a hundred miles of the
Azores. In the course of the following week, we

were becalmed for two successive days.   During
this tedious interval the motion of the ship was
most distressing, the swell being considerable, and
the vessel rolling unsteadily, at the mercy of every
wave. The passengers endeavoured to amuse themselves with reading and writing, and occasionally
with chess, draughts, and backgammon.   Many,
indeed, who had worn considerable dignity and
gravity of appearance when they first came on
board, now condescended to betake themselves to
the diversions of school-boys.   On the 4th of September, we were relieved by a brisk breeze from
the north-west, which carried us through the water
at the rate of ten miles an hour.   We were at the
same time gratified with the sight of several flying-
fish.   A shark was seen under our stern, and two
whales spouted within a mile of us.   In three days
from this period we approached the southern extremity of the great banks of Newfoundland, and
for a time were incommoded by a dense fog.

On the 8th the sea appeared luminous in the
evening, and broad streams of light flashed from
the bows of the vessel, like pure flame. The following morning a vast shoal of porpoises was seen
proceeding to the southward. These two phenomena
were regarded as indications of the approach of a
gale from the south.   Nor did they in this instance
deceive us.   The storm commenced with violence

at ten A.M., and its arrival was indicated by a sudden lurch of the vessel, by which many of the passengers were thrown down. All our sails were taken in with the exception of two, which being trebly reefed were allowed to stand. The cabin appeared dismal from the closing of the windows; but more dismal were the wailings of some of the affrighted passengers. On the deck the sea was pouring in torrents; and the captain himself, assisted by the mate, and clothed in a water-proof cloak, assumed the guidance of the vessel. On the following morning the tempest had subsided, and we were much amused by the gambols of several beautiful dolphins, which sported under the bows. One of them was taken on a hook, and drawn on deck, amid the acclamations of the delighted spectators. He was immediately hung up to perish, that the passengers might have the gratification of beholding the rapid and surprising changes of colour, which come over the skin of the dying fish. During the night we passed near an iceberg. The thermometer sunk a number of degrees, and we heard the hoarse and hollow sound of the waves dashing against the floating island. On the following day, September 14th, at the request of the captain, I read divine service to the passengers in the cabin [1];

[1] The Author was not ordained at the time.—*English Editor.*

a duty which had been unfortunately neglected on previous occasions, by reason of the weather, and other real or imaginary impediments.

On Monday we perceived indubitable tokens of our approach to land. The wind, too, was precisely in our favour, and we were advancing at the rate of eleven miles an hour. On Thursday, the 18th, at six o'clock in the morning, the great continent of the west was visible on deck. How eagerly did I scrutinize, with my telescope, every object of the New World that gradually arose above the blue horizon! Soon I distinguished trees, then a fallow field, and afterward a farm-house, the windows of which I was soon enabled to count. Then I perceived persons walking on the beach, and occasionally stooping down, as if engaged in picking up shells. About ten o'clock a tall lighthouse with white walls and a blue roof came in sight. Soon the lofty groves of Staten Island appeared; and soon afterwards a neat little village on the shore of Long Island. About noon, an elegant schooner-rigged boat was observed steering directly towards us. In a few minutes she came alongside, and her sails were lowered in an instant. A small boat then conveyed our pilot to us from this beautiful vessel. Other schooners of a similar description soon came up, from which issued the messengers of various newspaper establishments, all anxious to obtain the latest intelligence from Europe, together with accounts of our voyage, and of the number and names of the passengers. Our names, ages, professions, and allegiances were also entered in a book kept by the captain, and by him delivered to the proper authorities. About three o'clock P.M., we entered the Narrows, which constitute the southern approach to the harbour of New York. Two huge batteries frown upon the voyager from the opposite heights, and their numerous port-holes and long tiers of cannon appear sufficient to effect the annihilation of any unwelcome intruder. All at once, on turning a corner just within the Narrows, we were delighted at perceiving New York with its numerous steeples and crowded shipping full in view at the opposite extremity of the bay, and at the distance of four or five miles. Vessels of all sizes were lying on the unruffled bosom of this magnificent harbour, while country-seats, with neat gardens, studded the surrounding shores. Here the tide turned against us, and the wind also failing, we cast anchor.

Many of the passengers, including myself, now went on board the pilot-boat; but on account of the impediments already mentioned, we did not set foot on the American shore till eleven at night. We had left our baggage, with the exception of a few necessary articles, on board the Canada; so after a slight examination by the Custom-house

officers, who neither expected nor received any fee,
I proceeded with two others to the Adelphi Hotel,
a spacious edifice at the lower end of Broadway,
where, after partaking of an excellent supper we
retired to rest. During the night I suffered, for
the first time, the tormenting sting of the mus-
quitoes ; but happily soon lost all sense of their
provocations in a quiet and refreshing sleep, undis-
turbed by nautical cries and marine tactics. On
awaking in the morning, my first impulse was to
run to the windows and obtain a glimpse of the
New World. As my chamber was in the sixth
story, I possessed an extensive prospect. The bay
lay before me with numerous vessels at anchor, and
steam-boats continually passing and repassing.
Waggons, carts, hackney - coaches, and stage-
coaches, were driving up and down Broadway in
great numbers, while in the opposite direction, a
forest of chimneys reminded me that it was no inconsiderable city in which I had spent the night.
On going down stairs, I found an excellent breakfast on the public table, consisting of beef-steaks,
lobsters, fricassees, stews, boiled potatoes, eggs,
tea and coffee, bread and butter, warm toast, &c.
all very good in their kind. During the day I
visited some of the public buildings, and was agreeably disappointed in all that I saw. I went also to
the Custom-house, and obtained a permit to land

my baggage, which I accordingly transmitted to
my hotel in the care of a porter. The following
day was Saturday, and being anxious to proceed to
my destination, I busied myself in making inquiries
respecting the cheapest and most expeditious route
to Ohio ; and soon obtained such information as I
needed.

On Sunday, the hum of business was entirely sus-
pénded throughout the city ; and an agreeable stillness universally prevailed. At eleven o'clock, I went
to Grace Church, in Broadway, and obtained my
first impressions of the American Episcopal Church.
The appearance of the congregation was highly
respectable ; indeed it appeared to contain none of
the lower classes of society. The church itself was
beautifully clean and neat ; and handsomely carpeted throughout. The service is almost identi-
cally the same with that of the Church of England ;
but the Litany is somewhat retrenched, the Nicene
Creed is omitted in the Communion Service, the
Lord's Prayer is not so frequently repeated as in
England, and the President is prayed for instead
of the King. Some minor alterations, chiefly verbal,
are admitted ; some of which are unquestionably
improvements. As to the performance of the service, I observed no *clerk ;* and the responses were
made by the whole congregation. The singing and

B 6

chaunting were good, and conducted by skilful practitioners, assisted by an excellent organ. I perceived that the Prayer-book contained a collection of between 200 and 300 hymns, one of which was sung immediately before the sermon. The discourse was delivered by Dr. Wainwright, the rector of the church, and reminded me of some of the best sermons I had heard in England. In the afternoon I went to St. George's, where I observed the same peculiarities in the mode of conducting the service, which I had noticed in the morning; and heard an eloquent sermon delivered by a popular preacher, Mr. M'Ilvaine. In the evening, out of curiosity, I stepped into a large Methodist chapel. Here I found an immense congregation, the females seated on the left, and the males on the right. They appeared to be an entirely different class of persons from those whom I had seen at Grace Church and St. George's, and were listening with the most profound attention to a sermon in which I could discover neither point nor connection; but a bare repetition of the same phrases, with violent emphasis and gesticulation.

On Monday evening, September 22nd, I bade farewell to New York, and to the kind people who had received me, a perfect stranger, with the most generous hospitality. At 5 o'clock, P.M. I went on board the steam-boat " Chief Justice Marshall," and proceeded up the Hudson, or North River, at the rate of ten miles an hour.

The scenery as we advanced became beautiful. The banks of the river are finely wooded, and adorned with elegant country residences. Sometimes the opposite shores approach near to each other, and then gradually expand till the river assumes the appearance of a lake. Sometimes they rise into lofty, rocky, and extended precipices; and sometimes they sink almost to a level with the water, yet constantly retaining their clothing of forests, which form so striking a feature in American scenery. As night came on, the splendour of the prospect increased. The river was as smooth as glass, except where it was disturbed by some passing vessel. The moon shone so brightly that I amused myself till 4 o'clock in the morning with reading on deck. At seven A.M. we reached Albany, having travelled 145 miles in fourteen hours.

Immediately after landing, I proceeded with my luggage to an hotel, where I took my place in a huge stage-coach, containing three seats and nine inside passengers, and travelled sixteen miles to Schenectady where I arrived at one o'clock, just in time for the public dinner at the principal tavern. The materials of the repast were miscellaneous and abundant, and the meal was despatched in a remarkably short space of time. At two o'clock I took my passage on board a packet-boat on the great New York canal, which runs under the windows of the hotel. I paid three dollars and a half for my conveyance to Utica, 80 miles, being at the rate of a little more than two-pence sterling per mile, including board. These packets are very neat and convenient little vessels. They are each about 60 feet in length, 40 feet of which are devoted to the two cabins appropriated respectively to the ladies and the gentlemen. At meal-times the two cabins are thrown into one, and two long tables are extended from end to end. The fare is generally excellent and well cooked. A small library and a number of newspapers serve to beguile the tedious hours. The boat is drawn by three horses, and commonly travels about four miles an hour. Our route lay for many miles along the banks of the Mohawk river, and we passed through a long succession of picturesque scenery. The orchards were teeming with delicious fruit; and in many places the apple and peach-trees hung over the canal so near to us, that we gathered freely from the deck of the boat.

At night preparations were made for our sleeping accommodations, and I was amused at their ingenuity. Along the sides of the cabin, small narrow berths were fixed one above another,

partly resting against the wall, and partly suspended by strong wires from the roof. A third
row of berths was suspended from the centre of the
ceiling, and ran like the two others the whole
length of the gentlemen's cabin. These arrangements were made with wonderful celerity; and
about fifty passengers retired in good order to
repose. Early in the morning we found the boat
quite motionless; and on inquiring the cause, we
learned that a portion of the canal, four miles in
length, had been suddenly drained by the bursting
of one of the banks. We therefore procured waggons and horses at the expense of the captain, and
proceeded five or six miles over very rough roads
to a lock on the canal, where we found another
packet-boat ready to receive us. About noon we
reached the " Little Falls" of the Mohawk, a very
romantic spot. Here the river rolls foaming through
a deep glen between two lofty and rocky hills
clothed with verdure to the summit. The canal
passes many feet above the stream on the south,
while through the same glen, on the northern side
of the river, a turnpike-road winds laboriously over
bridges and along the margin of deep precipices.
We then passed through a highly cultivated region,
denominated the " German Flats," from the industrious people who inhabit it, and arrived at Utica
about seven o'clock P.M. Utica appeared to be a
neat and thriving town; and I was much struck

with the handsome aspect of its numerous places of
worship. Being inclined to change the mode of
travelling, I now took my seat in a stage-coach,
precisely similar to the unwieldy vehicle in which I
had journeyed from Albany to Schenectady.

I left Utica early in the morning, and, in the
course of the day, passed through a part of the
country occupied by a remnant of the Oneida Indians. These poor people had recently embraced
Christianity, and their condition was said to be much
improved. I noticed their dwellings, which were
ingeniously covered with the bark of trees. I saw
their council grove, which consists of twenty or
thirty trees of the walnut species. In the distance
their church was visible, and its spire rising above
the trees gave interest to the scene, and suggested
pleasing emotions. But from all I can learn, I
infer that the condition of the aboriginal inhabitants
of the United States is most pitiable. Their numbers are rapidly decreasing, and the government
seems to desire the removal of all Indian tribes
occupying any portion of its wide territory. I understand that the harmless people whom I have
just mentioned are soon to be transferred from their
present abode to some wild country beyond the
Lakes; and in that event, it is greatly to be feared
that they will lose whatever civilization they have
acquired.

I spent the night at Syracuse, a new town re-

sembling Utica in its general details; and the next
morning proceeded in a stage-coach on my journey
westward. We passed near some small lakes, eight
or ten miles in length, and bearing Indian names;
and soon arrived at Auburn, where there is a great
prison, conducted, as I am informed, upon an excellent system. Shortly afterwards we passed Lake
Cayuga, by means of a wooden bridge a mile in
length. This lake extends about forty miles from
north to south, and I observed a steam-boat plying
upon it. We dined at Geneva, a pretty town
situated on the banks of Lake Seneca, and then
proceeded sixteen miles to Canandaigua, a town
standing at the head of a lake of the same name.
The next morning we started for Rochester, where
we arrived early in the afternoon. Here I obtained a distant prospect of Lake Ontario, which
resembled the sea. Here, too, I visited the picturesque falls of the Genessee, where the river tumbles
over an abrupt precipice ninety feet in height. I
travelled the greater part of the night, and arrived
at Lockport about three o'clock in the morning.
Here the canal descends from a high level, to one
much beneath it, by a series of admirably constructed locks, from which the town derives its
name.

After breakfast, I took my seat in another stage
coach for the falls of Niagara, which I had deter-

mined to visit, although they lay a little out of my direct route. I arrived at Lewiston, on the Niagara river, about twelve o'clock. Upon the opposite side of the stream is Canada; and I was happy in again beholding British ground. There, too, I saw the lofty monument of General Brock, erected on the spot where that commander fell in the battle of Queenstown. We left Lewiston immediately after dinner, and, in little more than an hour, arrived at Manchester, a small town standing on the very brink of the falls. I cannot describe my sensations when, as I rode along, I first beheld the mighty and awful cataract through the trees at the distance of a mile, and heard its deep and hollow sound. I hurried from the inn to the water side, immediately on leaving the coach. I will not attempt to describe what I saw; I can conceive of nothing like it. A mighty river, nearly a mile in width, rolls over a precipice 170 feet in depth. The sublimity of the scene is heightened by the circumstance that a great portion of it is concealed, or but dimly seen on account of the thick clouds created by the spray. An island covered with tall forest-trees divides the cataract into two parts. A bridge has been built to this island, which conducts the passenger within a few yards of the precipice down which the Niagara makes its fearful plunge. I walked over this bridge, and almost became giddy when I saw the boiling waves rushing with prodigious velocity beneath. On the island I found warm springs and baths, with shady walks and alcoves for the convenience of those who visit this romantic retreat.

I would gladly have remained many days at the Falls; but my time was limited; and as soon as the horses were changed, I re-entered the coach, and proceeded on my journey. Reaching the canal in a short time, I took passage in a boat which happéned to be passing, and arrived at Buffalo soon after dark. I had no time for viewing the town, as I embarked early the next morning upon the blue waters of Lake Erie, in the steam-boat *Niagara.* I paid eight dollars for my passage to Sandusky in Ohio, a distance of 250 miles. After a voyage of thirty-nine hours, I arrived at that place; but found the stage-coaches so full that I could not obtain a seat for two days.

I spent that time in writing letters, in walking upon the beach of the Lake, and in talking with some Indians whom I happened to meet. Sandusky appeared to be a miserable place, and I was glad to leave it. I travelled slowly in the coach over dreadful roads, and through lofty and almost unbroken forests, till at night I arrived at a village called Mansfield, where I slept. Early the next morning, I again set out on my journey; and arrived at a town called Mount Vernon about noon.

Being now only five miles from my destination, I engaged the first waggoner I met in the street to convey me in his light two-horse vehicle to Kenyon College. In this conveyance I embarked with my luggage, and proceeded safely, though roughly, to my journey's end.

I have travelled 4000 miles in fifty-three days and three hours, (including five days and a half spent in New York and Sandusky) and at an expense of about fifty-four pounds.

CHAPTER II.

LETTER TO A FRIEND.—GAMBIER AND ITS VICINITY.

Caution necessary in judging of America.—History of Bishop Chase.—His appearance.—His labours.—Situation of Gambier.—Climate of Ohio.—People.—Inhabitants of Gambier.—Students in Kenyon College.—Their character.—Their Sunday-schools.

KENYON COLLEGE, *November*, 1830.

HAVING now resided nearly two years in this western world, I feel competent to the task of giving you a tolerably correct idea of life in the back-woods. Hitherto I have seen comparatively little of the eastern and more polished districts of the United States; you must therefore bear in mind, that my description of scenery and manners is applicable not to America in general, but to Ohio and this immediate neighbourhood in particular. I have already seen enough to convince me that different sections of this immense republic vary from each other in a number of respects; while the appearance and the society of every place are continually changing for the better. Consequently, to judge of the whole by a part, or of any one place by what it was a few years since, would be often both absurd and unjust. I shall devote this sheet to an account of Kenyon College and its occupants, together with a description of the scenery, the climate, and the population of the surrounding country.

Kenyon College owes its existence to the active and prudent zeal of Dr. Philander Chase, the first bishop of Ohio. This distinguished individual having been already before the English public, and his representations of the West having been my chief inducement in selecting this country as my home, you will, doubtless, expect that I should bestow upon him something more than a mere passing notice. Bishop Chase is a native of Cornish, a small town in the western part of the state of New Hampshire. His ancestors were English dissenters, and emigrated to America nearly a hundred years ago. He was himself educated in the Congregational or Independent persuasion, and continued his attachment to those principles until the year 1795, when nearly the whole of his father's family conformed to the Liturgy, and became members of the Episcopal Church. A candid examination of the Prayer-book, and of the important subject of an apostolical succession, were among the principal reasons which

1

led to this remarkable change. Philander Chase, then in his nineteenth year, being seriously inclined, and viewing with sorrow the feeble state of the Church, resolved to devote himself to the clerical office. Accordingly, after several years of close application to study, under the tuition of a member of the University of Oxford, then officiating as a parish minister in Albany, he received holy orders in 1798, and was appointed a missionary to extend the blessings of religion in the new settlements in the western part of New York.

I have described in my first letter the present flourishing condition of that portion of the country; but at the time to which I refer, the mighty forest was almost unbroken, the Indian remained master of his native woods, and the habitations of civilized men were few and far between. The zealous missionary, however, was not to be daunted by peril or difficulty, but persevered until he had planted congregations in Canandaigua, Utica, Auburn, and in several places on the banks of the Susquehannah, and on the borders of Vermont. In 1800, he became the rector of some parishes on the Hudson river; but in a few years afterwards, the declining health of Mrs. Chase led him to seek a milder climate; and he went, by the advice of his bishop, to the city of New Orleans, situated near the mouth of the Mississippi. While there, he organized an

Episcopal congregation; and was the first Protestant minister of any denomination that had officiated in that remote city.

After six years he returned to New England, and settled as rector of a church at Hartford, in Connecticut, where, also, he continued for six years, useful to his flock, and happy in himself. But the missionary work was dear to his heart. He heard of the religious destitution of the settlers in the new country of the West; he knew them to be exposed to the opposite dangers of enthusiasm and of infidelity; he was aware of the deplorable fact that scarcely a single duly authorised clergyman had as yet set foot upon the soil of Ohio, and he at length determined to make the sacrifice, and to devote himself to this distant region, then far more wild and inhospitable than at present. In 1817 he arrived in Ohio, and immediately returned to the delightful though laborious employment of his youth, the great and good work of establishing Episcopal congregations in recently built and fast increasing villages. His efforts were crowned with success, and two or three clergymen came to his assistance from other states. The number of Episcopalians continued to increase, and soon after Mr. Chase's arrival in Ohio, a diocese was organized in this State, and duly acknowledged by the General Convention of the Episcopal Church.

The Episcopalians in Ohio thus acquired the right of assembling in an annual Diocesan Convention, for the regulation of their ecclesiastical business; and Mr. Chase was selected as the first bishop by the votes of both clergy and laity. His consecration was performed at Philadelphia in February 1819, by Dr. White, Bishop of Pennsylvania; the Bishops of New York, New Jersey, and Maryland, being present and assisting. Bishop White had been consecrated at Lambeth in 1787 by the Archbishop of Canterbury; and thus the clergy ordained by Bishop Chase, in Ohio, derive their commission from the English hierarchy through only two connecting links.

In the course of 1820 Bishop Chase travelled on horseback through his diocese, a distance of twelve hundred and seventy-one miles, a fact which you will easily credit, when I tell you that Ohio is nearly as large as England: and that travelling by coach was at that period almost unknown. In consequence of the scarcity of religious means which he found to exist, he at length determined, with the sanction of his Diocesan Convention, upon visiting England in order to procure assistance. His object was to raise a fund for the purpose of erecting a theological college in Ohio; in order that young men might be educated on the spot, and trained up for the sacred ministry with a full knowledge of the

c

feelings and habits of western people. He was emboldened to undertake this expedition by the fact that at that time nearly one-third of the population of Ohio was supposed to consist of natives of Great Britain. He arrived in England in 1824, and was eminently successful; Lords Kenyon and Gambier, and others of our generous countrymen, contributing upwards of six thousand pounds. With this sum, in addition to what was given in America, Bishop Chase purchased eight thousand acres of land in a most eligible situation, and immediately commenced the erection of Kenyon College and of the village of Gambier.

In personal appearance the bishop is tall, portly, and dignified; he is also uncommonly active and powerful for one who has attained his fifty-sixth year. He rises at three o'clock every morning; and is engaged till night in superintending the workmen on the college buildings, and the labourers on the farms. Like most other persons of a sanguine temperament, he is occasionally subject to a painful depression of spirits; and this is more especially the case, when the want of funds and other difficulties retard the completion of the great work which he has so deeply at heart. He has stated to me that at such times he has been cheered by dreams, in which the countenances of his noble friends in England appeared to encourage him in his laborious undertaking. He expresses strong reliance on the divine help; and distinguishes the marked operations of a special providence in events which others would regard as the effects of accident.

From this imperfect sketch you will at once perceive that Bishop Chase is no ordinary character; and indeed, although I do not mean to claim for him that perfection which is not to be found on earth, I consider it a happy circumstance that I have formed an acquaintance with him. On every side I see the monuments of his untiring energy and perseverance. How different was the scene when I first arrived at Gambier only two years since. Then the lowest story of the college was not completed; the tall trees covered the face of the ground; the students occupied temporary wooden houses in which the frost of winter and the heat of summer alternately predominated; while the laborious bishop inhabited a little cabin of rough logs, the interstices of which were filled with clay. Now, on the contrary, I see the college complete, at least in part. Its massive stone walls, four feet thick, and four stories in height, lift themselves almost to the elevation of the surrounding woods; and a tall steeple, crowned with a shining weathercock, indicates its situation to the distant wanderer. Several hundred acres of rich

land, from which the trees have been removed,
supply grain in abundance and pasture for numerous
herds of cattle. A printer inhabits the bishop's
former domicil, and publishes a religious newspaper
denominated the Gambier Observer; while the
students are in part provided with commodious
dwellings, and in part supplied with lodgings in the
college, beneath the same roof with the bishop and
the professors. At the same time the conveniences
of older countries are fast flowing in; and a more
refined tone begins to pervade the habits and
manners of the community.

The situation of Gambier was chosen with much
discrimination. Remote as it is from any large
town, the young men educated here enjoy abundant
opportunities for quiet contemplation and study,
without great temptations to dissipation and folly.
The college and the adjoining village occupy the
flat summit of a hill, which slopes gradually towards
the east, and descends almost precipitously towards
the west and south. The upper part of the hill is
generally cleared of timber, although the good taste
of the bishop has retained a quantity of shade. The
slopes are still covered with trees and thick underwood, through which a number of agreeable walks
lead in various directions. At the foot of the hill on
the west and south, Vernon River holds its winding
course, and at a short distance below is employed

in turning a mill, the property of the college, and one of the grand means of its support.

The village of Gambier stands about 400 yards to the north of the college, with which it is connected by a long avenue of sugar maple-trees, planted by the students. It consists of four lodging houses for the young men, workshops for mechanics, a hotel for strangers, a post-office, a shop where goods of all kinds are sold, the printer's house mentioned above, and several out-buildings. North of the village the woods are as yet almost unbroken, and afford delightful walks of boundless extent. South of the hill, and along the river, are several hundred acres of rich bottom land, which yield 80 or 100 bushels of Indian corn per acre. Between the college and the village, I have erected a small house for my own occupation; and immediately adjoining me is a vegetable garden of several acres cultivated by a company of students formed for that purpose.

The sky in Ohio is exceedingly clear; and at night the stars shine with a brilliancy uncommon in England. Yet the extremes of heat and cold are great deductions from comfort. Several times I have seen the thermometer at 100° in the shade in the month of July; and in winter five or even fifteen degrees below zero is not unfrequent. The winter too is long, and the trees are not in full leaf before May. At that time summer commences, and vegetation advances with surprising rapidity. In the latter part of September, the leaves begin to fall, and by the first of November the woods are nearly bare. The latter month, proverbially unpleasant in England, is here one of the most agreeable in the year. Then comes the Indian summer, a phenomenon as yet never satisfactorily explained. The atmosphere, previously chilly and damp, suddenly becomes delightfully warm. A slight haziness overspreads the sky, through which the sun's rays diffuse a ruddy and not unpleasing light. The winds are still, and all nature combines to produce a calm and cheerful frame of mind. After continuing about a fortnight or three weeks, the Indian summer ceases, and winter commences in earnest.

During the cold weather the Aurora Borealis occasionally appears; but not so frequently as I anticipated before my arrival in America. The snow does not fall more abundantly than in the south of England; but it continues longer upon the ground, and, being hardened by severe frosts, generally allows of travelling in sleighs during a few weeks in January or February. Throughout the whole year, the number of rainy days is much fewer than in England; although the quantity of rain is, I think, much greater. The storms of rain, wind, and thunder, during the hot months are often tremendous. The sky, previously clear, quickly becomes overcast with black clouds ; the lightning flashes with terrific brilliancy ; the thunder instead of venting itself in half suppressed murmurs explodes at once with a crash like that of a hundred cannon simultaneously discharged. Then the wind comes howling through the forests, and the tallest trees are uprooted or broken down. The clouds discharge their contents in cataracts rather than in drops ; and the streams are quickly swollen to the size of rivers. In the autumn the foliage assumes an astonishing variety and brilliancy of colour. The brightest yellow and the deepest red are intermingled with green, orange, and brown in endless diversity, and the forests are then in their glory.

Having described the climate, you will doubtless expect me to say something of the people. I must then begin by stating that I have found my preconceived ideas upon this subject generally incorrect I expected to see many Indians in the country, and many relics of savage customs and superstitions. But, on the contrary, I find that the aboriginal inhabitants have almost entirely disappeared in Ohio; and I am informed that the whole number west of the Mississippi is exceedingly small. I have seen, perhaps, a dozen in the course of two years, and they were generally drunken vagabonds resembling the English gipsies in personal appearance and

c 4

complexion. The number of Indians residing in
Ohio does not exceed two or three hundred; while
the white inhabitants amount to nearly, if not quite,
a million. The latter are generally of British descent, although many Germans and Swiss are intermingled with them. From what I have heard
and observed, I should be inclined to estimate the
native European population at less than one-sixth
of the native American. The English language is
universally spoken, and with far more purity and
clearness than in the rural districts of the mother
country. At the same time the language of such
Americans as I have conversed with, is destitute of
that elegance of expression and melody of tone
which characterize the well-educated Englishman.
The appearance of the people, on the whole, is not
healthy; and though there are many exceptions, a
sallow complexion predominates. The men are frequently tall and muscular; but the females are
smaller than in England.

The costume does not materially differ from what
we are accustomed to see at home; but in summer,
broad-cloth suits are laid aside, and dresses formed
of the lightest materials are substituted in their
stead. As to the religious opinions of the people,
the greater part are more or less attached to the
Methodist, Baptist, or Presbyterian sects; and
probably not more than three thousand in all Ohio

at the present time acknowledge Bishop Chase as their ecclesiastical head. Many are destitute of scriptural instruction of any kind; and consequently for the most part are indifferent, if not absolutely hostile, to religion. The people seem to be above want; and in every town there are many who live genteelly, and to a certain extent handsomely. Although there are few finished scholars in Ohio, yet general knowledge and intelligence are evidently more diffused than in England. I have met with many true gentlemen; and have almost uniformly experienced great kindness and hospitality. The moral aspect of society also is far from discouraging to the philanthropist; indeed Ohio may, in this respect, admit of a comparison with older countries which have enjoyed superior advantages.

I will now give you a brief account of the inhabitants of Gambier. The bishop has been already mentioned. The Rev. William Sparrow is the Professor of Divinity, and receives a salary of six hundred dollars (135*l*.) a year, and a small house to live in. The Rev. C. W. Fitch is the Professor of Languages, the Rev. Mr. M'Elroy of Mathematics, and Mr. Kendrick of Mental and Moral Philosophy, &c. The three last receive even smaller stipends than the first, and indeed the situation of all the teachers in the institution at present requires much zeal and self-denial. A grammar-school is connected

c 5

with the college and preparatory to it, in which two
or three teachers are constantly employed. The
pupils in the school are principally quite young; but
in the college there are many between twenty and
thirty years of age, and even older. The students
generally are natives of various parts of the United
States, and the sons of episcopalian parents. There
are, however, a few Irish and Welsh, one Greek,
and one native of Hindostan. There have been
also three or four American Indians in the preparatory department; but they have recently quitted
the institution, and returned to their primitive
habits. The whole number of students is about
170, and perhaps twenty or thirty of these expect,
at some future time, to become clergymen. Their
parents do not send them here to educate them for
the sacred profession; on the contrary, they would
generally prefer them to enter upon a more lucra-
tive employment. Their own choice, and a sense
of duty, commonly determine the question; and
consequently a high standard of ministerial excellence prevails among them. Good sense, united
with great enterprise, and a willingness to endure
hardships, are qualities generally combined in those
who have dedicated themselves as candidates for
the sacred office. Perhaps in the whole institution,
about forty young persons are religiously disposed;
and the greater part of these are already engaged

in advancing the influence of religion and the
Church. They have about a dozen Sunday-schools,
from two to seven miles distant from Gambier,
each of which is under the care of two or three
students.

It may be interesting to you to hear a little more
on this subject: I will, therefore, give you an
account of my regular Sunday expedition, in which
I am accompanied by a worthy collegian, my inti-
mate friend. You must suppose the season to be
summer, when the country appears to advantage,
and the days are long. We rise early, and get a
light breakfast an hour or two before the ordinary
morning meal, and then sally forth with a few
books, and some frugal provision for the day. The
sun has risen about half an hour, and the dew is
sparkling on the long grass. We proceed about
half a mile through the noble aboriginal forest, the
tall and straight trees appearing like pillars in a
vast Gothic cathedral. The timber consists of oak,
hickory, sugar-maple, sycamore, walnut, poplar, and
chestnut; and the wild vine hangs from the
branches in graceful festoons. Occasionally we hear
the notes of singing-birds; but less frequently than
in the groves of England. Deep silence generally
prevails, and prepares the mind for serious contemplation. We soon arrive at a small clearing, where
a cabin built of rough logs indicates the residence

of a family. Around the cabin are several acres upon which gigantic trees are yet standing; but perfectly deadened by the operation of girdling. Their bark has chiefly fallen off, and the gaunt white limbs appear dreary though majestic in their decay. Upon the abundant grass, which has sprung up since the rays of the sun were thus admitted to the soil, a number of cattle, the property of the college, are feeding; and the tinkling of their bells is almost the only sound that strikes the ear. We climb over the fence constructed of split rails piled in a zigzag form; we traverse the pasture, and are again in the deep forest. The surface of the ground is neither flat, nor very hilly, but gently undulating. Our pathway is plain, and conversation enlivens our walk. Occasionally we pass a log hut surrounded by a small clearing; and after an hour we arrive at a roughly-constructed saw-mill, erected on a small stream of water. The miller is seated at the door of his cabin, clad in his Sunday suit, and reading a religious book lent him by us on a former occasion. We hold a short conversation with him; he expresses a growing interest in religion and the Church; and concludes by telling us that he wishes us hereafter to use his horse on our expeditions. We accept the offer as it is intended; my companion mounts the nag, and I walk by his side.

We then pass through the woods along the banks

of Vernon River; and in due time my companion descends from his seat, and I mount the quiet animal in his place. After another hour, we arrive at a small village, or rather a collection of log-houses, the scene of our labours. At the further extremity of the street is a school-house built of logs, with a huge chimney at one end, and a fire-place extending across one side of the apartment. Within it are a number of rough benches, and all around it is a kind of temporary arbour, covered with fresh boughs for the accommodation of those who cannot find seats within. Having tied our horse to a tree, we enter the school-room and sit down to rest. Soon the children come flocking from the cabins and through the woods; and with them their parents and many other grown up people, attracted partly by curiosity, and partly by a sincere desire of religious instruction. In a short time the school-room is filled, and a number of persons are standing without in the shade of the arbour; I then give out one of the hymns in the Prayer-book, reading two lines at a time on account of the scarcity of books. The people join in singing it, and then all kneel down to prayer. I repeat a large portion of the service by *memory*, knowing that my hearers, although belonging to no sect whatever, have at present all the prejudices of sectarians against " praying by a book." After prayer

my companion adds a few words of exhortation, to
which all listen with the deepest attention. This,
although not strictly regular, is permitted by the
bishop to candidates for orders, on account of the
exigency of the case. We then instruct the
children in the New Testament ; and about mid-
day we untie our horse, and set out on our journey
homeward, intending to eat our cold refreshments
on the way.

But scarcely have we left the village, when a
blacksmith runs after us and requests us to stop.
He tells us that he has felt deeply interested in the
services, that he desires more information, and that
he wishes us always to dine with him on Sundays
hereafter. We accordingly return to his cabin, and
his wife sets before us a plentiful repast, consisting of
chickens, potatoes, hot bread, apple-pies, and delicious milk. After some profitable conversation, we
bid them farewell, and about three o'clock arrive
at the miller's house, almost overcome by the ex-
cessive heat. When we have somewhat recovered
from our fatigue, we proceed to a spot on the bank
of the stream, where the grass is smooth, and where
the thick foliage produces a comparative coolness.
Here we find about a hundred persons collected, in
hope of receiving from us some religious instruction.
We conduct the service much in the same way as
in the morning. The effect of the singing in the

H. Caswell. del.

LOG-HOUSE in OHIO.

Published by J. G. & F. Rivington, London, Jan.ʸ 1838.

Day & Haghe Lith.ʳˢ to the Queen.

open air is striking and peculiar ; and the admirable prayers of our liturgy are no less sublime in the forests of Ohio than in the consecrated and time-honoured minsters of York or Canterbury.

The service concluded, we return on foot, and as we approach the college with weary steps, the fire-flies glisten in the increasing darkness. We arrive at our rooms fatigued in body, but refreshed in mind, and encouraged to new efforts. I have mentioned that a number of the young men are engaged in a similar manner ; and you will at once perceive that on account of the distance of their schools, they can but rarely be present at the regular morning and evening service at the college. The great majority of the students are however punctual attendants at Divine worship, and the bishop and professors are faithful in their sermons and exhortations.

I have already protracted my letter to an unreasonable length. It will, nevertheless, interest you to be informed that I have determined to remain in this country ; and if life and health are spared, to become a clergyman of the American Episcopal Church. I have accordingly been admitted as a candidate for holy orders, and shall be required by the canons to continue in my present state of probation for a period of three years, unless the bishop should think fit to shorten the term in my case.

But at all events, my candidateship must continue at least one year. I have prosecuted my studies of late with much satisfaction to myself, and have just taken my degree of A. B., after an examination in Greek, Latin, English composition, declamation, mathematics, natural philosophy, and political economy. In my next, I hope to give you some further information respecting this country and the Church.

CHAPTER III.

LETTER TO A FRIEND.—OHIO.

General description of Ohio.—Knox County.—Description of two townships.—Their inhabitants.—Character of the inhabitants. Author lost in the woods.—Log-cabin.—View of the country and people.—Newark.—Columbus.—Legislature of Ohio.— Episcopal worship at Columbus.—Antiquities at Circleville. —Chillicothe.—Cincinnati.—Return to Gambier.

KENYON COLLEGE, *June*, 1831.

OHIO, as I have already observed, is nearly equal to England in extent. It is bounded on the north by lake Erie, on the south by the Ohio river, on the east by the Ohio and Pennsylvania, and on the west by Indiana. Its shape is nearly square, and it contains seventy-two counties, chiefly laid off in the form of parallelograms. Its principal rivers are the Maumee, Sandusky, and Cuyahoga, which fall into Lake Erie; the Great and Little Miami, the Scioto, the Hocking, and the Muskingum, which fall into the Ohio. The soil is fertile, consisting of a rich vegetable mould ; and the face of the country is level, or gently undulating.

The staple production is wheat, and the principal exports are flour and pork. The chief towns are Cincinnati, Columbus, Chillicothe, and Zanesville. Columbus is the seat of the state government ; but Cincinnati is the chief town, and contains a population of nearly 30,000. The principal collegiate institutions are the Ohio University at Athens, supported by the state ; Kenyon College, which I have in part described ; and the Miami University near Cincinnati, under the control of Presbyterians.

I have mentioned the activity of some of the students in behalf of Sunday-schools. Another work in which they have also voluntarily engaged is the diffusion of the Bible. Shortly after my arrival here, they determined to supply with a Bible every family in the county destitute of one, and their determination was soon carried into effect. A benevolent society furnished them with the books, and the main business was the distribution. Knox county is thirty miles long by twenty wide ; and contains a population of about 15,000. It is divided, like the other counties, into square townships, of which it contains twenty-four. These townships were apportioned by the young men among themselves ; and to my share fell two, situated sixteen or seventeen miles from Gambier, and containing, perhaps, 250 families.

It was in the commencement of winter when I set out on my tour. The bishop's faithful old horse, Cincinnatus, was my only companion, and a pair of saddle-bags contained all that I thought it expedient to carry. The trees were stripped of their rich foliage, and the north-western blasts came keen and piercing from the region of the great lakes. The roads, such as they were, presented a long succession of stumps of trees not yet decayed, and deep miry sloughs in which the horse often sunk far above his knees. Thus I advanced at the rate of about three miles an hour, and had ample time to make observations.

I remarked that whenever I met a vehicle or a horseman it was expected that I should pass to the *right;* and this appears to be a general rule in America. I noticed also that none of the horsemen ever rose in their saddles while riding, which I account for by the fact that saddle-horses generally *pace*, by which peculiar step an easy motion is produced. As I proceeded I occasionally forded a creek, or small stream, the banks of which were rough and jagged from the frequent floods. The remains of a wooden bridge were generally visible, the crazy structure having been chiefly swept away. Sometimes I passed through cultivated

tracts, but my way was principally through unbroken woods. The axe has been busy for fifty
years, and yet the forest maintains an undisputed
right to nineteen-twentieths of the soil. Wherever a small clearing appeared, the dead stalks of
Indian-corn were standing in rows three feet apart,
their yellow blades waving in the wind at the
height of ten or even fifteen feet above the ground.
The farm-houses were variously built. Some were
mere log cabins, surrounded by log stables, log pig-
sties, and log barns. Others were constructed of
frame-work, covered with plank, and containing five
or six apartments. A few were convenient and
substantial brick buildings, which would appear
well even in England. In some cases where the
settler had rapidly advanced to prosperity, all the
three kinds of building were standing together.
The log-hut where the industrious owner had commenced his labours, and perhaps reared his family,
was now converted into a back-kitchen or a wash-
house. The frame-building, once deemed a palace,
was now employed to protect abundant stores of
Indian corn and wheat. The brick mansion was
the present abode of the family; and doubtless contained every thing essential to convenience and
comfort.

I continued my slow and unpleasant journey till
night came on. I was now within my appointed

sphere of labour; and seeing a light before me, I stopped at the house which contained it, and asked for refreshment and lodging. My request was readily accorded, and the farmer sending his sons to take care of my horse, piled huge logs upon his immense fire-place, and directed his wife and daughter to procure me some supper. I was plentifully supplied with coffee, eggs, fried pork, warm bread, fresh butter, &c., and after the repast entered freely into conversation with the family. Accidentally mentioning Gambier as my residence, I perceived the old man suddenly become silent and reserved. I was, however, furnished with a comfortable and clean bed; and in the morning was regaled with an abundant and excellent breakfast. I now prepared to depart, and offered to pay for my entertainment; but this was not permitted. As I was about to leave the house, the old man freely opened his mind, and in a manner which left no room to doubt the strength of his feelings. He told me that he regarded Kenyon College as imminently dangerous to the country. " I have fought the British," said he, " in the revolutionary war; I have again encountered them in the last war; and I know something of their character. I know they would not contribute so many thousands to build a college in Ohio without a sinister object. I am, therefore, convinced that Bishop Chase is an agent employed by them to introduce British domination here. The college is in fact a fortress, all you students are British soldiers in disguise, and when you think you have an opportunity, you will throw off the mask, and proclaim the king of England." I endeavoured to show him the absurdity of this opinion, but he only grew more angry, and I thought it useless to add another word. I therefore thanked him for his hospitality, wished him good morning, and departed. The old man's religion was that of the Calvinistic Baptists; his prejudices were not entirely peculiar to himself; while his hospitality is a common trait in the character of the western people.

I spent some days in the neighbourhood, and thoroughly explored the two townships. I found several schools in active operation, in which the elementary branches of education were taught. A Presbyterian minister, sustained by a Presbyterian Missionary Society, resided in the immediate vicinity, and had many followers, generally among the more intelligent. There was also a Baptist preacher, who evidently exerted much influence. A Methodist local preacher resided in one of the townships, and probably had more hearers than the other two. Episcopalians there were none, and the Church was generally viewed with suspicion and dislike. The Presbyterians had a small Sunday-

1

School, and had succeeded in establishing a Temperance Society. All the inhabitants of this rural neighbourhood evidently possessed the means of obtaining religious instruction in some form, and the majority were habitual attendants at the various services held in their log school-houses, and log meeting-houses. Four-fifths of the families were not only supplied with Bibles, but were well able to read them. Those who were destitute of a copy of the Scriptures, were principally the idle and dissipated; and only one family did I discover in which this destitution could be traced to poverty. This family consisted of a widow and four small children, who inhabited a wretched cabin in the very heart of the woods. The poor woman, when I stated my errand, took down from a wide chink between the logs of her hut, a few scattered pages, which were all that remained of her Bible. I presented her with a new and well printed volume, fresh from the press of the American Bible Society, which was received with tears of gratitude.

One evening I lost my way, and wandered for some distance through the forest without seeing a cabin, or meeting with a single human being. At length it became totally dark; and trusting to the instinct of my horse, I permitted the reins to lie loosely on his neck. After some time I perceived a

light occasionally glimmering through the trees, and
finally, wearied and exhausted, I arrived at the door
of a log cabin. I did not knock in vain, but was
hospitably received ; and the faithful horse was led
away to a good feed of Indian corn. On looking
about me I perceived that the cabin was one of the
rudest kind. The door creaked on wooden hinges
of a most primitive manufacture. The window was
a square aperture, cut in the logs which formed the
wall, and containing four small panes of glass. The
interstices between the logs were only partially filled
with clay, and the stars might occasionally be seen
twinkling through them. A huge fire was blazing
on a hearth ten or twelve feet wide, and was
occasionally replenished with billets five or six feet
long, and a foot thick. From the roof hung a rifle
and a powder horn, large lumps of dried venison,
together with small pieces of apples strung upon
lines for winter use. Huge pegs were driven into
the walls, by which were suspended farming utensils
and articles of clothing. A Bible occupied a shelf
in a corner, and near it was the only bed which the
cabin contained. My host was a strong and healthy-
looking man, evidently accustomed to hard labour.
His family consisted of a wife and three young
children, none of whom appeared to consider their
condition as one of hardship. All exhibited that

independence which is to be expected where every man is the owner of the land which he cultivates, and of the house which he inhabits.

Supper was soon prepared. It consisted of Indian corn meal, boiled to the consistence of hasty pudding, and eaten with milk. This is called *mush*, and is a deservedly favourite dish. After supper I began to wonder what accommodations would be provided for the night. I was, however, soon made to understand the arrangement which hospitality had designed. My host desired me to occupy the only bed ; and began to spread coats and cloaks on the floor before the fire, as a resting-place for himself and his family. I would by no means consent to this, and after some persuasion induced him to allow me the place on the floor. I accordingly lay down enveloped in my cloak ; and in a short time the whole family retired to their couch. As soon as it was supposed I was asleep, a soft step was heard on the creaking floor, and I found myself receiving the additional warmth of a coverlid, of which the worthy couple had, no doubt, deprived themselves.

In the morning they gave me a good breakfast ; and my host having fed and saddled my horse, brought him to the door, and held the stirrup while I mounted. All compensation was firmly, but civilly declined.

When I returned to Gambier, I compared notes
with the students who had explored the remaining
townships; and had reason to believe that the two
which I had visited presented a favourable specimen
of the agricultural population of the county. In one
township thirty or forty Roman Catholic families
were found, who positively refused to receive the
Scriptures. In another, drunkenness appeared to
be the besetting sin; while in a third, little or no
provision had been made for education or religious
services. On the whole, however, I am disposed to
regard the country people of Ohio as well-disposed,
kind-hearted, and anxious to improve themselves
and their children. They have chiefly emigrated
from New York, New England, and Pennsylvania;
and although not distinguished for cheerfulness,
they are generally active and industrious. Being
accustomed to think and act for themselves, they
evince more mind than the English peasantry;
while at the same time the possession of compe-
tence places them beyond the reach of many great
temptations.

You will now expect some account of the higher
classes of society in Ohio; and in order to give you
a few ideas on the subject, I will describe a tour
to Cincinnati which I undertook soon after the
excursion mentioned above. It was the depth of
winter when I mounted a horse hired for the pur-

pose, and descended from Gambier hill by the road which leads to Mount Vernon. After a cold and cheerless ride of twenty miles, I arrived at Newark, and sought the grateful shelter of a comfortable hotel. The next day being Sunday, I enquired for a place of worship, and was directed to the court-house, a brick building situated in the centre of the public square. Here I found a small congregation of Presbyterians assembled, and waiting for their minister. After some minutes he entered, and walked into the place occupied as a pulpit. He rose in his great coat, and gave out a hymn, in which a few persons joined, all sitting. He then made a long extempore prayer, all the congregation standing, but in a variety of attitudes. He then gave out another hymn which was sung as before. Next he read a part of a chapter in the Bible, and followed it by a familiar extempore sermon. Another hymn, and a short extempore prayer concluded the service.

As yet there is no Episcopal Church in Newark, although I am told that there are a few Episcopalians. On Monday I pursued my journey, and arrived at Columbus before night. Having brought letters of introduction from Bishop Chase, I was received by a most respectable family of Episcopalians with the greatest kindness and cordiality. How great was the contrast to the log cabins of the

forest ! Here all was neat and commodious. The
house was well carpetted and furnished; and all
things indicated the presence of taste and refinement. How little do we know the value of a
thousand comforts of life until we have been deprived of them ! How little are we sensible of the
real blessings of a highly civilized state of society
until we have been thrown among those who are
strangers to them ! I remained several days in
Columbus, which I spent most agreeably at the
house of the worthy family above mentioned. The
legislature of Ohio being in session, I availed myself
of the opportunity of being present at the debates,
to which all are freely admitted as spectators without distinction. The state-house is a large brick
building of no architectural pretensions. At the
summit is a cupola commanding a good view of the
town. The upper part of the house contains one
large chamber, well carpeted, and occupied by the
members composing the senate. Immediately un-
derneath a similar room is provided for the representatives. In each apartment the speaker is accommodated with a handsome and elevated seat, while
the members occupy convenient benches, and are
supplied with a number of small writing tables. The
senators and representatives were generally plain
farmer-looking men ; but evinced no destitution of
practical common sense. Among them were several

lawyers, who spoke with some eloquence, and appeared polite and well-informed.

On Sunday I accompanied my hospitable entertainers to church. The Episcopalians were few in number, and had not yet been able to secure the services of a clergyman. They had, nevertheless, obtained the sole use of a German Lutheran chapel, and here a zealous layman, with the bishop's approval, read prayers and a sermon every Sunday. The entire service was used, with the exception of the Absolution and the Benediction. The sermon was well chosen, and read with correctness and perspicuity. The responses were performed in a loud voice by the congregation, who also generally joined in the singing. The lay-reader neither wore any part of the clerical dress, nor entered the pulpit; but officiated at a table on a level with the congregation. All, in short, was conducted with extreme propriety and decorum. There are about fifty Episcopal parishes in Ohio; and as not more than fifteen or sixteen clergymen are at present in the state, lay-readers have been eminently successful in keeping the feeble flocks together.

At Columbus is the state-prison, in which those malefactors are confined who, in England, would be punished with transportation. The population of Columbus I did not ascertain, but should suppose it to be about three thousand. The buildings are

generally of brick, well built, and nearly as commodious as those in most English towns of the same
size. The furniture used by the genteel families
whom I visited, differed in nothing essential from
that of respectable houses beyond the Atlantic.
Altogether I was much pleased with the place and
its inhabitants.

Leaving Columbus, I proceeded about twenty-six
miles to Circleville, where I arrived in the evening.
This town derives its name from the curious fact
that it stands principally within an Indian fortification of high antiquity, which describes a perfect
circle, and contains perhaps ten acres. The fortification, if such it be rightly called, consists of a
moat and a wall of earth, and at the centre a lofty
mound formerly stood, which has been removed to
make room for a court-house. A narrow opening
on the eastern side of the circle, leads into a square
fortification, the sides of which face the cardinal
points, and contain an area not materially differing
from that of the circle. I found a clever though
eccentric antiquarian residing in the town, who gave
me an interesting account of American antiquities,
and considerably enlarged my views upon that most
curious subject.

The next day I reached Chillicothe, and was
cordially welcomed by the Episcopal clergyman of
the place. Here I found society more advanced

than in any part of Ohio I had yet visited, and consisting of several distinct grades. I enjoyed the satisfaction of being present at some evening parties, in which neither elegance, nor intelligence, nor politeness, were wanting. At Chillicothe the Episcopal Church contains many of the wealthier and more refined families ; but has not established itself in the preference of the great mass of the religious people, who are principally, as in other parts of Ohio, Methodists, Presbyterians, and Baptists. The population of the town is about 4000. Its name is derived from a celebrated Indian village, which once stood in the vicinity.

I left Chillicothe during a heavy snow storm, and made but slow progress. On the second day of my ride I lost my way, and wandered in the forest till after dark, the snow still descending abundantly. I knew no other resource than to trust as before to the instinct of my horse, who in due time conducted me to a house where I obtained refreshment and lodging. In three days and a half I travelled only a hundred miles, and reached Cincinnati more exhausted with cold than with fatigue. I put up at a large and convenient hotel, immediately fronting the Ohio river. The stream appeared nearly half a mile in width, and numerous steam-boats were passing up and down, although ice was beginning to descend in considerable quantities.

I remained a fortnight in Cincinnati, which I spent principally at the hospitable abode of an amiable and zealous Episcopal clergyman. Christ Church and St. Paul's are the titles of the two Episcopal parishes in Cincinnati, which together contain probably a hundred and eighty families. The great majority of the religious inhabitants are Presbyterians, Methodists, Baptists, and Roman Catholics, with some Swedenborgians, Unitarians, and Universalists. The population, as I have already observed, amounts to nearly 30,000, and is distinguished for industry and commercial enterprise. The houses are almost entirely of brick, and three or four stories in height. The streets are well paved and lighted; and cross each other at right angles. The public buildings are a number of houses of worship, a court-house, a college, a medical school, a theatre, a bank, two museums, and hotels and taverns almost without number. Society is more mixed than in Chillicothe; and business and speculation constitute the chief subjects of conversation. From 100,000 to 200,000 hogs are annually slaughtered here; and the pork is shipped in barrels for the southern market, to which the Ohio and Mississippi afford a ready access. The town is rapidly increasing, and promises before long to rival the cities in the Eastern States. The means of education are already considerable, and are constantly improving. I shall have occasion to mention Cincinnati again ; and shall therefore defer any further description until a future opportunity.

My journey homeward was performed by a route entirely new to me ; but affording few objects of interest. I arrived at Gambier near the termination of winter, having completed, under the worst of circumstances, a solitary ride of about four hundred miles. Although in many respects I had been much gratified, I resolved never again to undertake a winter journey on horseback in North America, if by any possibility it could be avoided.

CHAPTER IV.

RELIGION AND THE CHURCH.

Relation of the Civil Government to Religion.—General Christianity prevalent.—Relation of the Episcopal Church to the people.—Parochial organization.—Diocesan organization.—Convention of a Diocese.—Standing Committee.

In the preceding chapters I have given the reader, in the form of letters to a friend, a brief sketch of the people of Ohio and of the country which they inhabit. He must not, however, suppose that my observations have been entirely confined within those limits. On the contrary, since the date of the last letter, a period of seven years, I have voyaged and travelled more than 13,000 miles, and have seen a number of towns and cities, and conversed with a great variety of persons.

In the first place, I have paid a short visit to my native country. The rapidity of the travelling conveyances, by which I was taken in twenty-three

1

days from the centre of Ohio to the quiet paternal
home on the verge of Salisbury Plain, enabled me
to form a ready comparison between America and
England, and to correct my judgment of character
and habits. In the second place, I have spent
some time in New England, where I have seen
American society in its oldest and most established
form ; and have traced to their fountain-head most
of the opinions and customs existing in the free
states of the North-West. In the third place, I
have visited some of the slave states, and while I
have witnessed the evils of compulsory servitude, I
have experienced the hospitality, and admired the
generosity of the descendants of the Virginian Cavaliers. I am now in holy orders and married to a
niece of my bishop ; and consequently bound by a
twofold tie to America and to the American
Church. Although the reader may, perhaps, think
that I am no longer to be regarded as an impartial
witness, I shall still endeavour to state facts as they
have fallen under my observation, and to give him
the substance of the information which I have acquired from various sources. I consider my present
occupation of a parish minister decidedly favourable
to the task of giving a full description of the
American Church.

Religion sustains a nearer relation to the civil
government of the United States than is generally

supposed. Those who are accustomed to regard this confederacy as having renounced its allegiance to God, would be astonished to learn that Christianity is part and parcel of the law of the land. This will, nevertheless, appear to be the case from the following facts.

In the constitution of the United States we find the expression " Done in the Year of our Lord." In these words the representatives of the people of this Union date the ratification of their form of government from the Advent of Christ, and assert that Christ is their Lord. Again, the general government thus legislates in regard to Sunday ; " If any bill shall not be returned by the President within ten days (*Sundays excepted*) after it shall have been presented to him, &c." In accordance with this, not only the President, but both Houses of Congress, the officers of the state, treasury, navy, and war departments, are all discharged from work on Sunday. The Supreme Court of the United States is by law obliged to suspend its session on that day ; and further, the general government appoints and maintains chaplains in the Navy. By a law of Congress passed in 1800, it is enacted also " that the commanders of all vessels in the Navy having chaplains on board shall take care that divine service be performed in a solemn, orderly, and reverent manner, twice a day, and a sermon preached on Sunday: and that they cause all, or as many of the ship's company as can be spared from duty, to attend every performance of the worship of Almighty God." In the laws regulating the army " it is earnestly recommended to all officers and soldiers diligently to attend divine service." Punishment is provided for any officer or soldier " who shall behave irreverently at any place of divine worship." The officers and cadets of the military academy of the United States are required by law to attend divine worship on Sundays. By an act of Congress in 1808, the appointment of a chaplain for each brigade in the army was provided for. By another act in 1816, Congress determined on the appointment and compensation of a chaplain to each of its houses. And finally, when Michigan was a territory subject to the control of Congress, it was provided that " the first day of the week shall be kept and observed by the good people of the territory as a Sabbath, holy day, or day of rest from all secular employments."

This will suffice for the general government. The several state governments have taken similar and even stronger ground. The constitution of Vermont declares it to be " the duty of all Christians to observe the Sabbath, and maintain that mode of public worship, which to them shall seem most agreeable *to the revealed will of God.*" The constitution of

Massachusetts expressly assigns as a reason for certain provisions that " the encouragement of art, science, and all good literature, tends to the *honour of God and the advantage of the Christian religion.*" The constitution of New Jersey provides that " all persons professing a belief in the faith of any Protestant sect, shall be capable of being elected, &c." Maryland makes a declaration of belief in the Christian religion necessary to admission to office. North Carolina provides, " that no person who shall deny the truth of the Protestant religion, or the divine authority of the Old or New Testament, shall be capable of holding any office in the civil department of the state." It is said, on good authority, that twenty-three states, at least, have laws requiring the observance of Sunday as a Sabbath. In many of the states, if not in all, blasphemy is punishable at common law; while the method of administering oaths universally introduces the awful sanctions of religion. And lastly, in all the states, preachers of the gospel are authorized to solemnize marriages; while in some of them, ministers alone perform the nuptial ceremony.

But although Christianity is thus recognized by the civil authorities; although Christianity is, indeed, the basis of the common law; none of the existing religious denominations is preferred before the others. The chaplains appointed by the government are often Presbyterians and Methodists, sometimes Episcopalians, and occasionally Roman Catholics. The penal enactments above mentioned are seldom enforced ; and public sentiment, here almost omnipotent, is unfavourable to any attempt to sustain religion by prosecutions in a court of law. In consequence of this, the great mass of the Americans themselves are not aware of the extent to which Christianity, at least in theory, is acknowledged by their own government ; and an impression commonly prevails, that any legislation by which Christianity is distinguished from Mohammedism, paganism, or infidelity, is contrary to the first principles of American liberty. Yet, notwithstanding the government fails to exert any decided influence in favour of religion, a knowledge of the general principles of Christianity has been diffused by various means, throughout the country. A number of voluntary religious societies endeavour to act upon the principle of disseminating those doctrines, and those alone in regard to which all " evangelical denominations" agree. Hence it is that the Bible is found in almost every house in the land. Hence it is that tracts are circulated in endless profusion, strongly inculcating the necessity of personal religion ; although putting out of sight whatever relates to modes of worship, ecclesiastical authority, or outward ordinances. Again, the American people, especially those residing in the country, are in the habit of hearing a great variety of preachers, who agree with each other on certain points, and disagree on others. The doctrines on which they agree are believed, while those on which they disagree are disputed or denied. Hence it is, that amid much error and confusion, orthodox views are generally held on the doctrines of the Trinity, the inspiration of the Scriptures, the atonement of the Saviour, and a state of punishment hereafter. And, lastly, the Americans are a nation of travellers. In the most rural neighbourhoods, there are many who have enjoyed a religious education elsewhere, and are willing to communicate such information as they are able to bestow.

The Episcopal Church, for reasons to be stated hereafter, exerts, at present, but little influence on the population at large. Although many of the first families in the United States are enrolled among its members and friends, its field of usefulness is generally limited to the cities and towns. There is, however, a constant improvement in this respect. The number of its clergymen is rapidly increasing, the nature of its church government is becoming better understood, the sober and scriptural excellencies of its liturgy are more generally admitted, and many prejudices are fast wearing away.

I will now explain, as concisely as possible, our whole system of ecclesiastical polity.

A parish consists, in practice, "of all in any given place who prefer the Episcopal form of worship and government to any other, and who associate themselves in one body, in conformity with certain fixed rules, for the religious benefit of themselves and others." The parish, thus organized, applies to the Diocesan Convention for admission as a constituent part of the diocese, which is never refused when the articles of association are in proper form. In most of the states, a parish possesses the further advantage of incorporation, which, in Ohio, is granted by the state legislature without trouble or expense. The corporate body thus formed can sue and be sued in a court of law, can hold property, and can make all necessary contracts. In due time, a church is erected by voluntary contribution, a clergyman is settled, and arrangements are made for the performance of divine worship. On Easter Monday in every year, the male pew-holders assemble in the Church, and the clergyman opens the meeting with prayers. A vestry, not exceeding ten in number is then elected by ballot to serve for the ensuing year. The clergyman afterwards nominates one of the vestrymen as warden, and another warden is elected by the vestry themselves. The wardens and vestry then elect out of their own number, a treasurer, a secretary, and a delegate or delegates to the Diocesan Convention. Such is the general plan, although there are frequent variations.

The wardens and vestry manage the pecuniary affairs of the parish, and fix the salaries of the clergyman, sexton, organist, &c. To them is committed the care of the land, buildings, and other property owned by the parish; and by them the annual tax on the pews is fixed and collected. They also are empowered by their constituents to engage the services of a clergyman, in case of a vacancy; and, if the parish be large, to secure the additional labours of an assistant minister. Thus, the right of presentation, to use an English expression, is vested in them; and although they often elect a clergyman on the recommendation of the bishop, such recommendation is by no means deemed necessary. To the wardens more particularly is committed the charge of the communion plate, and of the vestments used in divine service. They also are required to collect the communion alms, to see that all things necessary for the decent performance of divine worship are provided, and to repress any improper behaviour which may occasionally interrupt the solemnity of the sacred ordinances. The wardens are commonly chosen from the most aged and respectable persons in the congregation, and are often re-elected to office for many years in

succession.   The income of the parish is sometimes
derived from endowments, as is the case in Trinity
Church, New York, which possesses landed property,
valued at several million dollars sterling.   More
generally, it is raised by means of an annual assess-
ment on the pews, often as high as 100 or 200
dollars on a single pew, and frequently as low as
thirty, twenty, or even five.   In some instances,
especially in infant parishes, a voluntary subscrip-
tion among the members is the only resource, and
this is often precarious and uncertain.

A diocese practically consists of "all Episcopalians
in a given state, organized upon a prescribed plan
as an ecclesiastical commonwealth."   When thus
organized it applies to the General Convention for
union with that body, and if the organization be
canonical, it is received and acknowledged as a
diocese.   The state of New York, in which Episcopalians are numerous, is soon to be divided by the
authorities of the Church into two dioceses, and
the same division will probably be soon effected in
other states.   Some dioceses contain from 100 to
200 parishes and clergymen, or even more ; and
some, especially in the west, as few as ten or twenty.
The ordinary ecclesiastical business of every diocese
is transacted in a convention.   The convention consists, first, of the bishop ; secondly, of all clergymen canonically resident in the diocese ; thirdly,

of the lay delegates appointed by the several parishes. In some dioceses each parish may send three delegates ; while in others, but one is allowed. The convention, thus constituted, assembles once in every year, or oftener, in case of a special exigency, at such time and place as it may determine. I will give a sketch of the proceedings at a recent diocesan convention, which will afford a good idea of all similar meetings.

The members of the convention assembled at ten o'clock, A.M., on Thursday, in a neat and substantial Episcopal church, lately erected in a considerable town. They took their seats in the front pews, the remainder of the building being occupied by a number of respectable persons attached to the Church. The bishop entered in his episcopal robes, and took his seat within the rails of the communion table. A clergyman, appointed by the bishop, then read Morning Prayers ; the bishop performed the ante-communion service, and a sermon was preached by another clergyman, also appointed by the bishop. After divine service, the bishop called the convention to order. A list of the clergymen entitled to seats was then read by a secretary, *pro tem.*, when about thirty answered to their names. The clergy then appointed, by ballot, one of themselves as secretary ; and the bishop nominated a committee of three to examine and report on the testimonials of the lay delegates. The lay delegates presented their papers to this committee, and in a short time the committee reported the names of about forty laymen entitled to vote. On motion of a clergyman the rules of order of the last convention were adopted as the rules of order for the present, and the bishop appointed one clergyman and one layman a committee on the unfinished business of the last convention. The clergymen then presented to the bishop written reports on the state of their parishes, which were laid on the table. The morning being now far advanced, the convention adjourned till half past two.

At the specified time all punctually assembled, and the bishop delivered his annual address from the reading-desk. He began by alluding to the sacred character of the business on which the convention had assembled, and urged upon the members the importance of improving the occasion by social prayer and devotional fellowship. He then referred to a death which had lately occurred in the clerical ranks, and deduced from it some serious reflections. He proceeded to give an account of his episcopal acts during the past year, and stated particularly what parishes he had visited, and the condition in which he had found them. Praise was judiciously bestowed upon those clergymen and laymen who had exerted themselves diligently in the cause of the Church, and notice was taken of the various improvements effected since the last convention. The ordination of nearly twenty deacons and priests, the confirmation of about 200 persons, and the consecration of five or six new churches were reported. The state of a college and of a theological seminary, belonging to the diocese was mentioned, and a full account was given of the number and progress of the students, and of their efforts to do good. The number and the names of clergymen who had been received into the diocese, and of those who had taken dimissory letters from it were stated, and a few appropriate remarks concluded the episcopal address. A committee was now appointed to receive the applications of new parishes desiring to be united with the convention; and the committee on unfinished business next made its report. Several resolutions respecting the diocesan college were then proposed and carried; and six clergymen and six laymen were appointed by ballot, to be trustees of the institution. The standing committee of the diocese, consisting of three clergymen and three laymen, was then elected in the same manner. The committee on new parishes reported that five such parishes had submitted the proper evidence of their canonical organization, and recommended that they should be received into union with the convention. The report was accepted, and the parishes were received. The Convention then adjourned till the next morning.

On the second day, Morning Prayer was read, and a sermon preached as before; but by different clergymen. The convention then elected, by ballot, four clergymen and four laymen as representatives of the diocese in the General Convention. Trustees of the General Theological Seminary at New York were afterwards appointed, according to the canons of the General Convention. The reports of the clergymen were now read. Each gave an account of the baptisms, marriages, and funerals, at which he had officiated during the past year: as well as of the number of communicants, Sunday scholars, and Sunday school teachers in his congregation. Many of them stated the amount of money raised for religious objects in their respective parishes during the past year; and gave such further accounts as appeared likely to interest and edify. The convention then adjourned till half-past two, when it assembled to hear an address on the subject of Sunday schools. It adjourned again till the next morning, when it assembled, and commenced with divine worship as before. A diocesan canon on the subject of Sunday schools was passed after some emendation; and a committee on missions and theological education within the diocese was appointed by ballot. The convention then fixed

the time and place of its next meeting. Some resolutions in favour of Sunday schools and missions
were passed, and 800 copies of the journal of this
convention were ordered to be printed at the expense of that body, and circulated through the
diocese and elsewhere. The members of the convention having been hospitably treated by the inhabitants of the place, a vote of thanks for their
kindness was unanimously carried, and the convention, after singing a Psalm, and receiving the episcopal benediction, finally adjourned.

A diocesan convention is wholly legislative in
its character, and empowered to pass any canons
or regulations not conflicting with those of the
General Convention. The clergy and laity commonly vote together ; but a vote, by orders, may
at any time be obtained at the call of a few members. In that case, the bishop and clergy give
their votes separately from the laity; and a
majority of both sides becomes necessary before
the canon or resolution before the house can pass.
Thus, the clergy can take no important step without the concurrence of the people ; and the people,
are, in like manner, kept in check by the clergy.
In some few dioceses the bishop is allowed a negative upon any of the acts of convention ; but the
episcopal veto, although defended with much learning, is generally unpopular in the Church, and little
exercised.

The canons for the election of a bishop vary a little in the different dioceses. Generally, it is by nomination of a majority of the clergy in the diocesan convention; and if such nomination be confirmed by a majority of the laity in the same convention, the person chosen is duly elected. But no diocese can elect a bishop unless it have contained, during the past year, at least six officiating presbyters, regularly settled in a parish, and six parishes represented in the convention electing. A diocese containing a smaller number of clergymen and parishes may yet obtain a bishop on application to the General Convention. In that case, the election is made by the bishops of the Church, subject to the approval of the General Convention; or during its recess, of a majority of the standing committees. Besides the election of a bishop, the diocesan convention is competent to the performance of the following acts, and others of a similar nature. During the vacancy of the episcopate, it may invite the bishop of a neighbouring diocese to officiate within its limits. It makes canons to determine the mode by which its clergy may be tried when charged with improper conduct or heretical doctrine. It regulates its parish elections, declares the duties of its wardens and vestries, and determines the ratio of its lay representation. It appoints the method by which its parishes shall be

E

organized, and the conditions upon which they may be admitted as constituent parts of the diocese. It declares the necessary qualifications and conduct of lay readers in such of its congregations as are destitute of the services of a clergyman. It provides for the appointment and support of missionaries within the diocese. It takes measures for the promotion of Sunday-schools, and of theological education. It elects trustees of any institution under its control. It chooses delegates to the General Convention; and, lastly, it appoints a standing committee.

The standing committee is a prominent and peculiar feature in the diocesan administration of the American Church. Every diocese is required by a general canon to appoint one, although the number of members composing it is not specified. In Pennsylvania it consists of five clergymen and as many laymen. In Ohio, three of each order are elected; while in Tennessee two of each are deemed sufficient. The standing committee serves for one year, appoints its own president and secretary, and meets at pleasure, by adjournment, or on the summons of its president. Its relation to the diocese resembles in some respects that of a vestry to a parish. It is also a council of advice to the bishop; and when the episcopate is vacant, it issues dimissory letters, institutes ecclesiastical trials, superintends by its clerical members all deacons in the diocese, and performs other functions not considered strictly episcopal within the diocesan limits. No bishop can be consecrated without the consent of the majority of the standing committees of all the dioceses in the United States. The only exception to this rule is when a bishop has been elected during the year preceding the triennial General Convention. In that case the standing committees are not consulted ; only the consent of the General Convention is obtained. No person can be admitted a candidate for orders in any diocese, nor ordained a deacon or a priest, until he has laid before the bishop testimonials of his fitness signed by a majority of the members of the diocesan standing committee, duly convened. If the applicant desires admission to the diaconate or to the priesthood, the testimonials must certify his religious and moral character during the last three years.

Such is the internal organization of an American diocese. In the next chapter I purpose to give some account of the General Convention, and of the respective functions of bishops, priests, and deacons.

CHAPTER V.

THE SAME SUBJECT CONTINUED.

General Convention.—Its various powers.—The Church wholly
   independent of the State.—Distinctions in the Ministry.—
   Probation of Candidates.—Deacons.—Priests.—Bishops.—
   Influence and standing of a Bishop.—Ecclesiastical Trials.—
   Mode of trial in Ohio.—Resignation of Bishops.—Assistant
   Bishops.

THE General Convention is the tie by which twenty-
two dioceses, covering an extent of about a million
of square miles, are bound together in one fellowship.
Its relation to the several dioceses is similar to that
which Congress sustains towards the different Com-
monwealths of the United States. It is an association of originally independent bodies voluntarily
established for mutual benefit, and for the effectual
promotion of the great ends which all are endeavouring to accomplish. The General Convention is
divided into two houses, the consent of both of
which is necessary, before any canon or resolution

can pass. The upper house consists of all the bishops of the Church, now seventeen in number, of whom the senior in point of consecration is president, while a presbyter, appointed for the purpose, acts as secretary. The lower house is composed of clerical and lay-delegates from every diocese, not exceeding four of each order, who appoint a president and secretary from their own body. In all questions, when required by the representation from any diocese, each order is allowed but one vote, and the majority of suffrages, by dioceses, is conclusive in each order, provided such majority comprehends a majority of the dioceses represented in that order. The concurrence of both orders is, in that case, necessary to constitute a vote in convention. The General Convention assembles once in three years, and commonly in one of the churches in Philadelphia. A special convention may also be called by the presiding bishop whenever a majority of the bishops may deem it expedient.

The General Convention, like those of the several dioceses, is exclusively legislative in its character, and wholly independent of the civil government. It possesses all those powers which cannot be conveniently exercised in the several dioceses

Thus, first. It enacts canons in regard to public worship, providing for uniformity, in that respect,

throughout the dioceses; making alterations in the
Prayer-book when deemed necessary; declaring how
Sunday shall be observed; appointing the mode of
publishing authorized editions of the Bible and
Prayer-book, and allowing every bishop to compose
forms of prayer for his diocese on extraordinary
occasions.

Secondly. It defines, to a certain extent, the duties
of bishops, priests, deacons, and candidates, as well
as of standing committees. Thus, it declares on what
conditions a person may be admitted a candidate
for orders, and how he shall conduct himself during
his probation. So also, it determines the age at
which a person may be ordained, making twenty-one
years necessary for a deacon, twenty-four for a
priest, and thirty for a bishop. It declares the
amount of learning which the candidate must possess, the testimonials to be produced by those who
are to be ordained, and the times of ordination. It
requires the clergy to prepare their people for
Episcopal visitations, to instruct the young in the
catechism, and the principles of Episcopacy, and to
keep a register of the baptisms, confirmations, communicants, marriages, and funerals within their
cure. It forbids any clergyman to officiate within
the parochial cure of another without his consent,
provides for the settlement of differences between
ministers and their congregations, and states how

and when the pastoral connexion may be dissolved.
It defines the offences for which clergymen may be
brought to an ecclesiastical trial, and the nature
and extent of the extreme penalty of degradation.
In like manner, it lays down the method of procedure against an offending layman, and the grounds
on which he must be repelled from the holy communion. It makes it the duty of bishops to address
charges to their clergy, and pastoral letters to the
laity from time to time; to visit all the parishes in
their care at least once in three years, and to deliver an annual report of their episcopal acts to their
diocesan conventions.

Thirdly. The General Convention legislates on
points touching the relation between the several
dioceses. Thus, it enacts that no congregation shall
receive a minister from another diocese, until he has
presented to the vestry a certificate from the bishop,
that he has brought satisfactory letters of dismis-
sion from the authorities of the diocese whence he
has removed. In like manner, it forbids a parish
in one diocese from uniting itself with any other
diocese, and declares that every congregation belongs to that diocese, within the geographical limits
of which its members reside.

Fourthly. It provides episcopal superintendence
for those districts of the United States not yet included in any diocesan organization. Thus it has

made a canon under which missionary bishops can be elected by the lower house of General Convention, on the nomination of the upper house. Bishops so appointed are required to exercise their functions under such regulations as the house of bishops may prescribe, and their support is to be provided for by the board of missions. As soon as a diocese is properly organized, it is admitted into the union by the General Convention, and entitled to representation.

Fifthly. The General Convention legislates on points relating to other denominations of Christians. No person is permitted to officiate in any episcopal congregation without producing evidence of his being an episcopal clergyman. A canon also prescribes the course to be pursued by a minister of any non-episcopal sect desiring to become a minister of the church. In this, the testimonials to be produced by him, and the examinations which he must undergo before ordination, are minutely stated.

Sixthly. The General Convention determines in matters relating to foreign Episcopal churches. For example, it was on application of the General Convention, as then constituted, that the English bishops consecrated the first American prelates. So also, a regularly ordained Episcopal clergyman, coming from a foreign land, is not allowed to take the charge of a parish until he has resided one year in

the United States, and produced evidence of his
good standing in his own country.

Seventhly. The General Convention directs the
operations of the Church in regard to heathen lands.
Thus, it can elect missionary bishops for Africa,
China, or any other pagan country, in like manner
as it appoints them for the states and territories at
home, not yet organized as dioceses. So also at
every triennial meeting it appoints thirty persons,
who, together with all the bishops, constitute a
board of missions. This board raises funds by
voluntary contribution, amounting to about 50,000
dollars (11,250*l.*) annually. Part of this sum is
devoted to missions within, and part to those without the United States. But on this subject I shall
speak more particularly when I come to describe
the missionary operations of the Church.

I have above given a sketch of most of the provisions found in the general constitution and canons.
Having been enacted only as circumstances called
for them, they are generally simple, practical, and
easily understood. As well as the diocesan canons,
they are, on the whole, conscientiously observed. I
cannot think that any civil legislation would add, in
the slightest degree, to the weight and authority of
the American canons. On the contrary, it would
probably tend to bring them into disesteem, even
among Episcopalians. It is the almost uniform

E 5

conviction of our people on this side of the Atlantic, that the Church is competent to take care of itself; that legislative interference would be a positive injury; and that the civil government will sooner need the protection of religion, than religion require the support of the state.

I now come to describe the ranks in the ministry. These are the ancient and primitive orders of Bishops, Priests, and Deacons; and beyond these no ecclesiastical distinctions are acknowledged. Consequently, there are no Deans, Archdeacons, or Archbishops in the Episcopal Church of the United States. Yet it would be incorrect to infer from hence, that ecclesiastical merit is deprived of due honour. There are various methods by which the clergy and people indicate their approbation of piety and talent. To say nothing of bishoprics, an obvious mode is by election to the standing committee, a post of great trust and responsibility, connected with no emolument. In like manner, clergymen, as well as laymen, of the highest standing, are usually appointed to represent a diocese in the General Convention, or to act as trustees of the General Theological Seminary, or of any other institution under the control of the Church. It commonly happens that every man, in due time, finds his level, and occupies that station for which his merit and his services have qualified him.

The Church has done as much as could be wished in order to preserve the purity of the ministerial body, both in regard to admission to the ministry, and rejection from it. In the first place, none can be ordained deacons without passing through a term of probation denomininated candidateship. This is generally of three years' duration, although in peculiar cases, the bishop, with the consent of the clerical members of the standing committee, is empowered to shorten it to one year. No person can be admitted, even to candidateship, without producing to the bishop of his diocese a certificate from the standing committee, that he is reputed pious, sober, and honest; that he is attached to the doctrine, discipline, and worship of the Church, and a communicant of the same; and that he is believed to possess qualifications which will render him fit for the exercise of the holy ministry. The candidate, during his probation, is under the special superintendence of his bishop, who is bound to see that he pursues his studies diligently and properly; that he does not indulge in trifling conduct; and that he avoids all amusements unfavourable to serious and studious habits. When his candidateship has expired, he must produce to the bishop a certificate from the standing committee, to the effect that for the last three years he has lived piously, soberly, and honestly, and that he is

thought worthy to be admitted to the ministry.
He may then be ordained a deacon, after having
passed an examination which I shall describe in a
future chapter. He still, however, remains subject
to the regulation of the bishop, without whose licence
he is not allowed to preach, and by whom the place
where he shall officiate is assigned to him.

After he has continued a deacon for one year, he
may apply for priest's orders, if he have attained the
canonical age. He is now required to produce fresh
testimonials from the standing committee, in the
same form with those already mentioned. He must
give evidence that he is engaged as minister of some
parish, or that he is employed as a missionary,
under proper authority, or that he is a teacher in
some seminary of learning duly incorporated. He
must pass a satisfactory examination before the
bishop and two presbyters; and finally, he must
subscribe a declaration of his belief in the inspiration and sufficiency of the Holy Scriptures, and a
solemn engagement to conform to the doctrines and
worship of the Church. Having complied with
these requisitions the bishop may ordain him to the
priesthood.

The stated times for ordination are on the Sundays following the Ember-weeks, although occasional ordinations may be held at such other times
as the bishop may appoint.

The relation which a priest sustains to his bishop is much the same as in England. He is bound by his ordination vows, " reverently to obey his bishop, and other chief ministers, who, according to the canons of the Church, may have the charge and government over him, following with a glad mind and will their godly admonitions, and submitting himself to their godly judgments."

The authority of the bishop is generally exercised in the way of persuasion and advice, and seldom in that of compulsion. His mere weight of character gives him great influence ; and without considerable weight of character it is almost impossible for any person to become a bishop. In the first place, he must receive the suffrages of at least a majority of all the clergy and of all the laity, in a diocese. In the second place, the consent and approbation of the General Convention, or of a major part of all the standing committees in the whole Church must be obtained ; and, lastly, a majority of all the bishops must declare their consent, before the consecration can be permitted.

Hence, a bishop possesses, from the first, the confidence and affection of those under his charge. Nor is his influence by any means confined to the clergy. The laity in general, the females, and the children, are accustomed to look upon him as their chief shepherd ; while even the members of

dissenting denominations treat him with a marked
attention and respect.   In every diocese, too, there
are very many, sometimes a great majority, both
among the clergy and laity, who habitually consider
their bishop as possessed of Apostolical authority
transmitted in an unbroken chain from the primitive
ages.   This opinion gives a dignity to the office in
the estimation of the religious, such as no temporal
wealth and no worldly titles could confer.   A
bishop is seldom troubled with contumacy or improper conduct on the part of his clergy.   Public
opinion, which rules with archiepiscopal as well as
sovereign sway, will not tolerate the careless or
vicious minister ; and a preacher of the Gospel will
more probably attempt too much, than rest content
with doing too little.

When cases of delinquency occur, which can
never be entirely prevented, the discipline of the
Church is promptly exercised.   Every bishop, priest,
or deacon, who is accused, by public rumour, of vio-
lating the canons of the Church, of criminal, im-
moral, or disorderly conduct, of wilfully discontinu-
ing his ministerial office, or of teaching heretical
doctrine, must be presented for an ecclesiastical
trial according to such mode as may have been
established in the diocese to which he belongs.   If
convicted, he must undergo the penalty of admonition, suspension, or degradation, as the nature of

the case may require. Should a bishop be tried,
there must be one or more of the episcopal order
present; and none but a bishop can pronounce
sentence of degradation or deposition upon any
clergyman. A layman, also, when repelled by his
pastor from the communion, possesses by the
rubric, the right of appealing to the bishop of the
diocese for an investigation of his case. Every
presbyter or deacon is amenable to the bishop ; or
if there be no bishop, to the standing committee.
In Ohio, the mode appointed for trying presbyters
and deacons is as follows.

Complaint having been made to the standing
committee by responsible persons, the standing
committee, if they deem the evidence sufficient to
demand a trial, make out a written presentment to
the bishop, specifying the offence or offences, with
particulars of time, place, and circumstances. The
bishop then causes a presentment to be served on
the accused, and nominates eight presbyters, from
whom the accused must select five, and notify their
names to the bishop within thirty days. These
five form a board for the trial, and meet at such
time and place as the bishop may appoint. They
may adjourn from time to time and from place to
place, provided they always keep within the diocese.
A written notice of the time and place of the first
meeting must be served at least thirty days before-

12

hand on the accused, as well as on the standing committee, who, by one of their number, prosecute the case, and produce such evidence as they can obtain. A majority of the board decides all questions, and renders judgment. Both parties may consult legal or other advisers, but no layman may be advocate for either party in the trial. Evidence must be reduced to writing by the secretary of the board, and signed by the witnesses respectively; and some officer, authorised by law, may, at the desire of either party, administer an oath or affirmation to the witnesses. The entire trial, if the accused desire it, may be in public. Depositions of absent witnesses may be taken by a person appointed by the bishop, both parties being allowed time to attend and examine the deponent. After considering the evidence, the board declares in writing, signed by a majority, their decision on the charges contained in the presentment. This is delivered to the bishop, accompanied with an opinion of the board as to what sentence should be pronounced. The bishop then passes sentence of admonition, suspension, or degradation, as he may deem proper, provided that he does not exceed the sentence recommended by the board. This sentence admits of no appeal, and is final, unless the bishop sees fit to order a new trial.

Such is the method of conducting clerical trials

in Ohio ; and similar to this, on the whole, is the course pursued in other dioceses. As yet, few dioceses have adopted any definite mode of procedure in regard to the trial of a bishop, influenced, no doubt, by the extreme improbability of such an event. A canon has been proposed in General Convention, which, if constitutional, and finally adopted, will place such trials in the house of bishops, on the presentment of two-thirds of the clergy and of the laity in the diocese of the accused.

A general canon has been passed by which a bishop is empowered to resign his jurisdiction, although under limitations which must preclude the possibility of such a resignation except in very peculiar cases. In the first place, two-thirds of the clergy and of the parishes in the diocese, must, in convention, express their assent to the proposed measure of their bishop. In the second place, a majority of each order in the General Convention, voting by States, must declare their consent, or in their stead, a majority of the standing committees of all the dioceses. And, lastly, a majority of the house of bishops must agree to the contemplated resignation before it can be valid. A bishop who has resigned his jurisdiction, does not thereby cease to be a bishop, but is still subject, in all matters, to the authority of a General Convention. It is not probable that many will have cause to desire such a resignation.   Infirmity cannot, generally, induce a wish to resign ; for when, by old age, or disease, a bishop is unable to discharge his episcopal duties, another bishop may be elected, by his diocese, to assist, and ultimately to succeed him.   Nor can a resignation be made desirable by a want of means to sustain the expenses of the episcopate.   A bishop is always supported respectably, either by some parish, of which he is the rector; or by a college, of which he is the president ; or by a fund raised for the purpose within his diocese.   Some controversy with his clergy and laity is almost the only conceivable circumstance which can lead to a separation ; and, in the ordinary course of events, this can occur but seldom.

I have thus given a tolerably minute delineation of the principal features in the American Episcopal Church.   It is now time to exhibit the system at work ; and I will begin with a brief history of the formation of my first parish, of Portsmouth, Ohio, and some account of my parishioners there.

CHAPTER VI.

THE LAY-READER.

Emigrants to the West.—Early years of Mr. Gunn.—He reads the Service in Connecticut and in New York.—He emigrates to Ohio, and reads the Service at Portsmouth.—Bishop Chase visits Portsmouth.—The Lay-reader's labours terminate.— He becomes blind.—He gives a third part of his property towards the building of a Church.—He addresses his descendants on his death-bed.—He dies.—Episcopal Parish at Portsmouth.—The Author resigns his charge.

THE rapid growth and increasing prosperity of the Western States afford a fit subject of admiration to the political economist and the statesman. Nor can the Christian behold the vast prospect without the deepest interest and solicitude. Sometimes he is tempted to fear that the means of education and religious improvement will never keep pace with the increase of the population; and again, he is cheered when he listens to the " church-going bell," in regions where but a few years since the Indian wandered, and the bear and wolf lay down. Of the many thousands who annually emigrate from the Eastern States and from Europe, the great majority, doubtless, are actuated solely by the hope of advancing their temporal interests. Yet there are not a few whose controlling motive originates in a higher source. Here are intelligent and pious settlers, who, while they seek a more genial sky, and a more productive soil, forget not that, wherever their lot may be cast, they are bound to use their utmost exertions in the cause of morality and religion. Such was the character of the humble individual by whom the episcopal parish of Portsmouth, in Ohio, was founded. I shall give a concise account of his efforts in behalf of the Church, as they will both serve to throw light on the system of American Episcopacy, and will at the same time afford a specimen of a large class of persons among the laity.

Samuel Gunn was born at Waterbury, in Connecticut, in the year 1763, and baptized by a clergyman sustained by the " Society for Propagating the Gospel in Foreign Parts." The war of the American Revolution commenced while he was a child, and consequently, he took no part in that fearful struggle. But the Church suffered severely during the momentous period in question, and became, in many places, but a name; a name, too, of obloquy and reproach. Yet Samuel Gunn continued faith-

ful to his spiritual mother. He loved the vine
which he believed the Son of God and his Apostles
had planted; and though now broken and spoiled,
he hoped to see the time when it would cover the
land with its spreading branches, and when its
leaves would be for the healing of the nations. The
war having at length terminated, the clergymen in
Connecticut rallied their remaining forces, and
elected a bishop, who was consecrated in 1784 by
the Scottish prelates. Bishop Seabury was soon
actively engaged in the great work of reviving the
enfeebled parishes committed to his charge. He
ordained pastors, and was the first who performed
the solemn ordinance of Confirmation in the United
States. Among the numbers who hastened to
receive this holy rite was the subject of our
memoir, who had now attained the age of manhood,
and had given unquestionable signs of a Christian
character.

The parish of Waterbury was, at that time,
without a clergyman, and Mr. Gunn, being a man
of unimpeachable morals, was appointed a lay-
reader. During the week he was engaged on his
farm, but on Sunday he occupied the desk, and
conducted the devotions of a few zealous Christians
according to the venerable forms of the liturgy.
Sometimes a clergyman visited the little flock; but
such opportunities were not frequent, and for ten

or twelve years, Mr. Gunn continued his useful labours without fee or reward. But his family was now increasing, and his circumstances were greatly straitened. At length he determined to seek a home in the western country, which already presented a wide field to enterprise and industry. He first removed, about the year 1793, to Windham, in the western part of the state of New York. Here he established a small shop, which yielded him a livelihood sufficient for his moderate wants. He soon found means to collect a few persons together, and to persuade them to unite with him in the performance of divine worship. He commenced, a second time, his vocation of lay-reader; and soon experienced the gratification of finding that his efforts were not in vain. The number of attendants gradually increased, until finally they organized a parish and obtained a clergyman. But Providence did not permit the subject of our memoir to enjoy the spiritual advantage of a pastor. He seemed destined to be a lay-reader; and by the silent influence of a blameless life, no less than by his direct exertions, he was to promote the truth among those who had few opportunities of hearing an official ambassador of God.

His circumstances becoming again embarrassed, he decided on removing into the fertile, but at that time, almost uninhabited region, bordering on the Ohio. Accordingly, having punctually paid his debts, he sallied forth with a light heart and a light purse, in quest of new toils and new means of usefulness.

It was in the autumn of 1805, that Mr. Gunn, with a wife and five children, commenced his long and fatiguing journey. An occurrence of a most distressing character soon wrung the affectionate heart of our lay-reader, and tried his faith to the utmost. While passing through the deep forest, one of his children fell from the waggon, and in a moment was crushed to death beneath the wheels. With his own hands the afflicted father dug a grave by the road side, and having read the solemn burial-service of the Church, committed the remains of his beloved offspring to their kindred dust. In the month of November he reached the banks of the Ohio, and embarked with his family and little property on the noble river which was to bear him to his destination.

No steam-boat then ploughed the western waters; and it was only in long and narrow vessels, propelled by poles or dragged by ropes, that the hardy boatmen could ascend the current. The passengers and goods destined for places down the stream were conveyed in flat boats of a temporary construction, which were broken up and sold when the voyage was completed. In a vessel of this latter kind, Mr. Gunn, with his little all, floated slowly to his future home.

At length, his boat was made fast near the village of Portsmouth, a place containing at that time not more than a dozen dwellings. There was, however, a dock-yard in the vicinity, where a large ship was afterwards built, which descended the river 1500 miles to the Gulf of Mexico, and was employed in the trade with Europe.

In so enterprising a neighbourhood, Mr. Gunn was not idle. He purchased a small farm, and diligently employed himself in felling the trees, breaking up the rich soil, and sowing the seeds from which he hoped to provide his children's bread. And now the liturgy was heard probably for the first time on the shores of the Ohio. Every Sunday, the lay-reader collected his family around him, and united with them in worship and praise. For many years, none but his domestic circle attended on these occasions; but a providential circumstance soon enlarged his congregation. He thought it expedient to sell his farm, and remove into the village of Portsmouth, where he established himself as a cooper. He soon found that he was not the only churchman in the place; but that there were a few others who had been taught to

believe in one Catholic and Apostolic Church. These
gladly attended his reading and assisted with their
responses. About this time, namely, in the year
1819, he received the grateful intelligence that a
diocese had been organized in Ohio, and a bishop
elected and consecrated. To complete his gratification, he learned that the new prelate was no
stranger to him. The Rev. Philander Chase, the
same missionary who, on more than one occasion
had slept under his roof, and dined at his table at
Windham, in New York, was now his bishop in the
Far West. Mr. Gunn immediately took his pen, and
wrote to his chief shepherd. He stated the importance of directly commencing regular services in
Portsmouth. He mentioned the comfort which
the few members of the Church in that increasing
village would derive from an episcopal visit; and he
concluded with earnestly requesting the bishop
either to come himself, or send some clergyman to
visit them at an early season.

Bishop Chase was engaged in highly important
business when this letter arrived. He therefore
sent the Rev. Mr. Morse, one of his most faithful
clergymen, who was received at Portsmouth with
unaffected cordiality. Once more, after an interval
of fifteen years, our lay-reader was permitted to
hear the word of life declared by a commissioned
ambassador of Christ. In about a month after-

F

wards, the bishop himself arrived. The court-house was immediately prepared for religious worship, and a large congregation, partly drawn by curiosity, and partly by a better feeling, soon assembled. The bishop delivered a plain and practical sermon, with that solemnity and that energy which seldom fail to produce a deep impression. Nor was this all. He remained in Portsmouth till he had gained the affection and respect of the people, had baptized and confirmed a number of persons, and had effected the organization of a parish, of which Mr. Gunn was elected senior warden. Having regularly appointed Mr. Gunn to the office of lay-reader, he left Portsmouth, and went onward to discover new openings for the Gospel and the Church.

For the third time, our lay-reader occupied the desk; but the people were, to a great extent, destitute of Prayer-books, and could not, of course, join in the responses. It was soon discovered that a printer in the village was in possession of a large number of these invaluable manuals of devotion, which he had long since laid away as unsaleable. They were immediately purchased, and some at high prices. Money was then scarce, and one person actually gave twenty bushels of corn for a single Prayer-book. For three years, Mr. Gunn regularly performed the services. During this period, the village was visited most severely by disease.

Many who had taken a deep interest in the church
militant below were removed to the church triumph-
ant above ; and after several unhealthy seasons,
few of the little congregation remained. In the
year 1823, a clergyman residing in Chillicothe, fifty
miles distant, consented to officiate once a month
in Portsmouth. This was a great benefit to the
people, and a great relief to Mr. Gunn, who had
now attained his sixtieth year. The latter, notwithstanding, conducted worship, and read a sermon
on the intervening Sundays ; and after two years,
when Mr. Kellogg, the clergyman, left Ohio, he
again took the entire labour upon himself. All
this, it must be remembered, was entirely gratuitous, and the only recompense was that of a good
conscience.

The congregation, now exceedingly small, was
often a subject of ridicule to the thoughtless and
the prejudiced. The members of other denominations also frequently importuned the few Episcopalians to unite with them, on the assurance
that a Church minister could never be obtained.
But the little community, attached by conviction
to the distinctive principles of Episcopacy, never
ceased to persevere in what they believed to be the
way of truth. In 1831, they obtained a convenient
room for their worship. They fitted it up with
commodious seats and a pulpit ; and here, after his

recovery from a severe illness, the aged lay-reader, with a trembling voice, continued to conduct their devotions. In the month of July, in the same year, he officiated for the last time.

Having been just ordained a deacon, by Bishop Chase, I was sent by him to Portsmouth, where I received and accepted an invitation to take charge of the feeble congregation. My compensation was fixed at 200 dollars (45*l.*) a year, which, with an additional hundred from the Diocesan Missionary Society, was enough to support existence at the low prices which then prevailed. But scarcely had I officiated once in my new sphere of labour, when a frightful accident befel the good Mr. Gunn, which hastened his departure from the world. A fire-engine had recently been purchased by the inhabitants of Portsmouth, and the old man, with many others, was observing its operations. The person who directed the jet unfortunately permitted the tube to fall, and in an instant the whole stream of water struck Mr. Gunn in the face, crushing his right eye, and completely destroying its power of vision. For some time his condition was extremely precarious ; and it was feared that a total loss of sight would be the result. At length nature rallied, and he recovered strength to walk. One eye was spared to him, but his former health was never restored. Yet the hope of immortality brightened upon him, and his conversation became more and more solemn and edifying. The Church, too, was dearer to his heart than ever; and it was not long before he gave a proof of his sincerity, which was the last crowning act of a life devoted to the service of God.

During the winter following the accident, he one day requested as many of the parishioners as could attend, to meet him on important business. A number of them accordingly assembled, and the old man, rising from his seat, represented to them in strong terms the importance of building a church. He showed them that no considerable accessions to their number could be expected until a distinct building, of sufficient capacity, and easily accessible to all, had been obtained. He concluded almost in the following words: "You know, my friends, that I am not rich, and that twice I have lost my all. Yet Providence has given me enough, and my property is now a little more than two thousand dollars. Of this, I will give *one-third* towards the erection of the proposed edifice, on condition that you will contribute the remainder of the necessary amount." This offer was accepted with admiration and gratitude, and a sufficient sum was promptly subscribed.

But the lay-reader lived not to see the Church erected, nor even its corner-stone laid. A few months after his generous gift, his form became emaciated, and he was soon confined entirely to his bed. Religious services were sometimes held in his room, which evidently afforded him great delight. On one of these occasions his children and grandchildren were present by his special request. I took for my text, *Eccles.* xii. 1. " Remember now thy Creator in the days of thy youth, while the evil days come not, nor the years draw nigh, when thou shalt say, I have no pleasure in them." At the conclusion of the service, the pious veteran raised himself a little on his pillow, and spoke a few words in the most pathetic manner, labouring to impress upon his offspring a deep sense of the necessity of pure and practical religion. He represented the comfort which he felt in resting all his hopes on the great Atonement ; and finally besought all his dear family to follow the narrow way of life, that he might ultimately enjoy the happiness of meeting them in heaven.

A clergyman, in priest's orders, visiting Portsmouth about this time, Mr. Gunn expressed his desire to partake of the holy communion. The sacred rite was accordingly administered to him, and he expressed the liveliest joy and consolation. Five days afterwards, he breathed his last in perfect peace, having almost completed his seventieth year. Many hundred persons accompanied his remains to the burial-ground; for he had been a friend to all, and had been long regarded as an example of uprightness and integrity.

My parochial charge in Portsmouth consisted of about twenty-five families. Four of these families were the descendants of Mr. Gunn, and four were, in like manner, the offspring of a worthy Lutheran couple, of German origin. The latter perceiving that the Episcopal Church closely resembled their own in rites and doctrines, had connected themselves with it at an early period, and had become devotedly attached to it. Previous to the erection of the church, my congregation, on Sundays, seldom exceeded fifty; although after that event, it considerably increased. My salary was paid quarterly with the utmost punctuality; and I contracted an affection for these plain, but worthy people, which time can never efface.

Portsmouth is beautifully situated on the Ohio, at the confluence of the Scioto with that majestic stream. The Ohio is here about one-third of a mile in width; and on the opposite shore, the hills of Kentucky rise precipitously from the bank, and terminate in rocky points. The frequent passing of steam-boats gives animation to the scene, which is further enlivened, at certain seasons, by the descent of immense rafts of timber, and flat boats loaded with produce for the southern market. The town, during my residence there, contained about twelve hundred inhabitants, although the completion of the Ohio canal, which enters the river at Portsmouth, has been the means of a considerable increase.

The Presbyterians were little more numerous than the Episcopalians; but the Methodists were abundant, and exerted the chief sway in religious matters. Nearly one-half of the population attended no place of worship whatever. On Sundays, I performed two services, and preached twice, sometimes adding a lecture at night. On Wednesday evenings I also conducted religious worship at my lodgings; and frequently my room was crowded. On Saturdays, the children assembled in my study, where they repeated the catechism to my wife, and heard a familiar explanation of its contents. On communion days, being only a deacon, I exchanged pulpits either with the Rev. Mr. Bausman, of Chillicothe, distant fifty miles, or with the Rev. Mr. Johnson, rector of St. Paul's Church, Cincinnati, distant a hundred and twenty miles. Both of these excellent gentlemen were at all times ready to assist in this way, and to encourage me by every means in their power. Altogether, my situation was one of great interest, and most gladly would I have continued to occupy it until the present moment. But the climate of the place, combined with extra exertions on my part, injured my health, and almost deprived me of voice, so that, ultimately, by the advice of physicians, I was induced to seek a purer air, and to retire for a while from parochial duty. Still I could not leave my flock without a pastor; but delayed my departure until I saw my early friend, with whom I had engaged in Sunday-school teaching at Gambier, established as minister of the parish, in my room. At length, after a residence of two years, I left Portsmouth, and commenced my journey to New England in a commodious boat on the Ohio canal. Many of my late parishioners accompanied us to the second lock, and here, with many painful emotions, I bade them farewell.

CHAPTER VII.

JOURNEY FROM PORTSMOUTH TO ANDOVER.

———

Liberality to Clergymen in America.—Ohio canal.—Moravians.—
Schooners on Lake Erie.—Cloud proceeding from the Falls
of Niagara.—Buffalo.—Rochester.—Report of St. Luke's
Church.—Albany.—New York.—President Jackson.—Hell
Gate.—Newport.—Episcopal Church.—Providence.—Boston.
—Convention of the Church in Massachusetts.—Ride to
Andover.

———

MY proposed journey to New England gave occasion
to an instance of generosity, which I cannot forbear
noticing. A gentleman of the Episcopal Church,
residing in Circleville, a connexion and name-sake of
the justly-celebrated nonconformist Dr. Doddridge,
was part owner of a commodious line of boats on
the Ohio canal. Hearing of my indisposition, and
of my arrangements for leaving Portsmouth, this
worthy man, though almost a total stranger, informed me that accommodations would be provided
at no expense, for myself and wife, on board one of

his vessels. Such offers are made, in this country, with the intention that they should be accepted ; and, accordingly, I did not hesitate to comply. The journey by canal was one of 330 miles, and would have cost us together about twenty dollars.

Instances of similar liberality to clergymen are by no means unfrequent in America. In travelling through Ohio, it has several times happened that after spending a night at an inn, and having taken supper and breakfast, the landlord has refused to accept any payment on hearing that I was a clergy-man. For the same reason, a drayman, whom I once engaged to remove my furniture from one house to another, resisted all my efforts to induce him to receive a compensation. There are captains of steam-boats who sometimes will carry clergymen at half price, or without any charge. Medical men also prescribe for the ministers of all denominations, and for their families, gratuitously. Such facts deserve to be mentioned, as they help to refute the unfounded accusation sometimes brought against the Americans, as a selfish and mercenary people.

We left Portsmouth on the 7th of May, 1833, in a remarkably agreeable canal-boat, where we were regaled with excellent cheer, and comfortably lodged. The canal is, in many places, extremely narrow ; and in passing through the locks the motion of the boat, as it dashes from side to side, is

very disagreeable. Yet I greatly prefer this mode
of travelling to jolting over American roads in an
American coach; and often, in the long run, it is
equally expeditious.

Our way was principally through deep woods
until we came to Chillicothe, where we arrived on
the morning of the second day. In the afternoon,
we crossed a beautiful aqueduct over the Scioto, and
arrived at Circleville, where I had an opportunity
of revisiting the remarkable antiquities already described. We soon returned to the boat, and proceeded on our way ; but were much retarded by
scarcity of water in the canal. On the following day
we passed through a wild, but romantic country,
and among other objects noticed a huge rock, on
which a colossal human hand, now defaced, had
been sculptured by the ancient Indians. During this
day we approached within eighteen miles of Gambier. In the evening we crossed an aqueduct over
the Walhonding, or Whitewoman River; and on
the morning of the fourth day arrived near Gnaden-
hutten, where the Moravians, or United Brethren,
once had a settlement among the Aborigines. This
settlement was destroyed during the revolutionary
war, and the converts to Christianity were mas-
sacred. At present there are no Indians; but two
congregations of German Moravians still exist.
The Moravians are acknowledged as Episcopalians

by the American Episcopal Church. Having a valid Apostolic succession, their ministers are allowed to preach in our pulpits ; and, in fact, they occasionally exchange with our clergymen. Their numbers are very small, and not rapidly increasing, as their peculiar system tends to exclude them from the rest of the world.

Our canal-boat now stuck fast; and we were obliged to wait for a rise of the water. I went on shore, and entered the nearest farm-house. It proved to be the dwelling of a Swiss, who, with his wife and family, were almost wholly ignorant of the English language. I conversed with him in French, which gave him great satisfaction. He was a Protestant, and had a bible and many religious books in his own tongue. His opinions appeared to be highly Calvinistic ; and he found great fault with the Moravians, who preached, he said, more of the law than the gospel. In the evening, to my great satisfaction, the Moravian clergyman, Mr. Higner, came on board, and took a passage to the next village. The water was now sufficiently deep, and the next morning we moved on again. Mr. Higner was a plain, but apparently amiable man, about thirty years of age. He pointed out to me one of his churches, in the very bosom of the forest. It was a rough log-building ; but he assured me that it contained a good organ. He also showed me the deserted site of Goshen, one of their first settlements, and the tomb of a missionary who lies buried there.

We were now approaching the highest point of the canal between the waters of the Ohio and Lake Erie. We passed another aqueduct in the afternoon, and entered a lake on what is called Portage Summit. Our horses crossed this lake at full trot by means of a long floating bridge. Soon afterwards we arrived at Akron, and immediately descended a steep hill by a long succession of locks resembling a stair-case. The next day, about noon, we arrived at Cleaveland, a flourishing town beautifully situated on Lake Erie, where the canal terminates. We now left our boat, and took passage for Buffalo on board the *Michigan*, a fine schooner of 180 tons. I had crossed the lake four times in steam-boats, and now desired to try a different mode of navigation. The vessel was heavily laden with flour, and there were no passengers besides ourselves. Every thing on board was comfortable, and the crew were civil and obliging. Late at night the wind, which had been contrary, shifted a few points, and enabled us just to weather the pier, and to run into the open lake. But a fearful tempest soon commenced, and before we had advanced seven miles our captain found it necessary to return. The tall lighthouse on Cleaveland Heights, and the smaller light on the pier head, directed our course through the darkness, and in a short time, we were again moored in still water.

The storm continued three days with unabated fury. The lake was one sheet of foam, and the pier at times was almost covered with the billows. At length the wind subsided, and we again put to sea. About thirty vessels, which had been detained with us, sailed at the same time, some for Detroit, but the greater part for Buffalo. They were principally schooners, with one brigantine, and the spectacle was extremely beautiful and animating as they glided together over the clear blue waves. They were all built for rapid sailing, but our schooner ultimately took the lead, and maintained her superiority. We were several times almost entirely out of sight of land, but it was never found necessary to take an observation. We met several steam-boats, crowded with passengers, going west-ward, and were occasionally overtaken by those on their voyage to Buffalo. I distributed a few Testa-ments among our sailors, which were thankfully received and attentively perused. I was told that a gentleman residing, I think, in Buffalo, had appro-priated a sum of money for the purpose of supply-ing all the sailors on Lake Erie with bibles, and that his plan would be shortly carried into effect.

1

On the second day of our voyage I observed a white cloud in the horizon in a north-easterly direction, which, though frequently altering its form, never changed its place. On pointing it out to the captain, I was informed that it was produced by the Falls of Niagara, now thirty miles distant. The clearness of the day gave a peculiar distinctness to this remarkable phenomenon, which I contemplated for hours with emotions bordering on the sublime. The steeples of Buffalo were soon distinguished with the telescope, as they rose one after another above the well-defined boundary of sea and sky. In the evening the whole town was before us at the distance of nine miles. The wind gradually died away; but aided by the current produced by the Niagara river, we continued to approach, until finally we came within the pier, and landed at the wharf. We had sailed 200 miles in thirty-six hours, which is twelve hours more than the time usually employed by the steam-boats in making the same passage. Dark as it was, we immediately embarked on a packet-boat, and commenced a voyage on the New York canal. Early next morning we reached Lockport, and descended the remarkable locks at that flourishing town. We spent Sunday with a friend, and attended the Episcopal Church, where we heard two excellent sermons by the rector.

The next day we embarked again, and on Tuesday arrived at Rochester.   Here are two handsome Episcopal Churches, in the Gothic style of architecture, one of which, St. Paul's, was erected at a cost of about 100,000 dollars, or 22,500*l*.   Of the flourishing condition of the other parish, St. Luke's, an idea may be formed from a recent official statement of its rector.   The report, *for one year*, delivered to the diocesan convention is as follows :

" Baptisms (adult, 27; infant, 85) 112; marriages, 26 ; funerals, 34 ; communicants (died 5 ; removed, 10 ; added, 93), present number, 374 ; bible and catechetical classes, 2 ; confirmed, 75 ; Sunday-school teachers, 50 ; scholars, 300.

COLLECTIONS.

Missionary.	Doll.	Cents.	Doll.	Cents.
Foreign department	226	25		
Domestic	157	..		
Diocesan	100	..		
Spirit of Missions	50	..		
			533	25
Education			270	..
Building of Churches			300	..
Episcopal Fund			10	..
Diocesan Fund			20	25
Charity School of St. Luke's				
Church			250	..
(equal to 312*l.* 7*s.* 6*d.*)			1383	50

" The vestry have taken measures for the erection of a third Episcopal Church, in the northern
part of the city, which, when finished, is to be connected with St. Luke's Church as a chapel, or established as a separate parish in communion with the
Protestant Episcopal Church, as may appear best.
The congregation has two *beneficiaries* ; the one in
the General Theological Seminary, the other at
College."

The above may be considered as a fair specimen
of the doings of Episcopal Churches in the larger
and wealthier towns of the United States.   Probably, the parish of St. Luke's contains not fewer
than twelve or fifteen hundred persons.   The
" collections" mentioned in the report are exclusive
of many private benefactions, communion alms,
repairs and improvements of the Church, wages of
organist and sexton, and a liberal salary to the
rector.   The minister of the parish is indefatigable
and systematic in his exertions, pleasing and gentlemanly in his manners, eloquent as a preacher,
and accomplished as a scholar.

Leaving Rochester the same evening, we reached
Syracuse in two days, and on Friday arrived at
Utica.   In both of the latter towns there are
flourishing Episcopal congregations, and the same
is true of nearly all the towns and villages along the
canal.   Numerous disorders and divisions among

sectarian bodies have, in this region, brought multitudes within the fold of the Church. On Saturday night we landed at Schenectady, having completed our canal voyage of 360 miles. We now took passage in a railroad-car, and were conveyed by horse-power sixteen miles to Albany. Here we spent Sunday, and attended divine service at the two Episcopal Churches. The landlord of the comfortable hotel where we lodged was an Episcopalian. He treated us with the utmost hospitality, and refused to accept any compensation.

After a brief sojourn in Albany, we took a passage for New York on board a steam-boat, and travelled the whole distance, 145 miles, in twelve hours. Our voyage was by day-light, and the magnificent scenery of the Hudson River appeared to the highest advantage. About sun-set we arrived at New York, and put up at a comfortable hotel near the North river. The population of this great city amounts to 230,000, and the number of Episcopal churches is twenty-five. At night the houses were illuminated in honour of President Jackson, then on a visit to the place. The next day we had an opportunity of seeing the President as he passed our hotel in his carriage. He was uncovered, and as he bowed to the multitude, he exhibited a pale and elongated countenance, expressive of determination, and intrepidity. The popu-

lace in the streets shouted " Hurrah for Jackson !"
and threw up their hats and caps; while the females
who thronged the windows waved their handker-
chiefs in compliment to the veteran chieftain. The
following day, June 14th, we left New York for
Newport, Rhode Island, in the steamer *President*.
As the boat passed Castle Garden, at five o'clock,
P.M., we observed an immense concourse of people
assembled in that place of resort, and were informed
that general Jackson was the grand object of attraction. A balloon, in the form of a fish was
floating over the crowd, and making sundry evolu-
tions in obedience to the string of its conductor. A
large balloon soon afterwards ascended, and accompanied our steam-boat for some distance on her
passage. We soon arrived at a narrow strait between the main land and the shore of Long Island.
This is denominated Hell Gate, and was the
terror of the ancient Dutch navigators. The tide
was running through with tremendous rapidity, and
the salt waves were boiling and foaming on every
side. Here and there black rocks lifted their
threatening forms above the billows, and a small
vessel lying upon a stony shelf indicated that the
dangers of the strait were not entirely extinct.
However, we passed this American Charybdis without accident, although at the very moment we were
maintaining a race with a Hartford steamer, and

the utmost power of our engines was put in requisition.

The immense vessels presented a curious spectacle as they shot, now to the right, now to the left, in order to avoid the hidden sources of destruction. We plunged through the mass of foam, and in a few moments were again in smooth water. During the night continued our course through Long Island Sound; and early in the morning, while off Point Judith, we felt the long and heavy swell of the Atlantic ocean. This, although very trying to most of the passengers, was not of long duration; for we soon floated on the quiet surface of Narragansett Bay, and at six o'clock in the morning landed at Newport, having accomplished a voyage of 160 miles in thirteen hours.

Newport is a neat and agreeable town, containing a population of 8000. It is quite old-fashioned in its general appearance, and presents a striking contrast to the cities and villages of the west. Its venerable and aristocratic-looking mansions carry the imagination a century backwards; while the quiet air of the place, and the absence of great commercial bustle, remind the traveller of the smaller watering-places in England. We put up at a very decent hotel kept by a quaker lady. It happened to be the period of a great meeting of the Rhode Island " Friends," and the spacious house was filled with the members of that respectable denomination.

All were clad in their appropriate costume ; and dignified solemnity was the order of the day. In the afternoon I went down to the beach, which is very fine, and affords a delightful promenade.

Five or six handsome carriages, containing fashionable parties, were driving on the sand ; while a number of vessels in the offing added to the animation of the prospect. The heavy Atlantic swell came thundering in, and the distant eastern horizon carried the thoughts to old England in a moment. The next day being Sunday I accompanied the rector of Trinity Church to his place of worship. The exterior and interior of the sacred edifice reminded me strongly of one of the larger village churches in England. The organ was a present from the renowned Dr. Berkeley, Bishop of Cloyne, who is said to have written his " Minute Philosopher" in Rhode Island. It still retains upon its summit the gilt crown which it wore in the days of British supremacy. A second Episcopal parish has been recently organized, denominated Zion Church, and is said to be in a flourishing condition.

On the following day we embarked on board a small steam-boat for Providence, distant about thirty miles. We had a smooth and delightful voyage over Narragansett Bay, and arrived at our destination early in the afternoon. Providence is a large town, containing a population of 17,000, and is beautifully situated at the head of the bay. It contains two handsome Episcopal Churches, St. John's and Grace Church, and the erection of a third is contemplated, in order to meet the increasing demand for our services. The Baptists have been hitherto the prevailing sect in Rhode Island ; but I understood that the Church is now beginning to take the lead throughout the state. We spent the night at Providence, and the next day proceeded by stage, forty miles, to Boston, over good roads, and at the rate of eight miles an hour. We put up at Shepherd's Temperance Hotel, where we found everything extremely comfortable.

Boston greatly resembles one of the best English towns. It contains a large number of handsome and costly edifices, many of which are built of granite ; and in every part of the city perfect cleanliness prevails. An ill-dressed person is seldom to be met in the streets ; while in literature and general education, Boston holds the foremost rank among the cities of America. Besides a handsome and conspicuous state-house, it has a picture-gallery, a fine market-place, an Athenæum, reading-rooms, fifty or sixty places of worship, and various charitable institutions. Its population is about 70,000, and it contains six Episcopal churches.

There are twenty-two Congregational, or Independent places of worship, thirteen of which are in
the hands of Unitarians, the prevailing denomination in Boston.   There is also a Roman Catholic
Cathedral, Boston being the see of a bishop of that
Church.   The Baptists are numerous, but Presbyterians, Methodists, and Quakers, are comparatively few.

It being the time of the Annual Convention of the
Diocese of Massachusetts, I went in the afternoon
to Trinity Church, where I was introduced to the
venerable Bishop Griswold, and many of the clergy
and lay-delegates.   Trinity Church is a massive
stone building, plain, but costly in its decorations,
and, altogether, exhibiting a good specimen of
Bostonian taste and refinement.   St. Paul's is also
an elegant edifice, built after the model of a Grecian
temple, though, unhappily, occupying a confined
position.   It was erected at a cost of at least
100,000 dollars, or 22,500l.   Christ Church is
situated in the northern part of the city.   It was
built before the revolution, and is one of the few
American churches containing a peal of bells.
The remaining Episcopal parishes are of less importance, although they are generally in an improving condition.

The convention opened in Trinity Church on
Wednesday, June 19th, at nine o'clock.   The

bishop took the chair, and the secretary called the roll, when thirty clergymen answered to their names. A committee of four was then appointed to examine the certificates of lay-delegates. The convention then adjourned for divine service at ten o'clock, A.M. Two clergymen officiated, as in the convention described in a former chapter, and the communion was administered by the bishop, assisted by two priests. A secretary and an assistant-secretary were then formally elected. Thirty-three lay-delegates being reported as having the canonical certificates, now came forward and took their seats.

Much difficulty now arose in deciding on the claims of some clergymen and laymen to seats, and several committees were appointed to consider the subject. The convention now adjourned till four o'clock, P.M. When it again assembled the committee reported, and a standing committee was elected by ballot. Considerable delay was produced by a resolution that the votes in this election should be taken by orders. After balloting three times, the standing committee, consisting of three clergymen and three laymen, was finally appointed. A committee of three was now appointed to inquire into and report on the condition of the fund for the support of the episcopate in Massachusetts. After a few unimportant resolutions, the convention adjourned until the next morning. On the second day the convention met, and attended divine service as before. A layman now moved the following resolution, which was passed :—" Resolved, that it be the duty of every clergyman connected with this diocese, with the consent of his parish, if he have one, to hold himself at the disposal of the bishop two Sundays in every year, to be sent to officiate in some parish where there is no settled minister. One-half of his necessary expenses being paid by the Episcopal Missionary Society of the state, and the other half by the parish to which he may be sent, unless such parish will defray the whole expense."

It was now resolved, on the motion of a priest, " That the bishop be requested to set forth a form of prayer to be used in our churches with reference to the disease called the cholera." The convention then proceeded to adopt several amendments to the constitution of the diocese, proposed at the last convention. Four clerical and four lay-delegates to the General Convention were then appointed, and the convention finally adjourned.

During the two days of the session there were meetings of the clergy and others at six o'clock in the morning for prayer and exhortation. There were also regular services and sermons after dark, but the people, generally, did not take that interest

in the proceedings which I had witnessed elsewhere; and very few, besides official persons,
attended the convention. Nor did there appear
among the clergy that hearty fraternal spirit which
characterizes our ministry in the west, and which in
Ohio renders a convention an occasion of real and
high enjoyment. I afterwards learned that unhappy differences of opinion had crippled the
energies of the diocese of Massachusetts, and had
materially checked the increase and proper influence
of the Church. At the period to which I refer,
namely, the year 1833, there were thirty-five
episcopal parishes in the diocese, of which nine
were vacant. The entire number of communicants
little exceeded 1900, the worshippers being probably about 10,000. This is not a sixtieth part
of the population, which, in 1830, amounted to
610,408.

The convention having closed, we proceeded, by
stage, twenty-three miles to Andover. The country
along the road is generally highly cultivated, although the soil is greatly inferior to that of Ohio.
We passed many agreeable villages, all of which
gave indubitable signs of the comfort and refinement of the people, although numerous small places
of worship, standing in the immediate vicinity of
each other, were a melancholy index of the prevalence of religious dissension. Our ride was per-

formed in about four hours, and early in the afternoon we were comfortably established in the "Mansion House," having completed a journey from Portsmouth of 1290 miles.

CHAPTER VIII.

NEW ENGLAND.

———

General description.—Religious divisions.—Unitarianism.—Harvard University.—Andover Seminary.—Episcopacy in New England.—Clerical Associations.—Visit to Bishop Griswold. His residence.—Description of Salem.—Marblehead.—Episcopal Parish near Andover.—Visit to Vermont.—Sleighriding.—Snow in New Hampshire.—Shakers at Lebanon.— Bethel in Vermont.—Episcopal Church.—Its Rector.— Return to Massachusetts.

———

New England is the general name applied to the six states of Maine, New Hampshire, Vermont, Massachusetts, Rhode Island, and Connecticut. It contains a population of little more than two millions, who are justly distinguished above all other Americans, for industry, intelligence, morality, and enterprise. The face of the country is greatly diversified; and the inland portions contain mountains exceeding 6000 feet in elevation. The soil is very inferior to that of the western states, and is best adapted to the production of grass. The raising of cattle, sheep, and hogs, is accordingly a leading pursuit of the New England farmer. Manufactures of various kinds have recently become an abundant source of wealth; while the commerce of the maritime districts extends to every coast. The climate in winter is excessively severe; and the summers are by no means so warm as in Ohio. It is stated, on good authority, that in the inland districts of New England travelling is performed entirely in sleighs during an average of ten weeks in every year. With the exception of frequent cases of consumption, the health of the people is excellent, and many live to a good old age. The fair complexions and ruddy cheeks of the inhabitants appear very striking to a person coming from the west. The neatness and convenience of their dwellings, and their comparative fondness for gardening, are circumstances which strongly prepossess an Englishman in their favour.

In politics, the New Englanders generally act in concert; but in regard to religion the case is far otherwise. The ancient Puritan establishment has been broken into a number of fragments, and although the old Congregational meeting-houses retain their place in almost every village, they have often passed into Unitarian hands, and are frequently rivalled by Episcopal Churches, or by the conventicles of Methodists, Baptists, Universalists, and other sects too numerous to mention. Still with all this division, the New Englanders as a body are a decidedly religious people. It is disreputable for a man to have no religious creed, and there are few who do not give their support to some mode of worship. Sunday is observed as a Sabbath with great strictness and decorum ; and among the aged people many complete specimens of the genuine Puritan are yet to be found. From the first settlement of New England, which took place more than two hundred years since, a universal provision has been made for the instruction of all classes. The country is filled with schools, academies, and colleges, and all parents are obliged by law to give their children an education.

The extension of the Unitarian doctrines among the descendants of the Puritans has been accounted for in various ways. The Unitarian himself ascribes it to the superior acuteness and intelligence of the age. The orthodox Congregationalist attributes it to certain local causes which he asserts have now ceased to exist. The Episcopalian discovers its origin in the same causes which he thinks have produced the apostasies in the Protestant churches of Geneva, France, and Germany, namely, a defective form of church government, and the want of an evangelical liturgy. Universalism, which consists in the denial of future or eternal punishment for the wicked, is a favourite doctrine in New England; and great numbers of the thoughtless and irreligious profess their adherence to this demoralizing delusion. Open infidels also exist, and put forth strenuous exertions to destroy religion altogether. Yet throughout New England generally, as in the rest of the United States, the weight of public sentiment among those professing any faith greatly inclines towards orthodoxy and practical piety.

The principal literary institution in Massachusetts is Harvard University at Cambridge, a venerable foundation possessed of considerable endowments and a valuable library of about fifty thousand volumes. The entire establishment has passed from the hands of the orthodox Congregationalists into those of the Unitarians, and is greatly instrumental in diffusing the tenets of the latter. The orthodox Congregationalists have accordingly seen the necessity of educating elsewhere the young men designed for their ministry, and the seminary at Andover is the result of their combined exertions. It was established in 1807, and is supported by private benefactions. One gentleman now living has contributed at different times 200,000 dollars (45,000*l.*) towards the institution. The endowments already amount to more than a million of dollars (225,000*l*.), and the library contains about 12,000 choice volumes, chiefly imported from Germany. There are five professors, each of whom is supplied with a commodious dwelling, and a salary of from 1200 to 1500 dollars (270*l*. to 337*l*.) The number of students is about 120, who have generally completed their academic studies at some college before entering the Theological Seminary. Besides these, several hundred boys pursue their studies at Andover in a classical school, and in Phillips's Academy, both of which institutions are under the same trustees with the seminary. The course of study in the Theological Institution occupies three years, a knowledge of Hebrew and other languages being necessary to admission. The qualifications of the teachers are undisputed, and the name of professor Stuart is almost as familiar to the divines of England as to those of America. No Episcopal institution of the same kind in the United States has yet attained the eminence of Andover.

Andover is one of the pretty villages for which New England is distinguished. It stands upon a hill about sixteen miles from the sea-coast, and is a cool and delightful situation in the warm season, although greatly exposed to piercing east winds in winter. From the seminary, which occupies the highest elevation, there is an extensive prospect of

a well-cultivated country, and of blue mountains in
the north and west from fifty to eighty miles distant.   Having letters of introduction, we were
kindly received by Professors Stuart, Woods, and
others, and in a few days established ourselves at a
boarding-house near the Seminary. The professors
politely allowed me the use of their valuable library,
and I found abundant and agreeable employment
in the perusal of the neglected writings of the
Greek and Latin fathers.

There being no Episcopal Church in Andover
(although one has since been erected) we often
attended the Seminary Chapel on Sundays, where
the services were conducted according to the usual
plan of the Independents.   While I could not but
lament the imperfect ecclesiastical organization of
these worthy people, I admired the energy of religious principle which developed itself among them.
To say nothing of the strict morality which prevailed among all classes, a number of the students
in the Seminary, possessed of fine talents and education, were preparing to act as missionaries in the
most wretched portions of the world, and the most
unhealthy climates. A regular system of correspondence was maintained with missionaries in every
land, by which means the students procured an
accurate knowledge of the habits, religious opinions,
and temporal condition of nearly all the nations on

the face of the globe. In this manner the peculiar
enterprise which characterizes the New Englanders
is turned to a good account, and made to accomplish noble ends. I cannot forbear stating in connexion with this, that the same spirit has been
manifested at Kenyon College from its first foundation. At the present moment many of its former
students are engaged as missionaries in America,
and one at least is labouring in the great work of
diffusing Christianity and Church principles among
the inhabitants of Africa.

Episcopacy has not yet taken deep root in any
part of New England except Rhode Island and
Connecticut. The former State, with a population
of 100,000, had, in 1835, twenty Episcopal clergymen, or one to every 5000. The latter with 300,000
inhabitants, contained at the same time eighty of
our ministers, or one to 3750; Maine, with a population of more than 400,000, contains only six or
seven; New Hampshire, with nearly 300,000,
about the same number; Massachusetts, with
more than 600,000, had fifty in 1836; and Vermont, with about 300,000, eighteen in 1835. The
dioceses of Connecticut and Vermont are provided
with bishops; but the four remaining dioceses of
New England are to a certain extent united in one
body, denominated the Eastern Diocese, and under
one bishop, the Right Reverend Dr. Griswold.

Each of these dioceses holds its annual convention, and in addition to this, besides the usual delegation to the General Convention, each sends its clergy and lay-deputies to an annual convention of the Eastern Diocese. This singular combination will, however, be dissolved on the demise of the present diocesan; and after that event, in all probability, New England will possess as many bishops as dioceses. Many efforts have been made to increase the efficiency of the Church in this region, some of which have been attended with success. In Rhode Island, monthly meetings of all the clergy, for prayer, preaching, and conversation, are said to have been chiefly instrumental in gaining for the Church the high stand which she at present occupies. In Massachusetts, a similar plan was adopted during my residence in that diocese, and about half the clergy assembled monthly in their respective parishes by rotation. Every clergyman who attended the meetings pledged himself to raise or to contribute annually a sum of money equal to one-tenth of his salary, to be applied to the support of missionaries within the limits of the diocese. By this means a parish was shortly established in the town of New Bedford; and missionaries were sustained in other parts of Massachusetts where it appeared probable that any persons could be induced to connect themselves with the Church. It

is said, that in the diocese to which I refer, these
meetings, or " convocations," as they are called,
have not produced the benefits which were at first
anticipated. Still, the idea is certainly good, and
under proper regulations, by which the promotion
of party measures should be effectually prevented,
similar associations might be followed by the happiest results upon both clergy and laity.

Having received dimissory letters from Bishop
M'Ilvaine, of Ohio, I determined on visiting Bishop
Griswold, in order to ascertain how I could render
myself useful to the Church during my residence at
Andover. Accordingly, taking a gig, I drove sixteen miles to Salem, over an excellent road, and
through a country which, in many respects, reminded me of England. Salem is a town of great
antiquity for America, being upwards of two hundred years old. I found the bishop residing in a
comfortable and handsome dwelling erected in the
fashion of former days. The house had been recently a scene of a dreadful tragedy, the former
occupant, an aged man, having been murdered in
his bed by some young men of the town for the
sake of his property. The premises had consequently much diminished in value, and the bishop
had obtained possession at a comparatively low
rent. The venerable prelate did not hesitate to
occupy the room where the fatal act had been per-

petrated, nor even to sleep on the spot where the blood of the former occupant had been shed. I was informed that the murdered man was an infidel in principle, and that the very day before his death he had commanded his servant to throw away a Bible which he had detected her in the act of reading.

The bishop very kindly pointed out to me some of the remarkable things in Salem. An old house overrun with ivy, and with its gable-end turned towards the street, was formerly the residence of a woman who had been punished for witchcraft. Another venerable mansion was the place where numerous supposed witches had been tried and condemned. These superstitions have long since passed away, and the people of Salem instead of believing too much, have now gone to the opposite extreme of believing too little. Unitarianism is very prevalent, as in Boston, and great numbers of the rich and fashionable are attached to its alluring doctrines. Episcopalians are comparatively few; but they have recently pulled down their old wooden church and erected a handsome stone edifice in its place.

I visited a highly interesting museum, consisting of curiosities obtained by the Salem merchants in all parts of the world during a long succession of years. The East India and China trade was formerly the chief source of wealth to the inhabitants of this ancient town ; but that branch of commerce having been engrossed by other places, the prosperity of Salem has declined. The appearance of the town is English, and the population amounts to 14,000.

Leaving Salem, I went onwards four miles to Marblehead, another venerable town, standing on a rocky promontory projecting into the sea. Here I found an Episcopal church, built in the form of a cross, and about a hundred and twenty years old. The congregation had been reduced very low, and most, if not all, of its male members had deserted it or died. Under these discouraging circumstances the ladies remained stedfast, and for some time supplied the offices of wardens and vestry from among themselves. Their perseverance met with its due reward, and at the time of my visit the parish was in an improving state, and all things had returned to their former channel. At present it may be considered as flourishing, for in 1836, the rector reported to the convention seventy-four communicants, and a hundred and twenty Sunday scholars.

After my return to Andover, my health being greatly improved, I commenced regular services, by the bishop's advice, at a place about seven miles distant from that village. Here an opening for the Church had been made in a singular manner, and not the most desirable. The majority of the Congregational population having determined to remove their meeting-house to a more convenient situation, the minority were displeased and withdrew from the congregation. For some time it was doubtful whether they would engage a Unitarian or a Universalist minister to preach to them; but ultimately they concluded on becoming Episcopalians, and, having drawn up articles of association, they elected a vestry and wardens, and were admitted into union with the Church in Massachusetts. They assembled on Sundays in a school-house to the number of about forty or fifty; but although attentive to the sermon, they generally took slight interest in the worship, and made little use of the Prayer-book. There were many amiable and worthy people among them, and a few decided Episcopalians; but I soon perceived that nothing but time and perseverance, with Divine help, could succeed in establishing the principles of the Church upon so uncongenial a soil.

Having connexions in Vermont whom we desired to visit, I procured the assistance of a gentleman who consented to officiate for me during my absence, and commenced a journey of a hundred and twenty miles in the depth of winter, the best time for travelling in New England. We hired a stout horse and a neat little sleigh adapted for two

persons, and having clad ourselves warmly, and
enveloped ourselves in buffalo skins, we set out by
moonlight, at five o'clock in the morning, and soon
crossed the line between Massachusetts and New
Hampshire. The frost was intensely piercing, but
we were well protected, and our infant daughter
slept quietly beneath the warm covering. Our
horse went forward at a rapid trot, and the collar
of bells round his neck sounded gaily as we glided
over the road on which the snow had fallen to the
depth of about six inches. Occasionally our horse
would break into a gallop of his own accord, and
the loose traces were a sufficient proof that the
sleigh and its occupants were but a small incum-
brance to him. I have often wondered why this
delightful mode of travelling is never practised in
England or Scotland, as the snow continues sufficiently long in both countries to allow of it during
a month or six weeks in almost every winter.
About sunrise we stopped to breakfast and to feed
our horse at a tavern, and immediately afterwards
continued our journey. As our distance from the
sea-coast increased, the snow became deeper, and
the country more hilly. Cedars and other evergreens profusely covered the elevated portions of
the ground, and gave a cheerful air to the desola-
tion of winter. We often met huge sledges drawn
by four horses, conveying pork to Boston, and occa-

sionally a public conveyance which rested on two sledges placed longitudinally for the convenience of turning. The track being extremely narrow, it was often difficult to pass other carriages without driving into the soft untrodden snow which lay on each side of the road three or four feet in depth.

We arrived at Concord, the capital of New Hampshire, about noon, having travelled forty miles. Here we dined, and suffered our horse to rest till three o'clock. We then started again, and continued gradually to ascend as before. The snow was still becoming deeper, and we were several times delayed by pork sledges returning from Boston, the drivers of which refused to make way for us, but continued to jog on a-head at a slow and tedious pace. At length, we managed to overtake them all, and our horse galloped forward as if aware of the approach of night. The snow now began to descend abundantly, and, together with the darkness, soon rendered the track invisible. The horse continued his rapid pace, and I confided in him. Thus we travelled for an hour until we drove up to the door of Shepherd's Hotel, at Salisbury, and gladly alighted, having completed our first day's journey of sixty miles. We found every comfort and accommodation, and the next morning were furnished with warm chocolate at four o'clock. We started when it was very dark, and I soon drove off the track

and upset the sleigh in snow five feet deep. I
speedily righted it, and we proceeded at a cautious
pace until we obtained more light.

We were now among lofty hills, and for many
miles passed through a succession of picturesque
scenery, where uncultivated nature appeared with all
the dreary accompaniments of winter. The branches
of the pine and cedar were weighed down by masses
of snow; valleys were filled to the level of the adjacent
hills, and the tops of trees often barely raised themselves above the shining surface. The broad tracks
of bears were occasionally seen, where these savage
animals had crossed the road in quest of food. The
snow-drifts rose in many places to the height of
eight or ten feet above the road, and we dreaded the
chance of meeting another vehicle. Every eminence
we deemed the last, but were continually disappointed, until about ten o'clock, when we reached
the highest elevation. We now began to descend
at a very rapid rate, and in a short time were
again among the abodes of civilization. We passed
through Lebanon, the residence of a sect denominated " Shakers," a people resembling in some respects the ancient Jewish Essenes. They live in
communities, abstain from matrimony, use dancing
in their worship, and support themselves by agriculture. We continued to descend until about one
o'clock, when we crossed the Connecticut river, and

entered Vermont. We dined and rested at the first inn, and then advanced twenty miles further along White River, to our destination, which we reached about six o'clock, having completed a journey of one hundred and twenty miles in two days. Our horse appeared more lively and active at the termination of his labours than at the commencement.

Bethel, Vermont, is situated among high and picturesque hills, and upon the waters of White River. The population is chiefly agricultural, and much attention is paid to general education. The soil in the neighbourhood is poor, and great numbers of the young and enterprising continually emigrate to the west. The people are much divided in religious opinion, and Universalism has of late extensively prevailed. There is, however, an Episcopal Church and parsonage; and many respectable Episcopal families reside in the vicinity, a large portion of whom are near relations of Bishop Chase. Mr. Thomas Russell, a nephew of the bishop, kept the congregation together for many years by lay-reading, assisted occasionally by the Hon. Dudley Chase, a senator in Congress, and a brother of the bishop. The present rector is a venerable English gentleman, once a strong dissenter, and the minister of an Independent congregation in the mother country. Having arrived in America, he formed an acquaintance with the Episcopal Church, and became convinced that the chief grounds on which the dissenters originally seceded from the Church of England had been fully removed in this country. After due consideration, he was received as a candidate for the ministry, and was ultimately ordained to the priesthood, and elected rector of Christ Church, Bethel. He is a faithful and laborious pastor, and a zealous defender of the Apostolic succession and other distinctive principles of Episcopacy. The Bishop of Vermont, Dr. Hopkins, is an able man and an eloquent preacher. He resides at Barlington, on Lake Champlain, where he is actively engaged in preparing young men for the sacred ministry.

After an agreeable visit we returned homewards. We took a different route from that which we had come, in order to avoid the New Hampshire hills. The way was more circuitous, and ultimately proved to be more fatiguing. We crossed the Connecticut river near Charleston, New Hampshire, and, proceeding by way of Nashua, arrived at our lodgings after a three days' journey.

CHAPTER IX.

THE CHURCH IN HARTFORD, NEW YORK, PHILADELPHIA, &c.

———

Author appointed to a Professorship in Kentucky.—Commences a tour in behalf of the Kentucky Theological Seminary.— Bristol.—Providence.—Church at Newton.—Good-Friday in Hartford.—Church in Hartford.—Washington College.—Its income and resources.—Voyage to New York.—Prosperity of the Diocese of New York.—Bishop's Address.—Episcopacy in New York and Brooklyn.—General Theological Seminary. —Character of the New York Episcopalians.—Journey to Philadelphia.—Diocese of Pennsylvania.—Episcopacy in Philadelphia.—Society in Philadelphia.—Return to Hartford.—Journey to the West.—Kenyon College revisited.—Arrival at Lexington.

———

A FEW weeks after my return, I received a communication from the trustees of a Theological Seminary just organized in the diocese of Kentucky, in which I was informed of my election to the professorship of Sacred Literature in that institution. This was accompanied by a request that I should act for a few weeks as agent for the seminary, in the necessary work of soliciting donations in the Eastern cities towards the collection of a library.

I accepted the appointment, and having resigned my parochial charge, immediately commenced my new employment. I left Andover early in March, 1834, and proceeded to Rhode Island by way of New Bedford. I preached several times in a new and beautiful Gothic church at Bristol, where a large Episcopal congregation is flourishing under the care of a devoted English pastor. Having brought the subject of religion in the West before the people, I proceeded the next day in company with the rector to ask for subscriptions. The pressure in the money market was considerable, on account, it was alleged, of the President's veto on the United States' Bank. Under these circumstances, the collection was not great, but as large as could be expected. I then went to Providence, where I remained two days under the hospitable roof of the rector of Grace Church. I addressed his overflowing congregation in the lecture-room, and endeavoured to impress upon them the necessity of strengthening the hands of the Western Church, and of building up such institutions as promise to become the sources of a wholesome religious influence. In answer to my appeal, I received a pretty good collection, and a few books. The rector of

Grace Church is the author of some well-written publications, which have served to promote the knowledge and love of the Church. Having returned to Andover, I called on the members of my late congregation in the vicinity, and bade them farewell. We then visited the agreeable village of Newton, ten miles west of Boston. Here we found a very neat Episcopal Church, surrounded by a burial-ground, which is quite unusual in America.

The worthy rector occupies a delightful parsonage immediately adjoining. The comfort of his residence, the taste displayed in his garden, and his well-worn pathway, leading to the church, reminded me strongly of former days, and of another country. These English ideas were materially increased when our reverend host informed us that the greater part of the residents in the vicinity were Episcopalians. I preached twice in the church on Sunday, and delivered a lecture on the wants of the West. A collection was made on the spot, which realized as much as could be reasonably expected.

In Boston I visited a few of the leading Episcopalians, and obtained a considerable sum, together with a few old and valuable books. We then proceeded by stage to Hartford, in Connecticut, where we arrived on the evening of March 27. The next day was Good-Friday, and we were agreeably surprised to find every shop closed, and the stillness of Sunday pervading the entire city. When the hour of service arrived, hundreds were seen flocking to their respective houses of worship, Congregationalists, Methodists, and Baptists, not excepted. Inquiring the reason of this unusual observance of the day, I was informed that the Governor of Connecticut had appointed the annual Fast-day, common throughout New England, upon Good-Friday, in order to meet the wishes of Episcopalians. Such an instance of courtesy in a high public functionary deserves notice, as it affords an evidence, not only of the numerical respectability of the Church, but of the liberality shown to it in a region where its services were formerly proscribed.

Hartford is delightfully situated on the river Connecticut, and is one of the most pleasant towns in America, both in regard to society and general appearance. It contains 10,000 inhabitants, 1000 of whom are Episcopalians. It was first settled in 1635, and consequently possesses many interesting memorials of the past. The church, in which Bishop Chase formerly officiated, being of wood, has been sold and removed, and the spot is now occupied by a Roman Catholic congregation. A splendid and substantial Episcopal church, of stone, has been erected in its stead, and presents the noblest specimen of Gothic architecture which I have seen

H

in America. At the time of my visit the tower
was not wholly completed; but when finished, I
should think that the expense could not fall short
of twenty thousand pounds. The interior is in perfect keeping with the exterior ; all is rich and solid,
without any superfluous or trifling decorations. In
one of the windows is a striking painting of the
Ascension, executed, as I was informed, in Italy.
Dr. Brownell, Bishop of Connecticut, resides in
Hartford, but without parochial cure, being sustained by an episcopal fund.   Here also is a literary institution, denominated Washington College,
under the control of Episcopalians.   The college
buildings are handsome, and pleasantly situated at
a short distance from the city, where they command
a delightful prospect of the winding Connecticut
and its fertile valley.

The institution originated in the same necessities
which soon afterwards gave birth to Kenyon College. The number of clergymen in Connecticut
was wholly inadequate to the wants of the vacant
parishes, and it was obvious that they could not be
usefully augmented without laying the literary
foundations, which in all ages have proved the nur-
series of the sacred order. A charter was accordingly obtained from the Connecticut legislature,
conferring ample and liberal privileges, and, agreeably to its provisions, fifty thousand dollars (11,250l.)

were immediately subscribed, chiefly by the inhabitants of Hartford and its vicinity. With the funds thus provided, fifteen acres of land were purchased in the suburbs of the city, suitable buildings were erected, and, in the autumn of 1824, the college commenced operations under the presidency of Bishop Brownell. To the well-directed and indefatigable exertions of that prelate, aided by the munificence of a comparatively small number of individuals, Washington College owes its existence. The first commencement was held in 1827, between which year and 1835, a hundred and fifteen young men, alumni of the college, received the degree of bachelor of arts, one half of whom were subsequently admitted to holy orders. In the autumn of 1831, Bishop Brownell resigned the presidency in order to devote himself more uninterruptedly to his episcopal duties. Dr. Wheaton was immediately elected by the trustees to the vacant situation, and took charge of the institution in the beginning of the following year.

The buildings consist of the college edifice, 150 feet long by 45 in breadth, and four stories high, containing 48 sitting-rooms and dormitories for the officers and students, and a large room for a literary club among the students, denominated " The Parthenon Society." There is also the chapel, 90 feet by 55, and three stories high, which, besides the chapel proper, 50 feet by 35, contains a library and museum, each of the same dimensions; a laboratory, and a room for chemical and philosophical instruments; a " Philosophical Chamber;" a room for the meetings of another club, called the " Athenæum Society;" and four apartments for officers and students. The college edifice and the chapel are both of stone.

The available sources of income to the institution are funds drawing interest, houses and ground-rents yielding a revenue of 1500 dollars (325*l.*), and college-bills, varying in amount with the number of students. To these must be added other resources not yet productive, amounting to 14,000 dollars, or 3250*l.* Still, however, the necessary expenses exceed the income, and appeals are consequently made from time to time to the liberality of the Episcopal public. One professorship has been already endowed with funds by voluntary contribution, amounting to 20,000 dollars, or (4500*l.*), and in 1835, considerable progress had been made towards the establishment of another. The entire amount raised for the institution up to that time was 105,000 dollars, or 23,625*l.* The library contains about 12,000 volumes, many of which were imported from Italy and other parts of Europe through the judicious care of the learned Dr. Jarvis.

The course of studies will be mentioned hereafter. The expenses of a student may be thus estimated:—

	Dollars.
College bills	56
Board (in private families) . .	50 to 70
Fuel, lights, and washing . .	16 .. 30
Use of books, stationery, and furniture .	10 .. 20
Taxes in classes . . .	5 .. 8
Total per annum .	137 .. 184

(or 31*l.* to 41*l.*)

I have been thus particular in my description of Washington College, since it stands in a relation to the Church in the East similar to that which Kenyon College occupies towards the Western Church. It has no Theological Seminary connected with it, the General Theological Seminary of the Church at New York rendering that department unnecessary.

After a short stay at Hartford, I took the steamboat for New York on Saturday, and had a delightful voyage down the Connecticut river. On the way I entered freely into conversation with a gentlemanly and intelligent passenger who proved to be a Unitarian from Massachusetts. Pointing to the Episcopal churches which appeared on both sides of the stream, he remarked, " Ah! if those churches had been in Massachusetts there would have been few Unitarians." He explained himself by expressing his conviction that Unitarians ob-

jected not so much to the doctrine of the Trinity
taught by the Church, as to the unpalatable, and
as he said, the revolting manner in which Christianity was presented by the orthodox congregational
divines.   We were detained by a storm during the
night at the mouth of the river, and did not reach
New York till nine o'clock on Sunday morning. In
the forenoon I went to St. George's, a church under
the pastoral care of Dr. Milnor, and in the afternoon attended a meeting of Sunday-scholars in the
same church.   A great number of children were
present, and the good doctor addressed his youthful
charge with much earnestness and simplicity.   In
the evening I preached at St. Ann's, in Brooklyn,
the congregation of which was formerly under the
care of Mr. M'Ilvaine, the gentleman mentioned in
my first chapter, and now Bishop of Ohio.   Brooklyn is to New York what Southwark is to London,
and contains several Episcopal churches.

I remained in New York a fortnight, and received much kindness from Bishop Onderdonk, the
Rev. Messrs. Jackson and Cutler, and others of
the clergy and laity.   The state of New York contained in 1830 nearly two millions of inhabitants,
and is the first among the United States for commerce, wealth, and population.   Its territory is extensive and fertile, and derives immense benefits
from inland navigation.   The number of Episcopa-

lians is great and rapidly increasing, and the Church still feels the beneficial effects of the zeal, talents, and uncompromising honesty of the late Bishop Hobart. In 1835, the total number of baptisms reported in the diocese was 2626; communicants, 10,630; confirmations, 643; candidates for orders, 46; ordinations, 32; number of clergy, 198; churches consecrated, 8; number of parishes, 215. The total amount of funds reported as raised in the diocese in the same year for various religious objects was 59,939 dollars (13,500*l.*) This is exclusive of the ordinary expenses for clergymen's salaries, building of churches, other current expenditures, and large amounts not reported. In the autumn of 1837, the bishop's address to his diocesan convention exhibited evidences of continued increase and prosperity. During the past year the bishop had ordained nineteen deacons and seventeen priests, in all thirty-six. He had instituted seven rectors and one assistant-minister. He had confirmed 1252 persons on ninety-two occasions; he had consecrated sixteen churches. There were in the diocese fifty-five candidates for holy orders, 239 clergymen, and 232 parish churches. Funds had been raised for the support of the episcopate to the amount of 101,732 dollars, or 22,890*l.*, so that the bishop is now released from all parochial charge.

The bishop made the following remarks in reference to the condition of the diocese.

" It has been to me a source of devout gratitude to God to perceive, in my visits to the congregations of the diocese, through the past year, evidences of a state of general prosperity,—*temporal*, far beyond what I feared would be the consequence of the prevailing temporal distress, but mainly *spiritual*, never, I believe, surpassed in the history of our diocese. Our parishes were never more generally supplied with ministerial services, and our clergy never more actively engaged in their Master's work. The blessed spirit of Christian unity and affection is strongly cherished, and extensively prevalent ; the spirit of true godliness is evidently increasing among us ; and certainly I have no recollection of a year in which the services connected with my visitations have been so uniformly well attended. God be blessed for this happy state of things."

The adjacent cities of New York and Brooklyn contain a population of about a quarter of a million. The entire number of places of worship, including three synagogues is about 150. Of these about thirty are Episcopal churches, thirty-eight Presbyterian, twenty-two Baptist, twenty Methodist, and five Roman Catholic. The number of Roman Catholics is estimated at 50,000. The communicants of the Episcopal Church are not fewer than 6000, and, estimating the worshippers at four times the number of communicants, the Episcopal population cannot be less than 24,000. One of the Episcopal churches is appropriated exclusively to black and coloured persons, and is under the pastoral charge of the Rev. Peter Williams, a respectable clergyman of African descent. Another is occupied by a French congregation, under the care of the Rev. Antoine Verren, who performs the church-service and preaches in his native language. A third is in like manner devoted to the Germans, and promises to be extensively useful. St. George's (Dr. Milnor's) contained 423 communicants in 1835, which was a greater number than any other Episcopal church in the city. The total amount of the benefactions of that congregation during the same year (exclusive of ordinary expenses) was 4055 dollars, or 912*l.* 15*s.* The number of its Sunday-scholars was 425.

The General Theological Seminary consists of handsome and capacious buildings, on the northern part of the city. It derives its name of " General' from the fact that the institution 'is under the control of the entire Church, instead of any particular diocese. It owes its origin and success in a great measure to the exertions of the late eminent Bishop Hobart, a prelate who will ever be regarded with gratitude by the American Church. The board of trustees consists of all the bishops of the Church, one trustee elected by every diocese, and one more in addition for every eight clergymen contained in the same. Besides these, every diocese can appoint a trustee for every 2000 dollars which it contributes to the Seminary, until the sum amounts to 10,000, and then one additional trustee for every 10,000. The bishops of the Church, the secretary and treasurer of the board, and six clerical and six lay gentlemen elected at an annual meeting of the board, constitute a committee which discharges the ordinary business of the institution. There are professorships of Church Polity, of Biblical Learning and Interpretation, of Systematic Divinity, of Oriental and Greek Literature, of Ecclesiastical History, of Pastoral Theology, and of the Evidences of Christianity. At the end of 1837, the number of volumes in the library was 6011, namely, 1085 folios, 953 quartos, and 3973 octavos and smaller volumes. Great and valuable additions of many hundreds have since been made by donations and purchase. As at Andover, there are three classes, and the course of study occupies three years. None can be admitted as students but those who are candidates for the ministry, who can produce good evidence of religious character, and who have passed through some college, or can stand a satisfactory examination in natural and moral philosophy, rhetoric, Latin, Greek, and Hebrew. The annual expenses of a student, exclusive of vacations, are about 106 dollars (24*l.*) for boarding, washing, fuel, and lights. As in other Theological Seminaries in America, there is no charge for room-rent or tuition. The number of students varies from time to time, but on the whole increases rapidly. In June, 1836, there were eighty-seven in the institution, who came from twelve different dioceses. There are twelve scholarships endowed by munificent individuals, four of which amount to 2500 dollars (562*l.*) each; five to 2000 (450*l.*); and one, the North Carolina Scholarship, to 2948 (664*l.*) Several of the professorships have also been endowed, in like manner, with sums amounting to 20,000 (4500*l.*) or 25,000 dollars (5625*l.*) respectively. The funds of the Seminary, all of which have been raised by voluntary contributions and legacies, amount already to more than 100,000 dollars (22,500*l.*)

The New York Episcopalians are pre-eminently distinguished for their disposition to assist all the institutions of the Church. If there is an infant parish established in the West, and unable to erect a place of worship, application is made to New York. If there is a new Episcopal school to be instituted in any part of the country; if there is a church burnt down; if there is a professorship to be endowed, recourse is instantly had to New York as the place where substantial tokens of sympathy may certainly be expected. Applicants after applicants come crowding in, and the fountain of benevolence still remains unexhausted, and even increasing in abundance. I have been credibly informed that many of the wealthiest merchants habitually devote a tenth part of their incomes, and sometimes much more, to religious purposes. Among these liberal people I met with much encouragement; and having effected the object of my visit, I proceeded to Philadelphia.

The journey, which is one of ninety miles, was performed in about seven hours. The first thirty miles were quickly accomplished in a steam-boat. The passengers were then transferred in a few minutes to a long train of railroad-cars, and whirled over the sandy plains of New Jersey at the rate of seventeen miles an hour. Reaching the waters of the Delaware, we were again placed on board a steam-boat, and arrived at Philadelphia in time for an early dinner.

Pennsylvania contained in 1830, a population of 1,348,233, and the state is rapidly advancing in agriculture and manufactures. The number of Episcopal clergymen in Pennsylvania was eighty-eight in the year 1837, and is constantly increasing.

Philadelphia is the second city in the United States, and is beautifully situated between the rivers Delaware and Schuylkill.   It is one of the most regular cities in the world, its streets uniformly crossing each other at right angles.   It is remarkable for its cleanliness, and is adorned with handsome public and private edifices.   Its population is about 200,000, and it contains some valuable public libraries, and many benevolent, scientific, and literary institutions.   There are at present thirty-three Episcopal clergymen in Philadelphia, and twelve churches, one of which, St. Thomas's, is designed for coloured persons.   There are twice as many Presbyterian houses of worship, ten Quaker, and ten Methodist.   Besides these there are nearly forty meeting-houses of various denominations, including six Roman Catholic churches and two synagogues.   The rector of the Episcopal Church of St. Paul's reported, in 1836, 449 communicants, and 480 Sunday-scholars.   The rector of St. Andrew's reported at the same time 361 communicants, 785 Sunday-scholars, and contributions during the past year to missionary and similar purposes amounting to 3506 dollars (789*l*.)   The entire number of Episcopalian worshippers in Philadelphia is probably 12,000 and of communicants, 3000.

Society in Philadelphia is of a high order in

regard to refinement and intelligence. The former ascendancy of Quaker influence still operates in checking the luxuriant growth of fashionable frivolity, and in imparting a tone of quiet and sobriety to the population at large. I met with substantial tokens of encouragement in Philadelphia, and was much assisted by the Rev. Messrs. Van Pelt and Boyd, and others of the clergy and laity. I had the further pleasure of meeting the venerable Bishop White, then in the eighty-seventh year of his age, and his assistant Bishop Onderdonk, brother of the Bishop of New York. The Episcopalians in the city were at that time deeply engaged in establishing a college of their own at Bristol near Philadelphia, yet this did not prevent the manifestation of great interest in the religious improvement of the West. Having remained a week among these estimable people, I took my leave of them and returned to New York, and thence on the following day to Hartford in Connecticut.

While in Hartford we did not omit to visit the Deaf and Dumb Asylum, and other objects of interest and importance. Nor did we neglect to ascend Wadsworth's Tower, a lofty elevation commanding a splendid prospect. But the New York canal being now open we determined to re-commence immediately our westward journey, and, accordingly, having proceeded to New York and

Albany by steam, we advanced to Buffalo by canal, and thence by steam to Cleaveland, Ohio. We then went by land to Gambier, where we found that immense improvements had been effected during our absence of nearly three years. The place had assumed the appearance of a neat New England village, and the comfortable abodes of the inhabitants were surrounded by gardens flourishing in all the verdure of an Ohio spring. Bishop M'Ilvaine inhabited a handsome dwelling, and the professors were chiefly accommodated in comfortable brick mansions in different parts of the village. Kenyon College had been enlarged by the addition of one wing; and Rosse Chapel was advancing towards completion. The appearance of the students had improved considerably, and all things seemed to promise that this favoured spot would hereafter become one of the most delightful places of resort in the western country. At the present time the number of students in the Theological Seminary is twelve, in the college fifty-six, and in the grammar-school ninety-four, making a total of 162. The authorities of the institution have the exclusive control of the lands belonging to the corporation, extending about a mile and a half in each direction from the college buildings. These lands are leased on such conditions and to such persons that no injurious influence from this source can be expected. The annual expenses of a student for tuition, board, room-rent, bedding, washing, fuel, lights, and medical attendance, are, in the grammar-school, 123 dollars (28*l.*) ; in the college, 100 (23*l.*) ; and in the Theological Seminary about 70 (15*l.*) ; no charge being made for instruction or room-rent. The college library contains between 4000 and 5000 volumes. At present the students sustain eighteen Sunday-schools in the vicinity, embracing about 1000 scholars.

After a short stay at Gambier, we proceeded to Newark, where we found a substantial Episcopal church erecting, and had the pleasure of meeting the worthy clergyman lately settled there. Travelling by canal, in two days we reached Portsmouth, where we were kindly treated by my former parishioners. I preached to them several times, and then taking a steam-boat we advanced sixty miles down the Ohio river to Maysville in Kentucky. We then took our seats in the stage-coach, and proceeded sixty-four miles over a delightful road to Lexington, where we arrived about the end of May, having completed a journey from Andover of nearly 1400 miles.

CHAPTER X.

HISTORY OF THE AMERICAN CHURCH.

General remarks.—First Settlement of America by Episcopalians.
—Emigration of numerous Dissenters.—Gradual increase of
the Church.—Opposition of the Puritans.—Cromwell's per-
secution of the Cavaliers.—Church established in Virginia.
—Sustained in New England by the Propagation Society.—
Character of the Clergy.—Disorders ascribed to the want of
Bishops.—Rapid growth of Dissent attributed to the same
cause.—Episcopalians endeavour to obtain Bishops without
success.—Puritans oppose Prelacy.—Ruin consequent on the
Revolution.—Episcopal candidates still ordained in England.
—Origin of the General Convention.—Consecration of Bishop
Seabury.

HAVING in the preceding pages given an account of
the present aspect of the American Church, I proceed to narrate the steps by which, through the
most disheartening trials, it has attained its existing state of comparative prosperity. Its eventful
history is replete with useful instruction to the
established churches of Christendom. Here may

be seen the deplorable effects which follow when the Church is left destitute of adequate Episcopal supervision. Here may be contemplated the ruin which ensues when the Church is suddenly deprived of that legislative aid on which it has been accustomed to rely. And here also it may be perceived that the Church, although cast down by such an event, is not destroyed; that its energies become contracted, its native resources developed, and, finally, its former days of happiness and usefulness more than restored.

The eastern shores of the country, now denominated the United States, were discovered under English auspices, and claimed by the English monarch, as early as the year 1497. Yet in deference to the authority of Pope Alexander VI., who had granted to the Spaniards all the territory more than a hundred leagues west of the Azores, no settlement was attempted prior to the Reformation of the Anglican Church. The feeble minority of Edward VI., distracted with factions, was not a more favourable period to schemes of doubtful utility; and the bigotry of his successor, Mary, disposed her to pay a sacred regard to that grant of the holy see, which vested in her husband Philip an exclusive right to the New World, It was not before the reign of Elizabeth that the English began seriously to form plans of settling colonies in those

H. Caswall inv.

Rev. C. Mayhew said "to the Queen."

RUINS of the FIRST CHURCH ERECTED in AMERICA

Engraved by J. & F. Tavistock, London. 1845.

parts of America which hitherto they had only
visited. Their earliest efforts proved abortive, and
no settlement was permanently established previous
to the reign of James I.

On the 26th of April, 1607, two years before the
settlement of Canada by the French, seven years
before the founding of New York by the Dutch,
and thirteen years before the landing of the Puritans at Plymouth, a small band of colonists disem-
barked on that coast denominated, in honour of
Queen Elizabeth, Virginia. They brought with
them the refined habits of the higher orders
of English society; they were members of the
Church established in the mother country, and they
were accompanied in their adventurous enterprise
by an exemplary clergyman (the Rev. Mr. Hunt),
whom they venerated as a father, and loved as a
friend. Religious considerations had conduced to
their voluntary expatriation. They had been required by their sovereign to provide for the preaching of the gospel among themselves and the neighbouring Indians, and they had been taught to regard their undertaking as a work which, by the
providence of God, might tend " to the glory of his
Divine majesty," and " the propagating of the
Christian religion." The piety of the emigrants,
stimulated by the exhortations of their pastor, led
to the almost immediate erection of an humble

building, dedicated to the service of the Almighty.
On the 14th of May, within three weeks after their
arrival, the colonists partook of the Lord's Supper;
and Virginia commenced her career of civilization
with the most impressive solemnity of the Christian
Church.   Upon a peninsula which projects from
the northern shore of James river, may still be seen
the ruins of the first Episcopal place of worship in
North America; and this, with its surrounding
burial-ground, is now almost the only memorial of
Jamestown.

Such were the fathers of the Church in the
newly-discovered continent; and it may be fairly
presumed that, if all succeeding emigrants had possessed a kindred spirit, the form of religion which
they introduced would have continued to prevail in
the United States until the present day.   But
various causes soon contributed to multiply a very
different class of settlers.   In the year 1614, New
York was colonized by the Dutch, who brought
with them their own confession of faith, and their
Presbyterian form of ecclesiastical government.   In
1620, the Puritans succeeded in colonizing New
England, and in establishing throughout that region
their peculiar doctrines and discipline. The Swedes
and Finns introduced Lutheranism into Delaware
and New Jersey in 1627; Maryland was settled by
Roman Catholics in 1634, and Pennsylvania by the

Society of Friends in 1681. Long before the termination of the seventeenth century, the members of the Church of England in the colonies were greatly exceeded in number by those of other persuasions. Nor was this all. From one denomination they soon experienced a violent and long-continued opposition. At a very early period a few persons withdrew from communion with the Puritans and assembled separately to worship God according to the liturgy of the Church. This was too much to be patiently endured by the dominant majority. The leaders of the party, two brothers, named Brown, were expelled from the colony of Massachusetts and sent home to England. A monument has been erected to their memory in St. Peter's Church, at Salem, which describes these worthy Episcopalians as the first champions of religious liberty in America. Heavy fines were inflicted on those who took part in the ceremonies of the Church; severe laws were enacted against "the observance of any such day as Christmas or the like," and (to use the words of an eminent New England jurist) "an Inquisition existed in substance, with a full share of its terrors and its violence."

As the country increased in population, the Church slowly advanced. Even in New England a few churches were at length established, and, under a load of obloquy, gradually gathered strength. New York having fallen into the hands of the English, a church was erected in that city. Philadelphia, under the tolerant influence of the Friends, was blessed with an Episcopal place of worship; and in Maryland several congregations were organized.

The Cavaliers and their descendants fled to Virginia during the persecutions of Cromwell's government; and in that country the Church maintained undisputed pre-eminence for nearly a century, notwithstanding the efforts of missionaries from New England to produce a defection.

Up to the period of the revolutionary war, the number of Episcopalians was very small, except in the southern colonies. In Virginia and Maryland a provision for the maintenance of the clergy was made by law, the territory was divided into parishes, churches were built, and glebes were attached. Here the Church possessed the authority, and commanded the respect, of a national establishment. But in the provinces north and east of Maryland the congregations were few and far between, and generally confined to some of the larger towns. It is believed that the only considerable endowment by the English government in favour of the Church in the northern colonies, was a grant of lands to Trinity Church, New York. These have become

1

immensely valuable, and are still retained by the original corporation, notwithstanding many efforts to procure an alienation. During the early part of the eighteenth century, a zealous friend was raised up to the Church in the English " Society for Propagating the Gospel in Foreign Parts." By means of this excellent institution, the greater part of the clergy resident in New England, New York, Pennsylvania, and New Jersey, were maintained, and the number of congregations considerably increased. To this society a very liberal grant was made by the colonial government, which under equitable management, might have sufficed to support the institutions of the Church to an indefinite extent. The territory of Vermont, when first surveyed, was divided into townships containing thirty-six square miles each, a hundred and fourteen of which were granted by Governor Wentworth, of New Hampshire, an Episcopalian. In each of these, one right of land, containing usually 330 acres, was reserved for the first settled minister, one right as a glebe for the Church of England, and one right for the Propagation Society. But the surveyors being unfriendly to Episcopacy, the lots reserved for the society, and for the glebes, were often located by them within the same identical spot, and often on mountains, rocks or morasses; in consequence of which, the grant promoted but little the cause which it was designed to subserve.

It is obviously important that something should be said in regard to the *character* of the clergy previous to the Revolution. It is the more desirable on account of the many misapprehensions which exist in regard to this subject. Let it then be remarked, that the Missionaries of the Propagation Society were generally men of holy, self-denying lives, and of blameless reputation. The venerable association, just mentioned, issued a notice in 1735 and subsequently, in which it besought those concerned, to recommend no man as a missionary, "but with a sincere regard to the honour of Almighty God, and our blessed Saviour." In the same circular the Society expressed its persuasion that any clergyman in America who had disgraced his character, must have gone thither without its knowledge, and concluded by promising to dismiss any one in its employment, against whom a just complaint could be preferred. It is true that many disorders prevailed in those districts, where the law, by assigning a considerable stipend to clergymen, without placing them under any ecclesiastical controul, held out an allurement to the unprincipled. And yet, even under these circumstances, the clergy and their people were free from many imputations

which must for ever attach to the memory of the
Puritans their chief opponents. The absurd superstitions which flourished in the north found an uncongenial soil in the southern colonies, and the
terrific excitements in regard to witchcraft had
little nourishment where the mild and scriptural
worship of the Church prevailed. The severe laws
of Virginia against dissent carry an appearance of
persecution; but these laws were seldom enforced,
and, in fact, were little more than a nullity.

The disorders which actually existed should in
all candour be traced to their proper source, the
want of an efficient episcopal supervision. This
destitution, again, should be assigned to its principal cause, namely, the opposition of the numerous
and powerful bodies of American Dissenters. For
though the Bishop of London was considered as the
diocesan of the American Episcopal churches, his
authority could not be effectually exerted at so
great a distance, and unworthy clergymen could
not be removed without serious difficulty. Other
causes contributed to render the appointment of a
colonial bishop necessary to the prosperity of the
Church. The only resources for a duly authorized
ministry were in emigration from the mother country, and in sending candidates to that country for
orders. The first could not be the channel of a
respectable permanent supply, and the second was

expensive and dangerous, many having perished on the ocean, or died by sickness, in their efforts to obtain ordination. The Church, too, was of necessity presented to the people in an imperfect form, the rite of confirmation being unpractised, and almost unknown. It was undoubtedly owing to the successful opposition of the Dissenters to the appointment of an American bishop, that, about the commencement of the eighteenth century, Baptists, Presbyterians, and others, obtained a footing in the Southern colonies. They availed themselves of all the unavoidable disorders among Episcopalians ; they multiplied their preachers as they were needed, and their congregations increased with rapidity and vigour.

Sensible of their necessities the adherents to the Church had taken measures to obtain an episcopate as early as the reign of Charles II., and had almost attained their object. The subject was agitated in following years, until the death of Queen Anne after many delays put a stop for a considerable time to all proceedings of this description. Still the poor neglected Church continued to advance, and several distinguished Dissenters were at different periods added to its ranks. Mr. Timothy Cutler, rector of Yale College in Connecticut, and Mr. Samuel Johnson, a tutor in the same institution, both congregational ministers, became convinced, after indefatigable study, that their ordination was invalid ; and shortly afterwards connected themselves with the Church of England. Being joined by several other persons of note, their defection was a great shock to the existing establishment. They proceeded to England for ordination, and on their return in 1723, Dr. Cutler was settled as pastor of Christ church in Boston, and Mr. Johnson as a missionary of the Propagation Society in Connecticut. In that colony the latter was for some time the only episcopal clergyman ; but distinguishing himself by his controversies in behalf of the Church, he was appointed, in 1754, President of King's College, (now Columbia) New York. By his writings, he succeeded in awakening general attention to the question of Episcopacy ; and about the year 1763 the applications for a bishop were renewed. At this, the dissidents from the Church in New England took alarm, and strongly resisted the introduction of the only means by which Episcopalians could fully practise the rites which their faith demanded. They also contended that the Propagation Society transcended its powers when it authorized its missionaries to settle in villages and sea-ports of New Hampshire, Connecticut, and Massachusetts. Dr. Mayhew, a congregational preacher in Boston, was the leader of this controversy in behalf of the Dissenters ; while a talented advocate for the Church was found in the Rev. East Apthorp, a missionary at Cambridge, Massachusetts, and afterwards a prebend of Finsbury, in England. Several others engaged in this discussion, among whom was Archbishop Secker, a devoted friend of the colonial Church.

The efforts to procure an episcopate continued to prove unsuccessful as before. Yet so obviously was it necessary, that, notwithstanding repeated discouragements, within ten years after the controversy with Mayhew another attempt was made, in the course of which the Rev. Dr. Chandler, of New Jersey, appealed to the public in favour of this great object. But the times were unpropitious. Difficulties had arisen between the colonies and the mother country ; and many of those who had previously desired an American episcopacy, now feared lest it should be made an instrument of accomplishing the political designs of Great Britain. Some of the clergy themselves were not free from this apprehension, and four ministers of the Establishment in Virginia actually protested against Dr. Chandler's plan, and received for their protest the thanks of the colonial government. The war of the revolution commenced shortly afterwards, and amid the clash of civil strife the whole subject was for a time forgotten.

At the commencement of the struggle between the colonies and the mother country, the condition of the Church, although far from flourishing, was more promising than it had been at any earlier period. In Virginia the number of clergy was above a hundred; in Maryland and the southern provinces it probably exceeded fifty; and in the colonies to the northward and eastward of Maryland it was not much less than eighty. As yet, however, the ministrations of religion were confined to the districts immediately bordering on the sea-coast; for the interior of the continent remained a pathless wilderness, tenanted only by savage beasts or still more savage men. But when the colonies were actually separated from Great Britain, the destruction of the Church appeared almost inevitable, notwithstanding the fact that the great Washington himself was an Episcopalian. A few years nearly overthrew the work which had been slowly carried forward by the exertions of a century and a half; and, had not Omnipotence interposed, the ruin would have been complete. The fostering hand to which the American Church owed a long continuance of care and protection, was withdrawn; and the Propagation Society no longer rendered its accustomed aid. Many of the clergy were thus left entirely destitute, and some were obliged to betake themselves to secular employments for support. In the northern states the clergy generally declined officiating, on the ground of their ecclesiastical

174 HISTORY OF

connection with the liturgy of the Church of England. In the south, many worthy ministers, conceiving themselves bound by oath to support the government of Great Britain, refused to enter upon a new allegiance, and quitted the country. By an unjust decision, the lands possessed by the Propagation Society in Vermont were confiscated, and applied to the purposes of education. An equally unconstitutional sentence, obtained through the united efforts of sectarians and infidels, ultimately despoiled the Church in Virginia of its glebes and houses of prayer; while, in addition to all these calamities, Episcopalians in general became subject to unmerited political prejudices. Most of their churches were destitute of worshippers; their clergy had departed, or were deprived of maintenance; no centre of unity remained, and no ecclesiastical government existed.

Yet even then the members of the Church did not despair. They recollected the promise of their Divine Head, and felt assured that the gates of hell could never entirely prevail against the principles which they professed. Accordingly, soon after the cessation of hostilities, several gentlemen embarked for England, and applied to Dr. Lowth then Bishop of London, for ordination as deacons and priests. The bishop could not ordain them without requiring an oath of allegiance inconsistent with their American citizenship, and found it necessary to apply for an act of parliament allowing him to dispense with requisitions of this description. In the meantime, the church of Denmark manifested a most gratifying and fraternal readiness to supply the wants of America. The bishops of that kingdom declared their willingness to ordain Episcopalian candidates, on the condition of their subscribing to those articles of the Church of England which are purely theological. This well-intended offer was for good reasons declined. The British parliament consented to the request of Bishop Lowth, and the candidates obtained their commission from that episcopate under which the American Churches had been planted.

The scattered condition of the Church now rendered it essential that some bond of union should be created to prevent the adoption of varying measures, and to secure the unity of the congregations and clergy that remained. Proceedings to this effect were accordingly commenced in Connecticut and Maryland in 1783, in Pennsylvania and in Massachusetts in 1784, which resulted in the framing of various articles of agreement among the respective clergy of these several states. But the first step towards the formation of a collective body of the Church in the United States was taken in May, 1784, by the distinguished Dr. White and a few other clerical gentlemen of New York, New Jersey, and Pennsylvania, at a meeting held in reference to a society for the relief of the widows and children of deceased clergymen. On this occasion it was determined to procure a larger assembly for the purpose of agreeing on some general principles of union. Such a meeting was accordingly held in New York, on the fifth of the ensuing October, and although the members composing it were not vested with powers adequate to the present exigence, they happily laid down a few general principles to be recommended to Episcopalians in the respective states as the ground on which a future ecclesiastical government should be established. These principles acknowledged Episcopacy and the Book of Common Prayer, and provided for a representative body of the Church, consisting of clergy and laity, who were to vote as distinct orders. It was also recommended to the Church in the several states, that clerical and lay deputies should be sent to a meeting appointed in Philadelphia on the 27th of September in the following year.

In the meantime, the Rev. Samuel Seabury, formerly a missionary on Long Island, had been elected to the episcopate by the independent action of the clergy in Connecticut, and had proceeded to England for consecration. Not meeting with success in that country, he had applied to the bishops in Scotland, and had there received the Apostolic commission. In the beginning of the summer of 1785, he returned to America, and entered on the exercise of his new function. Thus, at length, an American bishop had been obtained, and the Church, in one state, appeared in a complete form. But what was necessary in Connecticut was equally necessary in other regions, and although Episcopalians generally respected the new bishop, and few alleged any thing against the validity of his episcopacy, they still thought it most proper to direct their views towards that country from which they derived their origin as a people and as a Church.

CHAPTER XI.

THE SAME SUBJECT CONTINUED.

First General Convention.—Various opinions in the Church.—Influence of Dr. White.—Prayer-book altered.—Address to the English Prelates.—Reply from the English Archbishops.—Election and Consecration of two American Bishops.—Constitution of the Church revised.—Dr. Coke proposes a re-union of the Methodists with the Church.—Assistant Bishops appointed.—The House of Bishops acquires the right of negative.—Increase of the Church.—Western country nearly lost to the Church.—Diocese of Vermont organized.—General Theological Seminary and Washington College instituted. —Bishop Chase and others consecrated.—The Church quadruples its numbers in twenty-four years.—Missionary Society established.—Alexandria Seminary, Kenyon College, and Kentucky Seminary instituted.—General Convention of 1835. —Missionary Bishops.—Death of Bishop White.—His character.

On the 25th of September, 1785, the first General Convention was held in the city of Philadelphia. Seven states were represented, namely, New York, New Jersey, Pennsylvania, Delaware, Maryland, Virginia, and South Carolina. The Church had been thrown entirely on its own resources, like an infant deprived of the sympathy and guidance of a careful parent. It might, therefore, be expected that many crude opinions would exhibit themselves in this assembly, and that little unanimity would prevail in regard to the course necessary to be taken in future. The former was actually realized; the latter was providentially averted. In the north, the ideas of Churchmen on the subject of Episcopacy were generally correct and well defined, by reason of their frequent collisions with the dominant body of congregational dissenters. In the south, where church government had not been so much a subject of controversy, many singular views existed. In Maryland and elsewhere, the doctrine was held by Episcopalians, that a presbyter can perform all the functions of a bishop, excepting confirmation and ordination. The opinion was common among those of the middle states that the laity possessed a right to sit in convention with the clergy. This was defended as a natural consequence of the principle of following the Church of England ; and it was pleaded that in no other way could a substitute be provided for the parliamentary sanction to legislative acts of power. But on the other hand, it was maintained that the admission of the laity to an ecclesiastical synod was incongruous with every idea of episcopal government. This latter sentiment was held by Bishop Seabury and his clergy,

in common with the Episcopal Church of Scotland.
Some again were anxious to defer all measures towards the organization of the Church until a regular episcopate should have been obtained ; while
others were ready to establish an ecclesiastical
system, under the control of presbyters, until
bishops could be procured.

The moderate and conciliatory measures of Dr.
White, the Cranmer of the American Church,
and then president of the convention, contributed
much towards the settlement of difficulties, and
the first convention was concluded with a degree
of harmony greater than, under existing circumstances, could have been anticipated. During
this convention the articles of union were ratified
which had been proposed in the informal meeting
at New York. An ecclesiastical constitution was
likewise framed which provided for a convention
of the Church in each state, and also for a triennial General Convention, consisting of a clerical
and lay deputation from the several states. Considerable alterations in the Prayer-book were also
proposed, of which some were in accommodation
to the new government of the country ; others
were, perhaps, expedient as improvements, and a
few not only unnecessary, but altogether improper.
Finally, a document was drawn up by unanimous
consent, addressed to the English archbishops and

bishops, acknowledging the past favours received from them through the Propagation Society, declaring the desire of the convention to perpetuate the principles of the Church of England, and requesting the prelates to consecrate to the episcopate those persons who should be sent with that view from America.

This address was forwarded to the Archbishop of Canterbury through the American minister, John Adams, afterwards President of the United States. Early in 1786, an answer was received, signed by the two archbishops and eighteen of the twenty-four bishops of England, in which they declared their wish to comply with the request, but wisely stated that they must delay measures to that effect until they should have become fully acquainted with the alterations proposed by the convention. A letter soon afterwards arrived from the two archbishops, expressing their disapproval of several alterations, but stating that they expected to obtain an act of parliament, under which, if satisfaction should be given, they would feel at liberty to consecrate for America.

In consequence of the receipt of these communications, two special General Conventions were held in 1786, in the course of which, the constitution framed in the preceding year was adopted with some amendments, a second address was directed to

the English prelates, and several objectionable
alterations in the Prayer-book were removed. It
also appeared that Dr. Provoost had been duly
elected to the episcopate for New York; Dr. White,
for Pennsylvania; and Dr. Griffith, for Virginia.
The two former embarked for England in November in the same year, and on the 4th of February,
1787, were consecrated, according to an act of parliament, by Dr. Moore, Archbishop of Canterbury,
and soon afterwards returned to America. Dr.
Griffith was prevented by domestic circumstances
from prosecuting his intended voyage, and tendered
his resignation to the convention of Virginia by
which he had been elected.

The triennial convention assembled again in
1789, and was followed by a special convention in
the same year. During these sessions the constitution formed in 1786 was reviewed and new
modelled. The principal feature now given to it
was a distribution into two houses, one consisting
of the bishops, and the other of the clerical and lay
deputies. Bishop Seabury and the northern
clergy attended on this occasion, and a permanent
union of the Church was happily consummated.
The Prayer-book was arranged as it now stands
with the exception of a few minor alterations, and
the addition of some occasional services. The
canons were also established in a form which still

1

continues substantially the same; and the year 1789 must ever be considered an important era in the history of the Church.

In the year 1790, the Rev. Dr. Madison of Virginia, was consecrated bishop of that diocese, by the archbishop of Canterbury. The canonical number of bishops necessary for transmitting the Apostolic succession being now complete, Dr. Claggett was consecrated in New York as Bishop of Maryland; in Philadelphia, Dr. Smith, of South Carolina, and Dr. Bass, of Massachusetts; and in New Haven, Dr. Jarvis, of Connecticut, after the decease of Dr. Seabury, in 1796. In the meantime, a circumstance occurred which deserves to be recorded. In 1791, Bishop White received a letter from Dr. Coke, a superintendent of the Methodist connexion in America, proposing a re-union between that society and the Church. Dr. Coke stated his motive in this proposal to be an apprehension that he had gone further in the separation than Mr. Wesley had designed. Mr. Wesley himself, he was sure, went further than he would have gone, if he had foreseen some events which followed. Dr. Coke's plan unfortunately was impracticable; and, although a prudent answer was returned by Bishop White, the negotiation was soon broken off.

At the termination of the eighteenth century, the Church was completely organized, and was gradually recovering from the tremendous shock sustained during the revolution. Its members had learned in some measure to rely on their own resources, and its ministers were supported in some instances comfortably, by the voluntary contributions of their flocks. Yet the number of clergymen little exceeded two hundred; and these were widely scattered through the country bordering on the Atlantic. No great enterprises were undertaken, because a hard struggle was necessary to maintain the ground already occupied. It was reserved for another century to witness the rapid development of the energies of the Church, and the consequent increase of its numbers, piety, and zeal.

At the General Convention of 1802, a question was raised which created much discussion. Bishop Provoost of New York informed the house of bishops that, on account of ill health and domestic affliction, he had resigned his episcopal jurisdiction at the last meeting of his diocesan convention. It appeared also, that in consequence of this resignation, another person had been elected to succeed to the episcopate. The house of bishops, doubting the propriety of sanctioning resignations within their body, declined acting to that effect, but consented to consecrate an assistant bishop who might discharge any episcopal duties with the consent of his senior prelate. Conformably with a canon passed to this effect, several assistants have at different times been consecrated, who have succeeded to the entire episcopate on the demise of the senior diocesan.

In the same convention, after repeated debates, the thirty-nine articles of the Church of England were for the first time ratified, without even the change of their obsolete diction.

At the General Convention in 1808, the house of bishops acquired the full power of a negative upon the acts of the lower house. Previous to this, four-fifths of the clerical and lay delegates could accomplish any measure without the concurrence of the superior body. On this occasion, the version of the Psalter by Tate and Brady was sanctioned, and a number of hymns were added to the collection already in use. According to a canon of the last convention, a pastoral letter from the house of bishops to the members of the Church was drawn up by them, and read to the house of clerical and lay deputies.

The period had now arrived when the Church was to rise from its depressed condition, and to occupy a higher stand in the cause of religion. The greater part of those clergymen who had entered its ministry, supported by the laws or the beneficence of England, had now quitted the stage, and their places had been supplied by those who were not

only natives of America, but who had been trained
up under the influence of a Church relying solely
upon its own resources. The scepticism which had
been imported from France during the latter part
of the preceding century, was now rapidly giving
way throughout the continent, and many persons of
powerful intellect and devoted spirit were added to
the ranks of the ministry. In 1811, the number
of bishops was eight, two of whom were coadjutors
to the aged diocesan of New York. The clergy
were divided nearly in the following proportion:—
In the Eastern diocese (composed of Massachusetts, Rhode Island, Vermont, and New Hampshire), fifteen; in Connecticut, thirty; in New
York, forty-four; in New Jersey, seventeen; in
Pennsylvania, twenty; in Delaware, five; in Maryland, thirty-five; in Virginia, fifty; in South Carolina, fifteen; in Georgia, one.

About the same period, Dr. Bowden, of New
York, distinguished himself as a controversialist in
behalf of Episcopacy, and, like Dr. Johnson in the
preceding century, attracted much attention to that
neglected and unpopular subject.

The region west of the Alleghany mountains was
now rapidly increasing in population, and the necessity of supplying it with a valid ministry began to
appear. Various dissenting bodies had already
pre-occupied the ground to a considerable extent,

and only two or three clergymen of the Church
were to be found in the immense valley watered by
the Mississippi and its tributary streams. In 1811,
a letter was addressed to Bishop White by the
Rev. Joseph Doddridge, a clergyman settled near
the Ohio river, urging the appointment of a missionary bishop for the new country in which he
resided. The weakness of the Church with other
circumstances prevented immediate action upon
this important point; and the opportunity afforded
by the infancy of society in those vast regions was
for ever lost. The injury formerly experienced
through the want of an episcopate in the eastern
parts of the country was now more than realized in
the west, and vast numbers of the inhabitants
became the prey of cold indifference or enthusiastic
delusion.

About the same time the Church in Vermont
was organized, and admitted into union with the
General Convention. Measures were also taken to
regain to the Church, by a legal process, the lands
formerly held by the Propagation Society in that
state. These measures were delayed by the war
with Great Britain; but eventually, after a protracted litigation, they proved successful, and a
considerable portion of the property was recovered.

Hitherto all persons desirous of preparing for
the ministry of the Church had laboured under

great disadvantages. Few colleges were under episcopal control, and even there, theological education was neglected. The candidates were, therefore, compelled to pursue their studies under the direction of clergymen encumbered with parochial duties, or to resort to the institutions of dissenting denominations. Accordingly, about the year 1814, Bishop Hobart of New York issued proposals for the establishment of a divinity-school under the superintendence of himself and his successors. The deputies to the General Convention from South Carolina were also instructed by their constituents to propose a similar scheme. The subject was for some time under consideration; and finally, in 1817, it was resolved to establish a theological seminary at New York for the benefit of the entire Church, and under its control. In the same year the diocese of North Carolina was admitted into union with the General Convention, and measures were adopted to organize the Church in Ohio. The Rev. Philander Chase was consecrated to the episcopate of the latter diocese in 1819, and the Rev. J. S. Ravenscroft to that of the former in 1823. New Jersey had been provided with a bishop, the Rev. Dr. Croes, as early as 1815 ; and from this period, the advancement of the Church proceeded with almost unexampled rapidity. In 1814, the number of clergy was little more than 240, but in the course of twenty-four years, it has quadrupled itself, and the increase of congregations has been in an equal proportion.

The destitute state of the western country led to the formation of a missionary association in Pennsylvania about the year 1818. By this association, several missionaries were sustained in Pennsylvania and Ohio, and some churches were planted. In a few years this society assumed a more extended form, and, under the auspices of the General Convention, became known as the " Domestic and Foreign Missionary Society of the Protestant Episcopal Church." For many years its operations were extremely limited, and it was not until 1830 that it produced any considerable benefit. In the mean time, Washington College was instituted, the General Theological Seminary received a constant accession of students, and a second institution of the same kind was established at Alexandria, near Washington, designed especially to promote the interests of religion in Virginia and the other southern dioceses. Bishop Chase, as has been already stated, proceeded to England in 1824, in the hope of obtaining assistance towards the foundation of a similar institution in Ohio. His efforts, it is known, were successful, and in 1831 he had the satisfaction of beholding nearly 200 inmates of " Kenyon College and Theological

Seminary." Unhappy difficulties however having arisen with the trustees and professors of the Institution, he determined on resigning his episcopal jurisdiction in Ohio, together with the presidency of the Institution, which he had been instrumental in founding. The General Convention of 1832, after a protracted debate, concluded on legalizing his resignation, and the Rev. Dr. M'Ilvaine was consecrated to the vacant episcopate. At the present time, 1838, the number of clergy in Ohio is between fifty and sixty. Kenyon College has lately received from England, through Bishop M'Ilvaine, further donations amounting to about 12,000 dollars, besides many valuable books. In Kentucky and Tennessee, the increase of the Church has been as rapid as in Ohio. In 1825 there was but one officiating clergyman in the first mentioned state. In 1832 it contained eight clergymen, and in the same year the Rev. Mr. Smith of Lexington was consecrated bishop. In 1834 the " Theological Seminary of the Diocese of Kentucky" was incorporated; in the following year it received great pecuniary assistance from eastern Episcopalians, and in 1836 contained eighteen students. The clergy in the diocese now amount to twenty-one. So late as 1832 there were but three clergymen in Tennessee. There are now in that diocese about twelve, with Bishop Otey at their head, and a theological seminary in connection with a college is already in contemplation.

In the eastern states the progress of the Church has also been rapid and steady. The Church in Vermont had become in 1832 sufficiently strong to separate from the eastern diocese of which it had formed a part, and, accordingly, in the same year the Rev. Dr. Hopkins was elected and consecrated its bishop. It is highly probable, as I have mentioned in a former chapter, that before many years, Massachusetts, Rhode Island, New Hampshire and Maine will be provided with their respective prelates.

The General Convention of 1835 must be regarded as one of the most important events in the history of the Church. Bishop Chase was recognised as the head of the new diocese of Illinois. The Domestic and Foreign Missionary Society, the operations of which had now become extensive, ceased to exist as a separate body, and the Church, assuming its responsibilities, stood forth as one grand missionary association. It was resolved that missionary bishops should be provided for the states and territories destitute of episcopal supervision, and ultimately for the stations in heathen lands occupied by the American Church. The Rev. Dr. Hawks was accordingly appointed by the House of Bishops to the episcopate of Louisiana, Arkansas,

1

and Florida ; and the Rev. Dr. Kemper to that of
Missouri and Indiana. The former gentleman
declined his appointment. The latter was consecrated at Philadelphia, and immediately proceeded
to his destination.

The wisdom of the House of Bishops in the
nomination of Dr. Kemper has been abundantly
proved. The members of the Episcopal communion in the remotest parts of the west have been
strengthened and encouraged, and their numbers
have greatly increased. At the time of Bishop
Kemper's consecration there was but one clergyman in Indiana. Now there are eight, whose reports indicate a continued and rapid increase in
their respective congregations. The same is true
in regard to Missouri, where a prospect of future
prosperity gladdens the friends of the Church.
The indefatigable missionary bishop occasionally
extends his travels to remoter regions, sometimes
visiting the Indians of the western wilds, and sometimes the more refined population of Louisiana,
Mississippi, Arkansas, Alabama, and Florida. A
fund of twenty thousand dollars has been contributed in New York towards the establishment of a
college in Missouri under the superintendence of
Dr. Kemper.

In Michigan, an episcopal diocese has in two
years risen into great respectability and influence

under the charge of the active and zealous Bishop
M'Coskry. In Florida a diocese has been organized during the present year under promising
circumstances. In Virginia, the Church has nearly
recovered her former standing, and under eighty-
four faithful pastors, with the superintendence of
two excellent bishops, is a blessing to the country.
The course of events throughout the American
Church seems to promise that the neglect and de-
vastation of former years will yet be repaired, and
that the experience of the past will teach wisdom
for the future.

This narrative cannot be more appropriately
closed, than by recording an event still fresh in
the memory of American Episcopalians. Bishop
White, the good and great prelate, whose character
this portion of the Catholic Church will ever regard with reverence, died on the 17th of July
1836, in the eighty-ninth year of his age, the sixty-
sixth of his ministry, and the fiftieth of his episcopate. He was raised up by Providence at a crisis
when a person of his description was pre-eminently
necessary. Steady and sober from his youth, he
was prepared to advise in time of peril and excitement. Conciliatory in his measures, he was a man
perfectly adapted to the promotion of harmony, at
a time when diversity of opinions and high claims
respecting the independence of dioceses, threatened

K

to rend the Church in pieces. Under the influence of his blended meekness and wisdom, objections to the Liturgy and Articles melted away ; and many a root of bitterness was plucked up and allowed to die. The General Convention is the offspring of his prudence and brotherly love ; and from its first organization till the last meeting before his death, he was always at hand with his pacific counsels, superior to paltry manœuvre and selfish policy. His humility and piety were evinced more by actions than by words ; and he always acted on the maxim, that for any man to assume dictatorial airs, on the ground of ecclesiastical distinction, is in America most unwise, and in every country most unbecoming. Hence while he lived, he was venerated as a patriarch and loved as a man, and when he died, the event was regarded by the Church as an irreparable loss, and by the nation as a public calamity.

CHAPTER XII.

EDUCATION.

———

———

I ARRIVED at Lexington in May, 1834, and immediately entered upon my duties as professor of
Sacred Literature in the Theological Seminary of
the diocese of Kentucky.   It is my object in the
present chapter to present the reader with a concise view of education in America, and of theological education in particular.

If recent statistical reports may be credited, the
common rudiments of education are more generally
diffused in the United States than in England, but
less generally than in Prussia.   Yet between the

K 2

several states there is a great difference in regard
to the means as well as the diffusion of education.
In Massachusetts, for example, the laws have made
ample provision for the instruction of young persons.
Every district and every village in the state possesses the means of regular instruction in the
elementary branches, and, where there is wealth to
justify it, the further advantage of schools competent to the preparation of boys for college. The
money to maintain these schools is not levied by
the government, but granted at an annual meeting
of the inhabitants of the several townships, and
afterwards collected with the other taxes. The
result of this system is visible in the high degree of
intelligence possessed by all classes. Even in the
humblest walks of life a citizen of Massachusetts
will hardly be found incapable of reading and
writing, or ignorant of grammar and arithmetic;
while there are thousands, who, through the instru-
mentality of the higher schools sustained by public
expense, have acquired a respectable classical education. Throughout New England the same method
of supporting schools is generally prevalent, viz. by
a tax imposed by the people of the several districts
upon themselves in conformity with the requisitions of the law. In Connecticut, however, the
expense is met by a common fund, a method which
is said to be less efficient than where the voluntary

principle is encouraged. In the state of New York
a school fund of more than two millions of dollars
has been raised by the sale of lands appropriated
by the state to the purposes of education. Grants
from this fund are allowed to those districts alone
which have made some provision for themselves.
In the year 1832, New York contained a population of about two millions, half a million of whom,
(or one in four) were at school. None of the remaining states are equal to New York in this
respect. Pennsylvania is still very backward,
although active efforts are making to atone for past
negligence. The states in which slavery prevails
are likewise greatly inferior to the northern portions of the Union, both as to the means and the
character of education. In the free states of the
north-west large tracts of land have been set aside
for school purposes, from the first settlement of the
country. In Ohio, which sixty years ago was a
perfect wilderness, the school system has been thus
brought into full operation, and promises before
long to equal that of New York.

The schools above referred to, it will be recollected, are, with some exceptions in New England,
of a purely elementary kind, conveying little instruction beyond reading, writing, grammar, geography, and arithmetic. Yet, such as they are,
they constitute the strongest bulwark of the demo-

cratic government of the country ; and without
them the United States would soon be degraded
to the same level with Mexico and the republics of
South America. A conviction of this truth is
becoming more and more grounded in the public
mind ; and vast improvements in education are
consequently in daily progress. At present the re-
muneration of the teachers is unfortunately too
low to afford an adequate encouragement to persons
of high mental acquirements. It has been well
remarked by a recent English traveller, that
" where all sorts of ordinary labour find a liberal
reward, it is indispensable that the teacher should
be paid in proportion, or few will offer themselves
for that important vocation, and these few will
commonly be feeble and unfurnished."

Those parents who desire to give their children
greater advantages than the common school affords,
are provided with ample facilities towards the accomplishment of their object. Besides a multitude
of private establishments, many of the colleges are
supplied with grammar schools, which serve as a
connecting link between the common school and
the college. The grammar school of Kenyon College may be cited as an example. Here the boys
are instructed, 1st, in spelling, reading, writing,
geography, and arithmetic. 2dly, in English grammar, book-keeping, Latin, and Greek. 3dly, in

declamation, composition, sacred music, and the
Holy Scriptures. In this department the classical
books read by the more advanced pupils are Select
Orations of Cicero, and a compilation denominated
Jacob's Greek Reader.

The student, having completed his preparatory
education, is ready to enter college. In the United
States there are nearly a hundred colleges. It is
difficult to state the precise number, as new ones
are always in the course of formation in various
parts of the country. Of the existing number it
may be estimated that an eighth part are either
directly or indirectly under Episcopal influence, a
tenth Congregational, a third Presbyterian, a
seventh Roman Catholic, and the remainder Baptist, Methodist, Lutheran, and Unitarian. The
number of students in all these institutions, exclusive of those in preparatory departments, is probably between 6000 and 7000. The colleges referred
to vary exceedingly in regard to respectability, numbers, and endowments. There is for instance the
University, such as Harvard in Massachusetts, or
Yale in Connecticut, with its Academical, Medical,
Law, and Theological departments, its 400 or 500
students, its distinguished professors, its ample
funds, and its copious libraries. On the other hand
there is the infant college, just rising in the back-
woods, with its two or three teachers, themselves

perhaps but lately released from school; its twenty
or thirty students sustaining themselves by me-
chanical or agricultural labour, its log buildings, its
scanty salaries, and its library barely supplied with
the ordinary text books.   Yet in all these institutions, with very few exceptions, there are certain
features of agreement, and, as if by common consent,
the general arrangements are similar.

The course of study occupies four years. There are
four classes, in each of which the student continues
for one year. These classes are known as the Senior,
Junior, Sophomore, and Freshman.   The student
receives a degree of A. B. at the completion of his
four years' course, unless notoriously unworthy of
the honour. The professors are generally ministers
of some denomination of Christians, and exert
themselves more or less in disseminating religious
principles among the students.   They form a body
denominated the Faculty, and conduct the government of the institution by regulations and laws
established by themselves in " Faculty meetings"
from time to time.   The appointment of professors
and the control of the college property are in the
hands of trustees appointed by the legislature, if it
be a state institution, or if it be the property of a
religious denomination, by its ecclesiastical authorities.   The professors sometimes deliver lectures;
but are generally engaged in hearing the lessons or

" recitations" of the classes committed to their charge. The tutors occupy a rank subordinate to that of the professors. They reside among the students, explain their difficulties, hear their elementary recitations, and take charge of their general conduct. The students are often grown up men, whose youth perhaps has been spent in hard labour. Emulation is not so much encouraged among them as in England, the equal diffusion of knowledge, rather than its concentration, being the chief object of the instructors. A large portion of those engaged in qualifying themselves for the ministry, are supported as beneficiaries by education societies in their respective denominations. It is considered no disgrace to have been a beneficiary ; on the contrary many of the most respected preachers in America have been sustained in this manner while pursuing their collegiate course.

In regard to the colleges generally, it may further be remarked that the institutions which have been endowed and are sustained by the state, seldom prosper equally with those which have been established by the efforts of some Christian denomination. The history of Transylvania University at Lexington, in Kentucky, affords evidence that in America religious influence is essential to the success of a college. This institution was esta-

blished by the state at a very early period through
the efforts of some Presbyterians. A man of
infidel sentiments was afterwards appointed as a
professor by the trustees. Upon this, the Presbyterians withdrew their support, and established a
separate academy. This institution succeeded, and
the State University was completely prostrated.
The trustees, therefore, removed their infidel professor, and being convinced of the importance of
securing again the Presbyterian influence, proposed a union of the two institutions. This proposal was accepted, and the university flourished,
until the trustees appointed a Unitarian president,
and remodelled the institution on principles which
in a great measure excluded religious influence.
The Presbyterians with much effort then organized
another college in the neighbourhood, which soon
attained a respectable standing, while Transylvania
gradually decayed, and is once more in a state of
prostration.

The student having taken his degree of A. B.
is considered to be prepared for the study of
law, medicine, or theology. Omitting the law and
medical, as well as the military schools, I pass
to the theological seminaries. These institutions
have grown up in America entirely within the last
thirty years. The theological seminaries of all
denominations are between thirty and forty in

number. Of these four, or perhaps at the present time, six, are under exclusive Episcopal control, twice that number are Presbyterian or Congregational, and the remainder are Roman Catholic, Baptist, and Lutheran.

The General Theological Seminary of the Church has been already in part described. It has been found, however, that this admirable institution, notwithstanding its prosperity and advantages, is inadequate to the supply of the growing necessities of the Church. The numerous young men educated there are not sufficient to meet the demand for their services in the Eastern states, to say nothing of the vast regions of the West, which require the labours of the Christian ministry. Hence several of the dioceses have found it necessary to make provision for themselves. The first diocesan seminary of this kind was established by the Church in Virginia, at Alexandria, near Washington, and contains at present about thirty students. Next followed the Church in Ohio, with the Theological Seminary attached to Kenyon College, in which twelve young men are now preparing for holy orders. The Theological Seminary of the diocese of Kentucky was afterwards instituted, and contained, in 1836, eighteen students, although it is at present greatly depressed. In Massachusetts, Tennessee, and Vermont, similar Episcopal institutions are contemplated, and are perhaps already in partial operation.

The students of all denominations in the various theological seminaries of the United States amount probably to fifteen hundred; and of that number about a hundred and fifty are Episcopalians. Besides these, there are many who prefer a more private course of instruction, and pursue their theological studies under the superintendence of parochial clergymen.

Like the colleges, the theological seminaries greatly differ from each other in many respects. The chief of them in point of numbers are that of the Presbyterians, at Princeton, and that of the Congregationalists, at Andover, already described. The students in each of these institutions number from 130 to 150. The seminaries at Gambier and Lexington are examples of the smaller sort, although their advantages in regard to libraries are greater than in many institutions of more considerable note. The theological seminaries, like the colleges, resemble each other, with some exceptions, in many striking features. They are first established and afterwards maintained by voluntary contributions. The students are instructed free of expense, and are often supplied with books, clothing, and board, by societies established for the purpose in their respective denominations. They are generally natives of the free states, and comparatively few enter upon a theological course from the regions where slavery prevails. Certificates of pious and moral character, and of collegiate education, or equal literary advantages, are required from those who wish to enter. The course of study is three years, and there are three classes, denominated senior, middle, and junior.

The Scriptures are studied, more or less carefully, in the original Hebrew, Chaldee, and Greek ; sermons are composed according to the rules of criticism ; and instruction is given in pastoral duties. The trustees are nominated by the authorities of some Christian sect ; they appoint the professors, and they superintend the financial interests of the institution committed to their charge. The professors form a faculty, and govern the institution. They are also frequently employed in the unpleasant work of soliciting donations of books or money.

Theological seminaries confer no degrees, although at Gambier the college admits to a bachelorship in divinity those students who have completed their theological course. They are generally incorporated by the state legislature in the same manner and as readily as colleges and parishes.

Having thus described colleges and theological seminaries in general, it is not necessary to say much of Episcopal institutions of the same kind in particular. Their mode of government and their courses of instruction differ very little from those of non-episcopal denominations. The course of study in Kenyon College, Gambier, is very similar to that of Yale, and may be taken as a specimen of the whole. It is as follows.

Freshman Class.

First term. Sallust; Cicero de Contemnendâ Morte; Xenophon's Anabasis; English Grammar; Arithmetic Reviewed; Davies' Bourdon's Algebra; Porter's Analysis. *Second term.*—Folsom's Livy; Herodotus; Davies' Legendre's Geometry; Logarithms and Trigonometry. *Throughout the year,* Dilloway's Roman, and Cleveland's Greek Antiquities; Exercises in Reading, Declamation, and Composition; Translations from Latin to English, and from English to Latin.

Sophomore Class.

First term.—Iliad; Horace—Odes and Satires; Davies' Descriptive Geometry; Shades, Shadows, and Perspective; History. *Second term.*—Xenophon's Memorabilia; History; Cicero de Officiis; Quintilian; Davies' Surveying; Bridge's Conic Sections. *Throughout the year,* Compositions, Declamations, and Translations.

Junior Class.

First term.—Tacitus; Horace—Ars Poetica; Chemistry; Olmsted's Natural Philosophy; Blair's Lectures; Whately's Logic. *Second term.*—Whately's Rhetoric; Plato; Chemistry; Olmsted's Natural Philosophy; Demosthenes pro Coronâ. *Throughout the year*, Translations and Compositions; Declamations, selected and original.

Senior Class.

First .term.—Upham's Intellectual Philosophy; Natural Theology; Says' Political Economy; Œdipus Tyrannus and Medea. *Second term.*—Wayland's Moral Science; Bishop M'Ilvaine's Evidences of Christianity; Butler's Analogy; Constitution of the United States; Geology; Herschel's Astronomy. *Throughout the year*, Compositions and original Declamations.

Classes in the modern languages may be formed during any part of the college course by permission of the faculty.

Bishop M'Ilvaine is the president of Kenyon College, and professor of Ecclesiastical Polity in the Theological Seminary. Dr. Sparrow is the vice-president and professor of Divinity, and of Intellectual and Moral Science; the Rev. Mr. Muenscher is professor of Sacred Literature; the Rev. Mr. Wing, of Ecclesiastical History; and Dr. Colton,

of Pastoral Divinity and Sacred Rhetoric.   Besides
these, there are in the collegiate department a professor of Latin and Greek ; a professor of Rhetoric;
a professor of Chemistry ; and a professor of Mathematics and Natural Philosophy.   The preparatory department is under two principals and three
assistants.   Every student in both departments is
required to sign a promise that while in the institution he will neither use profane language, nor
gamble, nor drink ardent spirits.

The Theological Seminary at Gambier, equally
with the College, may be taken as a good specimen
of many others.   The course of study is as follows.

Junior Class.

Stuart's Hebrew Grammar ; Hebrew Chrestomathy, and Hebrew Course ; Biblical Geography ;
Biblical Antiquities ; Principles of Interpretation ;
Septuagint ; Stuart's Grammar of the New Testament Dialect ; Newcome's Harmony of the Gospels ; Lectures on Biblical Criticism and Biblical
Interpretation.   Exercises in Sacred Rhetoric
during the year.

Middle Class.

Interpretation of Scripture, continued ; Doctrines of Natural and Revealed Religion ; Ethics
and Evidences of Christianity ; Ecclesiastical History ; Sacred Rhetoric and Pulpit Eloquence ;
Recitations and Lectures in Pastoral Divinity.

Senior Class.

Systematic Divinity; Ecclesiastical History; Church Government; Pastoral Divinity; Sacred Rhetoric; Biblical Literature. The term of study in each of these classes is one year.

The education of females in the United States is more public than in England. Few private governesses are employed, and the number of boarding establishments and day schools is very considerable. In country places, and in early life, girls are commonly educated under the same roof with boys, and by the same teacher. Those whose parents possess the means (and they are very numerous) are afterwards transferred to schools of a higher order, which are generally the creation of individual effort. Of these there is a great variety. Many are temporary establishments under the care of male or female teachers indifferently, which, after continuing in operation half a year or a year, are abandoned through the caprice of parents or the migratory habits of the instructors. Others are organized on a permanent and extensive plan, bearing a close resemblance to the colleges, and under the care of Christian ministers. Such is St. Mary's Hall, a female school recently established by the indefatigable Bishop Doane, at Burlington, New Jersey. This institution is conducted on Christian principles, under the supervision and pastoral care of a prelate of the Church. There are seven teachers who instruct in all the English branches, the ancient languages, useful and ornamental needlework, domestic economy, French, German, Italian, Spanish, drawing, and painting; the piano, the guitar, the harp, the organ, and vocal music. There were fifty-two pupils in the institution in 1837. Full courses of lectures are delivered in botany, natural philosophy, and chemistry, with a complete apparatus. The *ordinary* annual expenses are 200 dollars (45*l*.), but the extra charges are considerable. The bishop has very considerately made provision for remitting the ordinary expenses to one pupil in every ten, being the daughter of a clergyman deceased or in necessitous circumstances.

In reference to American male students of all classes, it may be remarked that they are easily led by a judicious moral influence, while it is almost impossible to manage them by arbitrary or coercive measures. They are republicans from their early childhood; and experiments have actually been made to ascertain how far a strictly republican government would be admissible in schools. Such a method was adopted at an institution for boys denominated the Gardiner Lyceum, in the State of Maine. The legislative power was vested in a committee consisting of eight or ten, chosen by the boys from their own number. They met once a

week to transact such business as appointing officers, making and repealing regulations, and inquiring into the state of the school. The teachers had
a right of negative on their proceedings, but no
direct and positive power. They could pardon, but
they could assign no punishment, nor make laws
inflicting any. Such institutions have succeeded
for a time when the principal has possessed a sufficient share of *generalship* to enable him really to
manage the institution *himself*, while the power has
been left *nominally* in the hands of the boys.
Should this not be the case, as Mr. Abbott judiciously remarks, and should the institution actually
be surrendered into the hands of the boys, things
must be on a very unstable footing. And, accordingly, even in republican America, wherever such
a plan has been adopted, it has in every instance
been abandoned, and a more aristocratic system
established in its room.

Education in America is more general but less
thorough and accurate than in England. At the
same time, it seems to be well adapted to the present circumstances of the country, which require a
practical knowledge of many subjects much more
than profound scholarship in any single science.
Almost every American is more or less a working
man, dependent for subsistence upon his own exertions. Where all have something to do, a practical

education is in universal demand.   Hence it is that
the student in mathematics turns his attention to
surveying, rather than to fluxions ; because he contemplates the probability of deriving advantage
from the survey of some portion of the vast American continent.   The classical student aims at
acquiring a knowledge of ancient languages, not so
much that he may enjoy their beauties, as that he
may become conversant with the ideas on politics
and morals which prevailed in ancient times, and
apply his acquisitions to some beneficial purpose.
The student in rhetoric and declamation looks forward to the time when he can successfully harangue
the crowded assembly, and bend the democratic
multitudes to his will.   Learning, in short, is not
followed for its own sake, and for its indirect advantages, but for the purpose of accomplishing a direct
and immediate result.   It was, perhaps, a partial
view of this obvious truth which induced a respectable American to express himself in the following
quaint terms, in an address lately delivered before
a collegiate society in an eastern state.

" The multitude in this country, so far from
favouring and honouring high learning and science,
is rather prone to suspect and dislike it.   It feareth
that genius savoureth of aristocracy !   Besides, the
multitude calleth itself a *practical man*.   It asketh,
What is the use?   It seeth no use but in that

which leads to money or the material ends of life.
It hath no opinion of having dreamers and drones
in society. It believeth, indeed, in railroads; it
thinketh well of steam; and owneth that the new
art of bleaching by chlorine is a prodigious improvement; but it laughs at the profound re-
searches into the laws of nature, out of which those
very inventions grew; and with still greater scorn,
it laughs at the votaries of the more spiritual forms
of truth and beauty, which have no application to
the palpable uses of life. Then, again, the influence
of our reading public is not favourable to high
letters. It demands, it pays for, and respects,
almost exclusively, a lower style of production; and
hence a natural influence to discourage higher
labours."

CHAPTER XIII.

LEXINGTON, &c.

————

Incorporation of the Theological Seminary.—Its Professorships.
—Duties of the Professor of Sacred Literature.—The Stu-
dents.—Course of study in Sacred Literature.—Description
of Lexington. — Churches. — University. — Property of the
Seminary. — Inhabitants of Lexington. — Kentuckians. —
Population of Kentucky.—Slaves.—Sects.—Literary charac-
ters in Lexington.—Dr. Cooke.—His offices in the Church.
—Religious papers in America.—Episcopal papers.—Church
Advocate.—Christmas Address.

————

THE Theological Seminary at Lexington was
incorporated, on application, by the legislature of
Kentucky, in February, 1834. The act of incorporation is worded in terms similar to those of
another act by which a Roman Catholic institution
on a more extensive scale, had been previously
incorporated at Bardstown, in the same state.
This act acknowledges the trustees already existing, and authorizes them to pass such by-laws as
are not contrary to the law of the land. It also
confers on them the usual privileges of a corporation,

1

in regard to the tenure of property ; but requires
that the rents and proceeds acquired by them shall
never exceed 5000 dollars per annum. The trustees
are to continue in office for one year ; and the
nomination of their successors is left in the hands
of the bishop of the diocese ; subject to the approval of the convention of the Episcopal Church
in Kentucky. The property of the seminary is by
the same act exempted from all state taxation
whatever. The trustees are empowered to appoint
the necessary professors in all branches of learning
usually taught in theological seminaries. The professors are finally declared capable of exercising
such powers as the trustees may delegate to them
for the wholesome and faithful government of the
institution.

The professorships were arranged as follows :—
The bishop of the diocese took the department of
doctrinal theology and pastoral duties. The Rev.
Dr. Coit, a distinguished Episcopal clergyman then
president of Transylvania University in Lexington,
gratuitously acted as professor of the ethics and
evidences of Christianity. Dr. Cooke, a physician,
eminent in the Church for his writings in behalf of
Episcopacy, gratuitously lectured on the history and
polity of the Church, while to myself were committed the more onerous duties connected with
the professorship of Sacred Literature. I per-

formed likewise daily morning and evening prayer in the chapel of the Seminary, reading on both occasions the greater part of the Church services for the day. In addition to these occupations I was assistant to the bishop in the pastoral care of Christ Church at Lexington, and during his absence of eleven months in the eastern states, besides attending to my own engagements in the seminary and some of the bishop's, I read the services and preached two sermons every Sunday, conducted the Sunday school, and lectured every Wednesday evening. In reviewing these numerous duties, I am disposed to wonder that I did not entirely sink under them, in a climate where the thermometer in summer rises to 100° in the shade, and in the winter, although in latitude 38°, sinks to forty or fifty degrees below freezing. My compensation was fixed at 800 dollars per annum (180*l.*) 500 of which were promised by the trustees, and 300 by the bishop. Though this was a small stipend, I was fully satisfied with it in the infancy of the seminary, and notwithstanding much fatigue and occasional ill-health, I can truly say that I found my labour to be its own reward.

The students in the seminary were at first but three or four in number; but they subsequently increased as I have already stated to eighteen. They were chiefly from New England, Pennsyl-

vania, and Ireland, and only one was a native of
Kentucky. Unhappily the seminary had not taken
a high stand in regard to qualifications for admission, and hence the greater part of the students
not only had never received a degree, but were in
some instances unacquainted with more than the
mere rudiments of the dead languages. Still they
possessed the minds of men, and were generally
anxious to improve themselves as much as possible.
Hence, although my professional duties were various,
I was often highly gratified by the rapid progress
of my pupils.

It was my first care to see that they were
well grounded in the Greek and Latin gram-
mars. I then conducted them through the Greek
and Latin Gospels, explaining by the way the
chief difficulties in interpretation. Afterwards
they read the most striking portions in those
writings of the Greek and Latin fathers which we
possessed in our library, such as Clement, Hermas,
Ignatius, the Apostolical Constitutions, Jerome,
Cyprian, and Theodoret. They now carried their
Septuagints and Greek Testaments to chapel, and
were generally able to follow me in the reading of
the morning and evening lessons. Having laid a
tolerably good foundation in Greek and Latin, I
commenced instructing in Hebrew those to whom
the bishop had not granted a dispensation. They

were first taught to read accurately the language
with points, and were then taken five or six times
through the excellent grammar of Professor Stuart.
As soon as they had obtained a slight knowledge of
the grammar, and had committed to memory the
paradigm of the regular verb, they commenced
translating the short sentences in Stuart's Chrestomathy, and by the time they had read through the
grammar four times, the Chrestomathy was finished.
They were now able to construe with fluency a
chapter in the Hebrew Bible at every lesson, to
analyse the words, account for the vowel changes,
and explain most of the exegetical difficulties.   The
Chaldee grammar was soon acquired, and a few
weeks' practice in the Chaldee Chrestomathy of
Mr. Riggs enabled them to construe the Targums,
and all the Biblical Chaldee.   One young man of
fine talents afterwards commenced the Syriac grammar, and read many chapters in the Syriac New
Testament.   It was also his intention to study the
Arabic ; but unhappily he was induced to abandon
theology, and thus his promising abilities were
entirely lost to the Church.   During a part of their
course the students had daily recitations in Horne's
Introduction to the Study of the Scriptures, Ernesti
on Interpretation, and other works of a similar description.   The more advanced wrote weekly dis-
sertations on difficult parts of Scripture, and on the

meaning of remarkable Hebrew words. The Gospels and Epistles were also studied critically in Greek, with the aid derived from a knowledge of Hebrew, of the Septuagint, of the early Fathers, of Biblical Antiquities, and of the rules of interpretation.

Lexington is an agreeable town, delightfully situated in the richest part of Kentucky. It contains between 6000 and 7000 inhabitants, a quarter of whom are slaves. The houses are well built, and many of them are furnished with considerable elegance and taste. On the highest ground in the town is Transylvania University, a fine building with a Grecian portico, the most conspicuous object on approaching Lexington from the west and south. The locust tree or acacia lines the streets, and the poplar surrounds the green fronting the college, imparting a grateful sense of coolness, and giving to Lexington the appearance of a city in a wood. There is one Episcopal church containing accommodation for 800 persons, one Roman Catholic church, two Presbyterian houses of worship, one Methodist, several Baptist, and two African meeting-houses, Methodist and Baptist, erected by the slaves. The Presbyterians number more than 1200, and the Episcopalians, as in New York and Philadelphia, comprise about a tenth part of the population. The Methodists and Baptists are respectively nearly equal to the Presbyterians, or, if the negro congregations are counted, much superior to them in number. The Roman Catholics are as yet few, but their place of worship is the largest and handsomest in the town, and promises to be one of the most attractive. There is in Lexington a medical school, connected with the University, and furnished with ample and convenient buildings A short distance out of the town is the Lunatic Asylum of Kentucky, a noble institution, admirably conducted, and containing about a hundred patients.

The Theological Seminary is near the University, and occupies a beautiful situation. The buildings were arranged for an extensive school, under the tasteful superintendence of the Rev. Mr. Peers, an Episcopal clergyman afterwards president of the University. The grounds cover about two acres, and the various edifices contain accommodations for two professors and their families and about thirty students. The cost of the whole was 9000 dollars (2025l.) but the proprietor, Mr. Peers, generously remitted 1000 dollars (225l.) to aid in procuring a library. The purchase money was obtained partly by contributions in Kentucky, but chiefly by donations solicited in Philadelphia and New York, first by Dr. Cooke, and afterwards more extensively by the bishop. The salary annexed to the professorship of sacred literature was contributed for three years by the parishioners of the church of the Ascension at New York.

The people of Lexington are distinguished by their polite and agreeable manners, and by their attention to strangers. A large portion of the inhabitants are wealthy, and probably few towns of the same size in any part of the world contain so many persons in good circumstances. By wealthy persons I mean those possessing a quarter or half a million of dollars (56,000*l.* to 112,000*l.*) By persons in good circumstances I mean those whose income is not less than 2000 dollars (450*l.*) The number of handsome carriages and horses in Lexington is very great; and the other luxuries of life may be had in profusion. If the people have any striking defect, it consists in the fact that they are subject to sudden and violent excitements both in religious and political affairs, which have produced the natural effect of a division into a variety of parties. During the winter they are much engaged in amusements of various kinds. Balls and evening assemblies succeed each other in rapid succession, and there is no inconsiderable display of elegance and taste. In the summer, they have their races, their barbecues, and occasionally their camp-meetings, to enliven the monotony of existence, and to contribute to the excitement which is natural to them.

The same character which is seen in the people of Lexington is found more or less throughout Kentucky. A great misconception prevails in regard to the people of this important state. True it is that their ancestors were bold and rough men, little accustomed to conventional proprieties. But the present inhabitants have become rich, and with riches they have acquired a taste for polished society and for all the usual appendages of civilized life. In short, they greatly resemble the Virginians, from whom they are chiefly descended, and exhibit indications of constant and increasing improvement. They are becoming alive to the importance of general education, and many are already endeavouring to discover some scheme for the gradual abolition of slavery. The difference between the Kentuckians and the New Englanders is still exceedingly striking, and although an assimilation has been in progress for fifty years, the descendants of the Cavaliers, and those of the Roundheads, retain many of the distinctive features of their parents.

Kentucky, with a surface of 39,000 square miles, contained at the last census in 1830, a population, black and white, of 687,917. Since that period there has been little increase, by reason of the abundant emigration of the small farmers to Illinois and Missouri. A staple article of produce is hemp, which is prepared and made into coarse " bagging" by the slaves. This bagging is sold in the southern states, where it is employed in packing cotton for exportation. Great attention has lately been paid to road-making throughout Kentucky, and at the present time, besides a railway, five good macadamized turnpike-roads unite in Lexington, and afford delightful drives in every direction.

The slaves constitute about a third part of the population of Kentucky. They are said to be well treated, and have quite an independent air. On Sundays they appear dressed in the height of fashion, and very frequently are clad more expensively and gaily than their masters and mistresses. Still the system under which they live keeps them in great ignorance; and although there are many conscientious slave-owners, few general attempts are made to enlighten the descendants of Africans· The law peremptorily forbids any person to teach a negro to read without the express consent of his owner, and even Sunday school instruction is discouraged.

The prevailing sect in Kentucky is that of the Baptists, who are subdivided into many fragments, and contend with acrimony for their peculiar tenets. The Presbyterians are a numerous and increasing

L 4

body. The Roman Catholics possess more than
twice the strength of the Protestant Episcopalians,
and are supplied with a bishop and two co-adjutors,
who reside at Bardstown, their episcopal see. The
Protestant Episcopalians have a bishop and twenty
clergymen, many of whom have been students at
the seminary in Lexington. Their entire number
is probably about 3000, one half of whom at least
reside in the two chief cities of Lexington and
Louisville. Many of the parishes are still in an
infant condition, and their clergymen are sustained
in a great measure by the Board of Missions.

Lexington was formerly considered the Athens
of the west, but at present it can hardly be said to
merit that distinction. Still there is much literary
taste among the people ; and many persons of considerable talent have resided there at different
times. In the immediate vicinity is the seat of
Henry Clay, the distinguished orator and candidate
for the presidency of the United States. Dr. Holley,
the Unitarian president of Transylvania University,
was a gentleman of splendid abilities, but his peculiar tenets greatly injured his usefulness in his appropriate station. The Rev. Mr. Peers, the Episcopal
clegyman, before mentioned, was elected to the presidency in 1833, and manifested a most praiseworthy
zeal in the cause of general education. He was un-
ceremoniously dismissed from office by the trustees

after a short incumbency, under circumstances not discreditable to himself nor creditable to his opponents. After an interval of nearly two years, another Episcopal clergyman, the Rev. Dr. Coit of New England was appointed his successor. Dr. Coit had distinguished himself by his writings in favour of Trinitarianism, by his pungent essays on the history of the American Puritans, and by a useful and convenient edition of the Bible enriched with pithy annotations. He continued in office till the summer of 1837, when he resigned his charge and returned to New England. The predecessor of the present rector of Christ Church was Dr. Chapman, a zealous and talented advocate of the principles of Episcopacy. He published a volume of sermons on the " Doctrines, Discipline and Worship of the Protestant Episcopal Church," which has passed through several editions, and has been extensively useful. He has since issued a work entitled " Sermons to Presbyterians of all Sects," which has excited considerable attention to the real principles of Christian unity. Several professors in the medical school have in like manner become celebrated in their respective departments. Dr. Caldwell, a finished scholar and a polished writer, has chiefly distinguished himself by his works on Phrenology. Dr. Cooke has also become known to medical readers by his work on the Theory and Practice of Medicine.

But it is chiefly by his conversion to the Church, and his publications in defence of it, that the last mentioned gentleman is known to Episcopalians. Educated in Virginia, and connected with some distinguished families in England, Dr. Cooke spent his youth among the best society, and in habitual intercourse with the most cultivated minds. Sceptical opinions were then unhappily prevalent, and he imbibed the poison which has destroyed so many of the inconsiderate and unreflecting. While still a young man, he was induced, by a happy curiosity, to purchase of an itinerant book-pedlar, a work on the evidences of Christianity. He took it home, shut himself up in his room, and applied his whole faculties to the study of the interesting subject. His naturally strong mind felt the entire force of the argument, and his native straightforwardness led him to an instant avowal of the change which took place in his sentiments.

Knowing as yet nothing of church history, he was not adequate to make a proper choice of a denomination, but immediately connected himself with the Methodists, partly on account of their local proximity, and partly through a just admiration of their energy and zeal. For many years he

remained an active and influential member of that
sect, and some time elapsed after his appointment
as professor in the Lexington Medical School,
before any further change was effected in his sentiments. At length Dr. Chapman's sermons on the
Church were published, and produced on his mind
a strong apprehension that the American Methodists might be in a state of schism. He again shut
himself up in his study, and applied himself closely
to the perusal of such works on the subject as he
could procure.

During this investigation he attended no place of
worship, and determined to attend none until he
had succeeded in discovering the true Church.
Finally, he came to the conclusion that Scripture
as well as primitive antiquity concurred in requiring
an external commission derived from Christ through
his Apostles, as the only warrant for the performance of the ministerial office. He became convinced,
also, that the possession of such a ministry was a
necessary mark of the true Church, and that all
religious bodies destitute of that ministry are in a
state of separation from the primitive fold. By the
light of ecclesiastical history he now traced the
Apostolic succession through the early Church, and
found it still existing in the Greek and Roman
Churches, as well as in the Episcopal Churches of
England and America. A Romanist he could not

become, because ecclesiastical history had shown
him the origin of Roman Catholic errors, and the
superior purity of antiquity. He therefore connected himself with the American Episcopal Church,
since here he found all that is best in Romanism
without its corruptions; all that is valuable among
the dissenters, without their disorders.

He afterwards imported from abroad, at a great
expense, an admirable library, containing most of
the primitive fathers, and the voluminous writings
of former times on the subject of church history.
His convictions were complete, and he devoted his
time and money, with unsparing liberality, to the
diffusion of those important truths which he had so
providentially acquired.

Dr. Cooke was duly appreciated by Episcopalians
in Kentucky, and for many years represented the
parish of Christ Church in the Diocesan Convention, and the diocese of Kentucky in the General
Convention. He exerted much influence in framing the canons of the diocese, which were modelled
as nearly as possible according to primitive usage.
He was also a member of the standing committee;
a warden of Christ Church; a professor without
pay, as well as a trustee of the Theological Seminary. In the General Convention he was one of
the original proposers of the canon under which
missionary bishops have been elected and consecra-

ted, and in every situation he has always used his influence in promoting a close adherence to the spirit as well as the letter of ecclesiastical law. In the year 1835, with the consent of the bishop, he commenced, on his own risk, a religious paper denominated the *Church Advocate*. It appeared once a fortnight in folio form, the price was a dollar and half (6*s.* 9*d.*) per annum, and the design was to advocate the peculiar principles of the Church. After continuing the publication for nearly a year, he found it incompatible with his other engagements, and the editorship devolved upon myself.

The religious papers published in America are very numerous, and are conducted upon a great variety of principles, and with an immense diversity of spirit and ability. Every denomination of any numerical importance has its publications, which are diffused as extensively as possible. The general character of these productions, in a literary point of view, is not very high, and as many of them follow the example of political papers in abusing and misrepresenting their opponents, it may be doubted whether, on the whole, they promote to any considerable extent the knowledge and love of truth. With a few exceptions, the Episcopalian publications are, notwithstanding, moderate and candid, and many of them contribute to throw light upon antiquity and Church principles. *The*

Churchman, The Spirit of Missions, The New York Review, The Sunday-school Visitor, The Children's Magazine, and *The Gospel Messenger,* are published in the diocese of New York. *The Christian Witness,* in Massachusetts; *The Missionary,* in New Jersey; *The Episcopal Recorder,* and *The Protestant Episcopalian,* in Pennsylvania; *The Southern Churchman,* in Virginia; *The Gospel Messenger,* and *Southern Episcopal Register,* in South Carolina; *The Gambier Observer,* in Ohio; and, finally, *The Chronicle of the Church,* in Connecticut.

The Churchman is conducted with singular ability, by a grandson of Bishop Seabury, and is a powerful instrument in promoting the influence of Episcopacy. It contains the choicest extracts from *The British Critic,* and *The British Magazine,* and elaborate essays designed for intellectual minds on doctrinal theology, church ordinances, and ecclesiastical polity. *The Christian Witness, The Episcopal Recorder, The Gambier Observer,* and *The Southern Churchman,* are designed for general readers, and are conducted on ecclesiastical principles resembling those of the London *Christian Observer. The Sunday-school Visitor, The Gospel Messenger* (of New York), *The Children's Magazine, The Missionary, The Protestant Episcopalian, The Gospel Messenger* (of South Carolina), and *The Chronicle of the Church,* generally agree in principle with *The Churchman.* *The Spirit of Missions* is the organ of the board of missions, and *The New York Review* is almost wholly literary. The principles of *The Church Advocate* may be gathered from the following Hudibrastic effusion, printed in Lexington and distributed by the little boy who carried the paper to the subscribers living in the town.

CHRISTMAS ADDRESS OF THE CARRIER OF THE CHURCH ADVOCATE TO ITS PATRONS.

Old Thirty-five is nearly gone,
Good Churchmen all, in Lexington!
Soon Thirty-six will be our date,
Good patrons of the *Advocate!*
We pray you, lend a little time,
To listen to our humble rhyme;
And get a little information
Without much trouble or vexation.

"What is the Church?" all men inquire:
Some say " *A building with a spire,*
Where gentlemen and ladies go
To lounge away an hour or so."
Some say, "THE CHURCH, THE KINGDOM COME,
Is every sect in Christendom,
Quakers, and Shakers, and Socinians,
As many CHURCHES as OPINIONS."
Some say (to whom great praise is given)
"Tis all GOOD FOLKS in earth and heaven;
But who they are we cannot tell,
The Church is quite INVISIBLE."

If such be then their doubtful state,
What says the "little *Advocate?*"
" The Church is *all that mighty host,*
In every land, in every coast,
Baptized and *taught* (through heavenly love)
By those COMMISSIONED from above,
To spread the tidings of salvation
In EVERY AGE and EVERY NATION."

But, hark! we hear our neighbours cry,
" What prejudice and bigotry!
Surely that rule *unchurches us,*
How monstrous and incongruous!
What *arrogance,* what zeal *intrusive,*
For a *small sect* to be *exclusive !*"

EXCLUSIVE! did our neighbours say?
Tell us, good reader, what are THEY!!!
Should we be deem'd *exclusive,* when
ELEVEN-TWELFTHS of Christian men
Within our limits are *included,*
And only ONE SMALL TWELFTH excluded?
A twelfth which left the way we go
Less than three hundred years ago ;
But now, in mercy meek and civil,
Rank us with Antichrist and Devil;
Or, even with that wicked one,
The scarlet dame of Babylon.

Yet even these we trouble not,
But wish them all a happier lot;
Again repeating, and again,
" We hate the ERRORS, not the MEN."
Fain would we meet them on the ground
Where holy men of old were found;

Where Peter held the heavenly key,
Where blessed Paul rejoiced to be :
Where Christians long in UNION trod
The peaceful path that leads to God ;
In UNION ate the Gospel feast
For fourteen hundred years at least.

But, mark, *we* never can come down
To the low ground *they* stand upon ;
We cannot leave our noble craft
To sail upon *their* crazy raft,
Which, tost by faction's stormy breezes,
May in a moment fall to pieces.
Our lot within THE ARK is cast ;
We nail our colours to the mast ;
Our banner to all eyes unfurl'd,
" THE ARK ALONE CAN SAVE THE WORLD."

CHAPTER XIV.

PRAYER BOOK OF THE AMERICAN CHURCH.

————

Propriety of alterations.—First plan of an altered Prayer Book.—
  Objections of the English bishops.—Further deliberations in
  Convention.—Subsequent alterations.—New Offices.—Com-
  parison of the American Prayer Book with that of England.
  —General inference.

————

EXCELLENT as are its general arrangements, and
venerable as are its services, the Prayer Book in
America as in England constitutes no essential
part of the ecclesiastical fabric. It rests solely
upon the authority of the Church, by which it may
be altered, newly arranged, or made to give place
to another form of worship as circumstances render
desirable. The Church of England in the Preface
to the Prayer Book has laid down a rule that
" the particular forms of divine worship, and the
rites and ceremonies appointed to be used therein,
being things in their own nature indifferent and

alterable, and so acknowledged, it is but reasonable, that upon weighty and important considerations, according to the various exigences of times and occasions, such changes and alterations should be made therein, as to those who are in places of authority should, from time to time, seem either necessary or expedient."

The same Church has likewise in the articles and homilies declared the necessity and expediency of occasional alterations and amendments, and, accordingly, we find that "seeking to keep the happy mean between too much stiffness in refusing and too much easiness in admitting variations in things once advisedly established, she hath, in the reign of several princes, since the first compiling of her liturgy in the time of Edward VI.   .   .   .   . yielded to make such alterations in some particulars, as in the respective times were thought convenient."

When the American states became independent with respect to civil government, their ecclesiastical independence, on Protestant principles, was necessarily included. The American Episcopal Church was therefore left at full liberty, in conformity with the rule of the Church of England, to arrange its forms of worship in such a manner as might be most conducive to its future prosperity. The attention of the General Convention was first drawn to those

alterations in the liturgy which became necessary
in the prayers for civil rulers, in consequence of the
revolution.   But while these alterations were in
progress, the Convention thought it proper to take
a further review of the public service, and to establish such other amendments as might be deemed
proper.   The following brief history of these alterations is chiefly derived from Bishop White's valuable " Memoirs of the Episcopal Church."

When the General Convention first assembled in
September, 1785, very few, if any, of the members
thought of altering the liturgy further than to
accommodate it to the revolution.   In the course
of the debates, however, arguments were adduced
in favour of a further change, from the fact that
some points not dependent on doctrine, were universally regarded as exceptionable.   Some topics were
also started which gave rise to much painful controversy.   Thus, one of the lay-members proposed
that the first four petitions in the litany should be
struck out.   This motion was lost without a division.   A motion was then introduced for framing a
service for the anniversary of American independence.   This service it was understood would be a
test of the political opinions of the clergy, as it was
designed to imply a retrospective approbation of
the revolutionary war.   Dr. White, and other decided republicans in the Convention, opposed the

measure on account of the notorious fact, that many of the clergy could not use the service without subjecting themselves to ridicule and censure. It was notwithstanding carried, but the service was read in but few places, and was finally abolished. On the subject of the articles, disputes arose in regard to those on justification, predestination, and original sin, which many desired to alter or set aside ; and, accordingly, the 17th article was so modified as to express no definite idea whatever. A committee appointed for the purpose reported a great number of further alterations, which were allowed by the Convention with little controversy, and ordered to be printed. The book thus produced is commonly known by the name of the " Proposed Prayer Book," and corresponds greatly with the plan laid down by the commissioners of the King of England in 1689.

It will be recollected that all these proceedings took place before any bishops had been consecrated; and it soon appeared that they had been conducted with too much precipitancy and too little discretion. The report of the alterations above mentioned reached the English prelates almost simultaneously with the application of the General Convention for the consecration of bishops. This report being accompanied by private statements somewhat exaggerated, produced on their minds unfavourable im-

pressions in regard to the doctrine and discipline
advocated by the American clergy. In a letter to
the committee of the General Convention they declared that, besides their seeing no occasion for
some smaller alterations, they were dissatisfied with
the proposed omission of the Nicene and Athanasian Creeds, and of the descent into hell in the
Apostles' Creed. They stated also that before
they could consecrate for America they expected
that satisfaction would be given in regard to the
subjects mentioned.

On the receipt of this letter a special meeting of
the General Convention was summoned, and the
question came before the house, how far it would
be proper to accede to the requisitions of the English prelates. The omission of the Nicene Creed
had been generally regretted, and, accordingly, it
was now without difficulty restored to the Prayer
Book, to stand after the Apostles' Creed, with permission to use either. The clause in the latter
creed of the descent into hell, occasioned much debate, but was eventually restored. The restoration
of the Athanasian Creed was negatived.

The result of the deliberations of the Convention
was addressed to the Archbishops of Canterbury
and York, with thanks for their fatherly attention
to the welfare of the Church. All obstacles being
now removed, the bishops elect proceeded to Eng-

land, received consecration, and soon afterwards began the exercise of the episcopal functions.

Still the alterations in the Prayer Book were not considered as wholly complete. In the year 1789, the house of bishops proposed that the Athanasian Creed should be restored to the Prayer Book; but the proposal was negatived by the house of clerical and lay deputies. In 1792, it was ordered that a rubric should be inserted before the Apostles' Creed, allowing any Church to omit the article respecting the descent into hell, or to use in its stead the words, " He went into the place of departed spirits."

Selections from the reading psalms were also adopted and prefixed to the Psalter, with permission to use them instead of the ordinary psalms for the day. In the service for the administration of the Communion a great change was made, by restoring to the consecration prayer the oblatory words, and the invocation of the Holy Spirit, left out in King Edward's reign.

Some few alterations in the ordinal of the Church of England, required by local circumstances, were prepared by the bishops in the Convention last mentioned. There was no material difference of opinion, except in regard to the words used by the bishop at the ordination of priests, " Receive ye the Holy Ghost," and " whose sins thou dost forgive

1

they are forgiven, and whose sins thou dost retain, they are retained." It was finally determined that the alternative of another form should be allowed to those bishops who might desire it. This form is as follows:—" Take thou authority to execute the office of a priest in the Church of God, now committed to thee by the imposition of our hands; and be thou a faithful dispenser of the word of God, and of His holy sacraments; in the name of the Father, and of the Son, and of the Holy Ghost."

In the Convention of 1795, a service was appointed for the consecration of a church or chapel. It is substantially the same with a service composed by Bishop Andrews, in the reign of James I., and commonly used by the English bishops in such consecrations.

In 1799, the review of the thirty-nine articles was moved in the lower house of Convention, and a committee was appointed to draw up a new body of articles which were to lie over for the consideration of the next Convention. Accordingly, in 1801, the subject was for the first time authoritatively acted on. After repeated discussion, it was found that the thirty-nine articles of the Church of England, with the exception of local matters, were more likely to give general satisfaction than any new form which might be devised. They were accordingly adopted *verbatim*, with those changes only which political circumstances required, and which the exclusion of the Athanasian Creed made necessary in the eighth article.

In 1804, an office was framed and ordered to be used at the induction of clergymen to the rectorship of churches. In 1808, this office was changed in name to "the office of institution," and rested on recommendation, not on requisition as before. At the same time thirty hymns were added to the *Book of Psalms and Hymns.*

In 1811, an amendment to the constitution of the Church was adopted, by which all further alterations in the Liturgy were restrained, except such as should be proposed at one Convention and ratified three years afterwards at the next. Since that period very few changes have been effected; and those few have been chiefly of a minor description. The Hymns set forth by the authority of the General Convention are now 212 in number, and have been chiefly selected from the best English sacred poetry. A selection from the metrical Psalms, with many alterations and improvements, has also been authorized and substituted for the entire version of Tate and Brady. There is at present an increasing disposition to avoid unnecessary changes and to keep as close as possible to the Liturgy of the Church of England.

As there are many to whom this subject will

M

prove interesting, I here subjoin a list of the chief alterations which have been admitted. A few very trifling verbal changes are not specified.

The general contents of the American Prayer Book, as well as their order, are nearly the same with those of the Church of England. The Creed of St. Athanasius, the Commination, and the Forms of Prayer for the 5th of November, the 30th of January, the 29th of May, and the 29th of January, are all omitted. Between the " Churching of Women" and the " Psalter" are inserted " Forms of Prayer to be used at Sea;" " A Form of Prayer for the Visitation of Prisoners;" " A Form of Prayer and Thanksgiving to Almighty God for the Fruits of the Earth, and all the other Blessings of His merciful Providence;" " Forms of Prayer to be used in Families;" " Selections of Psalms to be used instead of the Psalms for the Day, at the discretion of the Minister." The following are always printed after the Psalter, though not contained in the table of contents:—" Articles of Religion;" " The Form and Manner of making, ordaining, and consecrating Bishops, Priests, and Deacons;" " The Form of Consecration of a Church or Chapel;" " Prayer to be used at the Meetings of Convention;" " Office of Institution of Ministers into Parishes or Churches." After the selection from the metrical Psalter the Hymns are always inserted.

The *Preface* differs from that of the English Prayer Book, having been drawn up with the design of vindicating the alterations admitted by the American Church.   In the *Order for the Psalter*, the injunction to repeat the Gloria Patri at the end of every Psalm is omitted, as well as the *note*.   Permission is also given to use the Selection of Psalms, and on days of fasting and thanksgiving, such psalms and lessons as the minister may consider expedient, unless any have been appointed by the ecclesiastical authority.   A few alterations are also made in the table of " Proper Psalms on certain Days."   The arrangement of *Lessons* from the Old Testament for Sundays is altered.   From Septuagesima to Easter, passages from the Prophets, of a penitential character, are read; from Easter to Whitsunday, chapters from the Prophets, adapted to the season; and from Trinity Sunday to the 22nd Sunday after Trinity, selections from the Historical Books.   While in the English Prayer Book the lessons from the New Testament are those appointed for the day of the month, in the American there are lessons specially appointed for every Sunday in the year.   Lessons from the Apocrypha are read on holy-days, but never on Sundays.   In the " Table of Vigils, &c." the vigils are wholly omitted; but the fasts coincide with those of the Church of England, a peculiar distinction being given to Ash Wednesday and Good Friday. The first Thursday in November, unless the civil authority should appoint another day, is set apart as a day of *Thanksgiving* for the fruits of the earth.

The *first Rubric* is omitted, because parts of it have become obsolete, and because custom is considered to have sufficiently established the use of the surplice, the gown, and other usual ornaments. Three additional sentences, namely, *Hab.* ii. 20, *Mal.* ii. 11, and *Psalm* xix. 14, are prefixed to those which stand at the commencement of the Morning and Evening Services. In the *General Confession,* and in all other places where it occurs, the expressions " them which," and " them that" are altered to " those who." After the usual *Absolution,* which is denominated the *declaration* of Absolution, is inserted the Absolution belonging to the Communion Service, which may be used instead of the former at the discretion of the minister. In the *Lord's Prayer,* the American service reads, " Our Father WHO art, &c." After the Lord's Prayer, the words, " O God, make speed to save us. O Lord, make haste to help us," are omitted. The four last verses of the *Venite* are omitted, and the 9th and 13th verses of the 96th Psalm inserted in their stead. After the Psalms are finished, the *Gloria Patri* or the *Gloria in Excelsis* must be said or sung. In the *Te Deum,* as well as in the Psalms, the metrical punctuation is set aside. The 16th verse of the former reads thus, " When thou tookest upon thee to deliver man, thou didst humble thyself to be born of a virgin." In the *Benedicite*, the address to Ananias, Azarias, and Misael, is omitted. The last eight verses of the *Benedictus* are omitted. In the *Apostles' Creed* is to be noticed the variation already mentioned on the descent into hell, which has occasioned so much controversy. The expression, " he rose again," is also changed to " he rose." Then follows the *Nicene Creed*, which may be substituted for the former at the discretion of the minister. Subsequently to the Creed, immediately after the words " let us pray," the whole of the versicles, as well as the Lord's Prayer, are omitted as far as the prayer, " O God, make clean our hearts within us." The *first Collect* is omitted when the Communion Service is read.

The *Prayer for the President* is slightly altered from the Prayer for the King. The expression "our most gracious Sovereign Lord " is changed to " thy servant the President of the United States." The words, " High and Mighty, King of Kings, Lord of Lords, the only Ruler of Princes," are altered to " the High and Mighty Ruler of the Universe." " Health and wealth," is altered to " health and prosperity ;" and the petition for victory over his enemies is wholly omitted. This prayer is *always*

M 3

used at Morning and Evening Service. The Prayer
for the Royal Family is of course entirely set aside.
In the prayer for the *Clergy and People*, the phrase
" who alone worketh great marvels," is changed to
" from whom cometh every good and perfect gift."
After this are inserted the prayer " for all Conditions of Men," and the General Thanksgiving.

In the *Evening Service*, besides the alterations
above specified, the " Magnificat," and the " Nunc
Dimittis," are omitted, and the " Bonum est confi-
teri," and " Benedic, anima mea," are substituted.
In the Collect for *Aid against Perils*, the words
" Lighten our darkness, we beseech thee, O Lord,
and "—are changed to—" O Lord, our heavenly
Father, by whose Almighty power we have been
preserved this day."

In the eighth petition of the *Litany*, the American service reads " from all inordinate and sinful
affections." This alteration was made in order to
avoid the appearance of countenancing the distinction between venial and deadly sins. In the thir-
teenth petition, "wealth" is changed to "prosperity."
A petition for all Christian rulers and magistrates
is substituted in the place of those for the king,
royal family, and nobility. " Love and *dread* thee,"
is changed to " love and *fear* thee ;" and in the
29th petition, the American service reads, " All
women in the perils of childbirth." From the

second solemn invocation of the Lamb of God, the minister is at liberty to omit the whole of the prayers as far as the expression, " we humbly beseech thee, O Lord." The General Thanksgiving is again inserted immediately before the prayer of St. Chrysostom.

Of the *Occasional Prayers*, the first is for *Congress*, to be used during the session. This is slightly altered from the prayer for Parliament. The second is for. *Rain*, and is the same as in the English Prayer Book. The third is for *Fair Weather*, and is almost entirely changed. The fourth is to be used in time of *Dearth and Famine*, and is but slightly altered. The fifth is for times of *War and Tumults*, and omits the expressions, " abate their pride, assuage their malice, and confound their devices." The sixth and seventh are the two prayers for those who are to be admitted to *Holy Orders*. The eighth is for times of great *Sickness and Mortality*, and differs entirely from that in the English Prayer Book. The ninth is for a *Sick Person*, and is taken from the Visitation Service. The tenth is for a *Sick Child*, and is derived from the same source. The eleventh is for a person or persons *Going to Sea*. The twelfth is for a person *Under Affliction*, and the last is for *Malefactors after Condemnation*.

Of the occasional *Thanksgivings*, the first is that

of women after childbirth.　The 2nd, 3rd, 4th, 5th, 6th, and 7th, are the same as the corresponding ones in the English Prayer Book.　The 8th is for a recovery from sickness, and the last is for a safe return from sea.

The *Collects*, *Epistles* and *Gospels*, excepting a very few trifling alterations, are identical with the English.　After the Collect for Ash Wednesday, are inserted the three last Collects prescribed in the English Prayer Book for the Commination Service, to be used immediately after the Litany.

In the *Ante-Communion Service*, the Lord's Prayer may be omitted if Morning Prayer have been said immediately before.　After the *Ten Commandments*, may be read, at the minister's discretion, the two great Commandments given by our Saviour as the substance of the law.　The Collects for the King are omitted, and in their stead is substituted the second of the six Collects placed in the English Liturgy, at the end of the Communion Service.　Before the reading of the Gospel the people are enjoined to say " Glory be to thee, O Lord."　The Nicene Creed after the Gospel is omitted when it has been read immediately before in the Morning Service.　In the prayer for the Church militant, the petition for the King and Council is changed to a prayer for all Christian rulers.　The word " curates" here, as elsewhere, is altered to " minis-

ters." In the first exhortation, the allusion to
Judas is omitted. In the third exhortation, the
first parenthesis is omitted, and also the paragraph
between "unworthily" and "judge therefore your-
selves." The expression, "devoutly kneeling," is
also substituted for "meekly kneeling upon your
knees."

A substitute is provided for the proper preface
upon the feast of Trinity. The prayer of Consecration is somewhat different from the English service,
and, agreeably with the first book of King Edward
and the Scotch Liturgy, is immediately followed by
the Oblation, commencing, "Wherefore, O Lord
and Heavenly Father," concluding with the first
prayer in the English Post-Communion, and containing the invocation of the Holy Ghost omitted
in the present English Prayer Book. At the end
of the service the rubric is omitted requiring every
parishioner to communicate at least three times in
every year. The protestation in regard to kneeling
is also omitted, being considered no longer necessary.

In the *Public Baptismal Service for Infants*,
parents are allowed to become sponsors for their
children, if they desire it. The Apostles' Creed is
omitted in the questions to sponsors, and this in-
quiry is substituted for it, "Dost thou believe all the

M 5

articles of the Christian faith, as contained in the Apostles' Creed?" The rubric permits either immersion or affusion, giving precedence to the former, but without any conditions annexed. The sign of the cross may be omitted when parents or sponsors particularly request it. The declaration at the end of the service respecting the salvation of baptized infants is omitted.

In the form of *Private Baptism* the first prayer is somewhat longer, and the examination of sponsors is omitted. In the *Catechism*, the word "sponsors" is substituted for "godfathers and godmothers;" "all the people of God," is the substitute for "all the elect people of God;" "spiritual enemy," for "ghostly enemy;" "both of the soul and body," for "ghostly and bodily;" "civil authority," for "king;" and "spiritually taken," for "verily and indeed taken."

In the *Confirmation Service* the bishop says, "the solemn promise and vow that ye made or that was made in your name," and "which ye then undertook, or your sponsors then undertook for you."

The service for *Matrimony* is greatly abridged. Of the exhortation, only part of the first sentence is retained together with the last paragraph. The phrase "with my body I thee worship," is omitted. The Lord's Prayer is introduced immediately after the giving of the ring. The service terminates with the blessing which follows the completion of the marriage covenant.

In the *Visitation Service*, the special confession of the sick person, together with the absolution, are omitted, and the " De Profundis " is substituted for " In te, Domine, speravi." A prayer for all persons present, and another for cases of sudden surprise, are added to the discretional prayers.

In the *Burial Service*, a selection from the two psalms is used instead of both. " To take out of this world the soul of our deceased brother," is substituted for " to take unto himself the soul of our dear brother here departed," and " looking for the general resurrection in the last day, and the life of the world to come," for " sure and certain hope," &c. The Little Litany before the Lord's Prayer is omitted. In the last prayer but one the American service reads—" We give thee hearty thanks for the good example of all those thy servants who having finished their course in faith, do now rest from their labours." It also omits the petition for the accomplishment of the number of the elect.

In the *Churching of Women*, the 6th, 7th, 8th, 9th, and 10th verses of the first psalm are omitted, as well as the second psalm, and the Little Litany.

In the *Forms of Prayer to be used at Sea*, the necessary alterations in regard to the government have been made, and the expression, " prevent us," is changed, as elsewhere, to " direct us."

The form for the *Visitation of Prisoners* is taken from the Irish Prayer Book.

The forms of prayer for families are abridged from the excellent family prayers of Bishop Gibson.

In regard to the articles, the declaration at the beginning is omitted, as well as the 21st article. The eighth is accommodated to the omission of the Athanasian Creed.   The 37th, being political in its nature, is of course laid aside, and another article substituted, which declares that the power of the civil magistrate has no authority in spiritual things.

The alterations in the ordinal are very slight. After the services for the consecration of Churches, follows an admirable form of prayer to be used at meetings of Conventions.   The institution service has been already noticed, as also the metrical psalter, and the hymns, with which the book concludes.

The above minute account will fully justify the following assertion of the American Church contained in the Preface to the Prayer Book.   " This Church is far from intending to depart from the Church of England in any essential point of doctrine, discipline, or worship ; or further than local circumstances require." And, indeed, considering the circumstances in which the Church was placed, the discerning reader, far from objecting to the number of these alterations, will be disposed to wonder that amid discordant opinions and conflicting wishes, so great an agreement has been successfully maintained.

CHAPTER XV.

MISSIONARY OPERATIONS OF THE CHURCH.

———

Trial of the Bishop of Kentucky.—Author becomes a Mission-
ary.—Madison described.—Indiana.—Bishop Kemper's early
zeal for Missions.—Domestic and Foreign Missionary Society.
—Its resources.—Present organization.—Systematic offerings.
—Their results.—Missionary operations.—Importance of
Domestic Missions.—Account of the Rugby Missionary.

———

I HAD resided in Lexington between two and three
years, when events occurred of an exceedingly unpleasant description. For various reasons, I forbear mentioning occurrences which may ultimately
lead to important consequences, and may form
a striking portion of the history of the Western Church. Suffice it to say, that the bishop was
brought by his Convention to an ecclesiastical trial
before three other bishops; that the proceedings,
in default of a better precedent, were conducted
after the manner of a court-martial; that judgment
was pronounced; and that, although the bishop

was not displaced, a penalty was inflicted. This was the first trial of an American bishop, and it is devoutly to be wished that it may be the last. During the continuance of these troubles, I received an invitation to take charge of a recently-formed Episcopal congregation at Madison, in Indiana, within the jurisdiction of Dr. Kemper, the missionary bishop. I immediately accepted the offer, and proceeded with my family to this new sphere of labour.

Madison is agreeably situated on the northern bank of the Ohio river. It is about eighty miles from Lexington, the same distance below Cincinnati, and fifty miles above Louisville. Its inhabitants amount to between 4000 and 5000, and are characterized by industry, enterprise, and general morality. On an average about six steam-boats daily stop at the wharfs. There are daily packet-boats to Cincinnati and to Louisville, which, besides numerous passengers, carry the mail-bags and a quantity of freight. There are seven places of worship in the town, viz. one Roman Catholic, one Episcopalian, two Presbyterian (old school and new school), two Methodist (Methodist Episcopal and Protestant Methodist), and one Baptist.

Indiana, which a few years since was a wilderness inhabited by savage tribes, is now a prosperous and improving state with a population of half a

million.   The Indians from whom it derives its
name, have been almost entirely removed, and
emigrants are constantly pouring in from the
eastern and middle States. The prevailing religious
denomination is that of the Methodists ; but the
Presbyterians and Baptists are also numerous.
Vincennes, the old capital of the State, is the see
of a Roman Catholic bishop, who has fifteen clergymen under his charge.   In 1835 there was but one
Episcopal clergyman in Indiana. The appointment
of the missionary bishop has produced the happiest
results, and as I have already stated, there are
now eight clergymen and as many congregations in
the State. The parish of Christ Church at Madison
is barely three years old, and already about forty
families are connected with it, and the number is
rapidly increasing. Nearly one third of these Episcopalians have emigrated from England.

As the clergy in Indiana are partly sustained by
the board of Missions of the General Convention, I
consider this a proper place to introduce an account
of the Missionary system of the American Church.

Previous to the General Convention of 1835, a
zeal for the promotion of the Gospel in connection
with the Church had been long increasing among
American Episcopalians.   Having derived their
existence in a great measure from the English
Society for Propagating the Gospel, they had long

been accustomed to regard missionary operations
with respect, and were consequently aroused with
the greater facility to the great work of evangel-
izing the world. In the year 1812, a great impulse
was given to this growing interest by the efforts of
the present Bishop Kemper, then a young man in
deacon's orders, and residing in Philadelphia. He
originated an eminently useful missionary association denominated " the Society for the Advancement of Christianity in Pennsylvania," and was
actively instrumental in carrying it into effect. He
became himself one of the missionaries of that
society for a season; and undertook a mission to
the extreme western parts of Pennsylvania, an
object at that time most important to the Church.
But the new States west of Pennsylvania possessed
strong claims upon the Church; the Indians of the
wilderness ought not to be neglected, and the
pagans of foreign lands were thought to deserve a
share of sympathy and attention. Accordingly, in
the year 1820, a more extensive society was instituted under the title of the " Domestic and Foreign
Missionary Society of the Protestant Episcopal
Church." This society was composed of the bishops
of the Church *ex-officio*, and of all others who should
contribute three dollars (13*s.* 6*d.*) annually, or thirty
dollars (6*l.* 15*s.*) at one time. As there was a considerable difference of opinion in regard to the com-

parative claims of domestic and foreign missions, it
was provided that all subscribers might specify to
what particular missionary object they desired their
contributions to be applied. The presiding bishop
of the Church was president of the society, and the
other bishops, according to seniority, vice-presi-
dents. A secretary and twenty-four directors were
chosen by ballot at a triennial meeting held at the
same time and place with the General Convention.
The directors possessed authority to establish missionary stations, to appoint missionaries, to dispose
of funds, and to make general regulations. They
could not, however, establish auxiliary societies in
any diocese, without the consent of the bishop. In
like manner those domestic missionaries who were
supported by them, within the limits of any organized diocese, derived their appointment solely from
the bishop of that diocese, and acted under his
direction. All missionaries, whether foreign or
domestic, were required by the directors to conform to the canons, rubrics, and liturgy of the Church
in the performance of all the offices of their ministry.
No clergyman could be appointed a missionary without a recommendation from the bishop of the diocese
to which he belonged.

The resources of the society were derived from
the annual payments of members, from auxiliary
societies, and from occasional donations. Yet for

many years it continued in a feeble state ; and as late as 1829, its annual income was only 1500 dollars (337*l.*) Great efforts being then made by a few active clergymen and laymen, the society was relieved from its embarrassments, and its funds were materially increased. During the year ending in May 1832, the receipts were 16,443 dollars; in 1833 they were 19,957 ; in 1834, 26,007 ; and in 1835, 27,621. At the last mentioned period, viz. at the General Convention of 1835, the organization was greatly amended. The principle had by this time gained currency, that as missions were originally committed to the Church, so the Church in its collective capacity should assume the responsibility of carrying them forward. It was, therefore, proposed that the General Convention should exert its prerogative of authorizing missionary operations ; that it should create a society which should be subject to it, instead of independent of it ; and that it should adopt the broad principle of comprehending in this society all who by baptism had become members of the Church. This great and momentous measure was carried successfully and harmoniously by the joint action of the old society and of the two houses of Convention. The Church now originates and sanctions all missionary measures, and all the steps taken are to be reported to the Church, as existing in its assembled representatives. The object now to be attained is, that every baptized person should contribute his proportion to the extension of the Gospel; that every parish should be itself an auxiliary association; and that the clergy, with the bishops at their head, should be the agents in causing this great work to be done with energy and effect.

The society, as now established, therefore, consists of all the bishops, clergy, and members of the American Episcopal Church. These, acting through the representative medium of the General Convention, appoint by a concurrent vote, on nomination by a joint committee of the two houses, a board of thirty members, who, together with the bishops, are called the " Board of Missions." This board performs the functions of the old board of directors, and superintends the general missionary operations of the Church both at home and abroad. The presiding bishop, as before, is its president, and in his absence the senior bishop present. It meets triennially, on the second day of the General Convention at the place of its meeting, and also annually at such time and place as itself may determine. It appoints four clergymen and four laymen as a committee for domestic missions, and the same number of clergy and laity as a committee for foreign missions. To these two committees is referred, in their respective departments, during the recess of the board, the whole administration of the general missionary work of the Church, subject to the general regulations of the board. Every bishop has a right to attend the meetings of the committees. The board appoints for each committee a secretary and general agent with a suitable salary. This agent collects information for the committee, conducts its correspondence, devises plans of operation, and executes the purposes of the board, submitting his measures for approval to the committee for which he is appointed. No clergyman can be appointed a missionary by either of the committees without the recommendation of his bishop, nor can any missionary be sent to officiate in any diocese without the consent of the diocesan authority. The appointment of any missionary, whether domestic or foreign, may be annulled at any time by the written order of a majority of the bishops. It is emphatically declared, that the missionary field is always to be regarded as one, the WORLD— the terms domestic and foreign being understood as terms of locality, adopted for convenience. Domestic missions are those established *within*, and foreign missions are those established *without* the territory of the United States.

Since this new system came into effect, the missionary income of the Church has greatly increased. In June 1836 the income for the pre-

ceding year was 55,249 dollars (12,431*l.*), and in
1837 (a year of great distress throughout the
country) 48,674 (10,950*l.*)

This increase is to be ascribed in a great measure
to the growing prevalence of systematic contributions, in the form of weekly or monthly offerings.
To Bishop Doane of New Jersey belongs the credit
of having brought the latter subject fairly into notice.
It had become sufficiently obvious that with all the
complicated machinery of agencies, charity sermons,
newspaper appeals, and other expedients, the amount
contributed to missionary purposes was exceedingly
small, compared with the actual capabilities of the
Church.   It was plain also that the benevolent
public was not so much indisposed to give, as under
the influence of bad habits in giving.   Excitement
was a grand resource, and when this failed, the task
of arousing to liberal action was difficult.   Under
these circumstances Bishop Doane and other influential clergymen conceived the plan of establishing a more ample, permanent, and effective supply.
The idea was derived from the system recommended
to the Corinthian Christians by St. Paul, when
pleading in behalf of the impoverished Churches of
Judea; " Now concerning the collection for the
saints, as I have given orders to the Churches of
Galatia, even so do ye.   Upon the first day of the
week, let every one of you lay by him in store as

1

God has prospered him, that there be no gatherings when I come." It was justly concluded, that if but a comparatively small portion of the members of the Church could be induced to adopt this primitive practice, the funds thus raised would be sufficient to sustain on a liberal scale the missionary operations of the General Convention. Accordingly in 1833 Bishop Doane introduced the system into the diocese of New Jersey, and it was soon afterwards recommended and partially introduced in other dioceses.

In commencing this plan in any parish the clergyman calls upon each of the members of his flock, and requests him to lay by on every Sunday a certain sum according to his means. The names of the persons consenting are enrolled in a little book, ruled with twelve columns for the months in the year, which is kept by the clergyman himself. During morning service on the first Sunday in each month, the sums laid by in store are collected by the proper persons directly after the reading of the Gospel, and placed upon the holy table with the alms for the poor and other devotionary offerings of the people. The contribution of each person is tied up, or sealed in a paper marked with the name of the contributor. These parcels being opened by the clergyman the several sums are credited to their respective contributors in the proper column for the month, and remitted quarterly to the treasurers of the two committees.

Nothing can be more satisfactory than the results of this system wherever it has been established. To take the small diocese of New Jersey for an example, it may be stated that although the annual missionary contributions of that diocese had previously amounted to only 266 dollars a year; immediately after the system of offerings was introduced, and before it had been fully carried into effect, they amounted to 905 dollars a year. The following table exhibits the average of five years contributions on the old plan from six parishes in New Jersey; together with the receipts of Church offerings during the first year, on the new plan.

Parishes.	Average for five years.				Offerings of the Church for the first year.			
	Dls.	Cts.	£	s.	Dls.	Cts.	£	s.
St. Mary's, Burlington ..	75	94	17	7	271	59	61	4
Trinity Church, Newark ..	49	52	11	3	149	20	33	1
Christ Church, New Brunswick	13	46	3	0	79	98	18	0
Christ Church, Newton ..	5	0	1	2	50	0	11	5
St. Mark's, Orange	7	54	1	15	49	15	11	1
St. Peter's, Morristown ..	12	36	2	15	32	6	7	4

In 1835 the Convention of the Church in Kentucky, by a unanimous vote, urged every clergyman to adopt this admirable system. Accordingly I immediately introduced the plan in Christ Church, Lexington, (of which I was then in charge,) with the most complete success. I visited only the *communicants*, in my efforts to procure subscriptions, and from these I obtained pledges of weekly offerings amounting to 600 dollars (135*l.*) a year. This too was in a congregation which gave its rector 1000 dollars per annum, and his assistant 300 ; besides contributions for many other purposes.

I now proceed to give an account of the present missionary operations of the American Church ; and in this I am guided entirely by the official statements of the secretaries of the two committees. And first, in regard to the domestic department. In this department the number of missionaries is *fifty-six*, and of teachers *five*, total *sixty-one*. Seven of these, including the five teachers, are engaged among the American Indians at a cost of 3000 dollars per annum. Five are stationed in infant parishes of New England at a cost of 1300 dollars per annum. Twelve are in Ohio, Michigan, and Wisconsin, for whom the annual expenditure is 3000 dollars. Sixteen are in Indiana, Illinois, and Missouri, at a yearly expense of 7000 dollars. Ten are in Kentucky and Tennessee, for whom the expenditure is 3000 dollars. Eight in Alabama and Mississippi cost the society annually 2500 dollars. The annual extra expenses of this depart-

N

ment are 3000 dollars, and the outfits of missionaries cost from 1000 to 2000 dollars, making the
whole expense, at present, about 25,000 dollars
per annum (5625*l.*) The domestic committee has
nearly forty vacant stations, which ought to be immediately supplied. Most of these stations are in
the remote west, where, in many cases, every
month's delay in supplying them with missionaries,
is a year's delay in the final establishment of the
Church.

In regard to the foreign missions, it may be
stated that the missionaries are *ten* in number;
and that assistants and native teachers swell that
amount of persons in the employ of the committee
to *forty*. Three missionaries and two or three
teachers are in Western Africa. At Cape Palmas
they are forming their first post, and calling for
help to enter the interior. Their expenses are
about 4500 dollars per annum. At Batavia and
Singapore three missionaries are preparing to exert
themselves among the Chinese, and a small school
of thirty pupils, under two teachers, is now in its
second year. The annual expenses of this mission
are about 3000 dollars. Three other missionaries
are employed at Athens and Syria, in Greece, and
in the island of Crete. At Athens *eight hundred*
children are receiving Christian education from
American Episcopalians; at Syria a press has long

been in useful operation ; and in Crete a school has been commenced under promising auspices. The expense of the Greek and Cretan missions is 11,500 dollars a year. One missionary is now exploring the interior of Persia at an annual cost of about 1500 dollars. The annual expenses of the foreign committee are about 26,500 dollars (5962*l.*)

The importance of the domestic missions of the American Church can hardly be estimated too highly. America itself is a missionary field of the most interesting character. The population of the United States advances with almost incredible rapidity, and doubles itself in little more than twenty years. This surprising enlargement is to be chiefly ascribed to natural increase, and very little, comparatively speaking, to emigration. Hence it follows, that unless some unexpected calamity should intervene, the increase will continue nearly in the same ratio, until the vast territories now embraced within the limits of the Union are over-spread with an abundant population. It may then be safely estimated, that in the year 1900, a hundred millions of persons, speaking the English language, will inhabit these fertile and highly favoured regions. It is a question of tremen-dous import, whether these unborn myriads will present the spectacle of a vast Christian com-munity, diffusing happiness throughout the world, or whether, under the blighting influence of heresy and atheism, they are to forget the true end of their being, and become a degenerate and degraded people. From the latter frightful alternative nothing can save them, but the present general diffusion of Christian principles. The civil government, by its constitution, can render little aid in promoting this great work, and whatever is done, must be done by Christians as individuals, or as organized into associations. Much has been effected in the latter method; many sacrifices have been made, and great self-denial has been undergone; but still the supply of religious instruction is by no means commensurate with the wishes, and still less with the necessities of the people. The American Episcopal Church is becoming sensible of its duty in reference to this subject, and through its board of missions is doing something, though as yet but a little, towards rescuing the American people from the impending danger. Missions to China or to Persia, though commenced under the influence of excellent motives, and though destined possibly to accomplish much good, appear of small importance when compared with those which are to determine, in a great measure, the future character of perhaps the mightiest nation upon earth. And surely those persons may be pardoned, who, without depreciating foreign efforts, still maintain that the energies and the means of American churchmen should be chiefly devoted to the diffusion of pure religion in that interesting country, for which in a peculiar manner they are responsible.

Throughout the western part of the United States, there are multitudes who have been baptized and educated in the Episcopal Church. Yet by far the greater part of these, after waiting perhaps for many years in the hope of obtaining the services of a clergyman, have been swept away by the prevailing current of popular sentiment and have united themselves with dissenting denominations. Still a few remain stedfast, and these few constitute the germs of future congregations, which are certain to be established when missionaries can be obtained.

The Episcopal missionary occupies, of necessity, a post requiring much patience and perseverance. In the first place, on entering upon his station, he must rally the almost expiring energies of the few resident Episcopalians. A temporary place of worship must then be secured by him until a church can be erected, and even this is often a matter of difficulty. Sometimes he conducts his ministrations for years in private houses, in taverns, in schools, in the borrowed or hired meeting-houses of different sects, or in disagreeable and dirty court-houses. His allowance from the board of missions seldom exceeds 250

dollars (56*l.*), and the stipend afforded him by his
little flock is of course always small, and often paid
irregularly or defectively.   Hence he is frequently
harassed with pecuniary difficulties, especially in
those places where the expense of supporting a
small family cannot be much less than a thousand
dollars per annum.   Frequently he finds it necessary to establish a school, and to devote to education the time and labour which should be given to
the Church and the Gospel.

The worthy missionary at Paris, in Kentucky,
affords a fine example of indomitable perseverance.
Mr. Cleaver is a native of Rugby in England, and
was educated a Baptist.   Having emigrated to
America he became convinced of the superior
claims of Episcopacy, entered upon a course of
theological study, and in due time was admitted
to holy orders.   He was stationed in the town of
Paris, where he determined with divine help to
establish a congregation.   Most of the respectable
inhabitants of the place had been baptized in the
Church in Virginia and elsewhere ; but through
the want of a pastor had become Presbyterians,
Methodists, or Baptists, according to their respective inclinations.   Only one or two families remained
who called themselves Episcopalians, yet upon this
foundation the missionary resolved to commence.
He performed divine service, by permission, in the

court-house, and very frequently with a congregation of only four persons. He purchased a piece of ground in a favourable situation, and here, with his own hands, assisted by his two sons and a hired negro, he commenced the walls of a church. His private means soon failing, he performed several tours through the United States, and by dint of repeated applications succeeded in raising about 5000 dollars, including a small portion subscribed in Paris. With this amount he finally erected a handsome house of worship after six years of untiring labour. He superintended the work himself, in order that every part should be done with symmetry and stability. During the progress of his labours, about ten or twelve families became gradually interested in the church, and a parish was organized at an early period. After the completion of the edifice, about twenty pews were disposed of, and the patient missionary expects that in the course of years the church will be filled with worshippers. And what compensation, it will be asked, has he received? During a part of the time the board of missions has allowed him 250 dollars a year, and on an average his congregation has contributed about eighty dollars per annum. But of this he has expended annually from 100 to 200 dollars, and has sustained himself partly by teaching a few pupils, and partly by a small private income.

I would not, however, produce the impression that all domestic missionaries, or even the greater part of them, are required to labour and deny themselves equally with the gentleman just mentioned. On the contrary, there are many instances in which a congregation grows to maturity in a few months, erects a handsome church from its own resources, and relieves the board of missions from all expense in the support of its clergyman. Yet it may be laid down as a general rule, that the domestic missionary must expect many hardships, and comparatively few earthly comforts. And while the devotion and the zeal of the foreign missionary receive due credit ; the domestic missionary must expect little applause from men, and in all his trials must rest satisfied with the approbation of his conscience and his God.

CHAPTER XVI.

CHURCH BUILDINGS IN AMERICA.

Erroneous ideas in England.—Real condition of Church edifices.
—Variety of places of worship.—Scene in an arbour at
Gambier. — Log-church. — Village Churches. — Organs. —
Pulpit and Desk.—Altar and Font.—Pews.—Sign of the Cross.
—Christmas decorations.—Parsonages.—Burial grounds.—
City churches.—Western churches.—Splendid decorations.—
Church Building Society.

It is, I believe, a common impression in England
that the places of worship in America are almost
entirely of a temporary description, and that little
expense is bestowed upon their erection or embellish-
ment.   Such, at least, were my own ideas previous
to crossing the Atlantic ; and my surprise was considerable when I found myself mistaken.   The
architecture of churches and meeting-houses im-
proves, at least, in an equal ratio with that of the
private dwellings.   So long as all the tenements in
a village are log-cabins, a log-church may naturally

be expected. But when the industrious inhabitants have erected more convenient abodes ; when the frame building and the brick mansion occupy the site of the former contracted domicil, a corresponding and frequently a superior degree of improvement may be traced in the houses of worship. As the place advances in wealth and population, the churches assume a more imposing and ornamental appearance. The Gothic tower and the Grecian portico begin to arrest the attention, the organ performs its part in softening the feelings and correcting the taste, and hundreds of thousands are expended where a few hundreds were formerly considered a sufficient outlay. Yet in different parts of the United States different feelings and habits prevail in regard to this subject. The New Englanders, and their descendants in the west, pride themselves not more on their showy and convenient dwellings, than on their elegant, neat, and commodious churches. The Virginians and their offspring, on the other hand, are less attentive to external appearances. They are willing to reside for years in the most ordinary habitations, provided they can furnish a comfortable interior and an abundant table. Hence in the south and southwest the churches possess few architectural pretensions, but the clergy who occupy them are the more liberally supported and the more punctually paid.

Of places of worship there is an almost endless diversity. The Methodists and Baptists on extraordinary occasions conduct their devotions at camp-meetings in the depths of the forests. A square of perhaps 200 feet is cleared from all underwood, and covered with rough benches formed of split logs. Around this square are erected a number of canvas tents, or temporary log-houses, and at one side is a large platform for the preachers, connected with a shed provided for their accommodation. Within the area the lofty aboriginal trees are allowed to stand, and at each corner tripods or similar contrivances are erected, upon the top of which large fires burn by night at the elevation of five or six feet above the ground. Such places of worship are truly romantic, and in the hot weather of summer would afford delightful occasional retreats, but for the wild enthusiasm which too often actuates the assembled multitudes.

Camp-meetings, as such, are never held by Episcopalians. Yet occasionally, for want of a church, our services are performed in the open air, and I recollect with pleasure an interesting occasion of this kind in Delaware county, Ohio. The place of worship was a beautiful orchard, and the time was the month of May, when the abundant blossoms of the apple and the peach filled the air with their delicious odour. A table for the communion was

N 6

placed on the green grass and covered with a cloth of snowy whiteness. Adjoining the rustic altar, a little stand was erected for the clergyman, and a number of benches were provided for the congregation. A large number of persons attended, who behaved with the strictest decorum and propriety. Besides the service for the day, baptism was administered by the missionary to three or four adults, a stirring extempore sermon was delivered, and the Lord's Supper completed the solemnities.

I happened to be witness of a curious scene in a similar place of worship near Kenyon College. It was the time of the annual convention of the diocese of Ohio, and the clerical and lay delegates assembled at Gambier. It was also the period appointed for the annual commencement of the college, and a great gathering of the neighbouring population was expected. Rosse chapel being incomplete, there was no room in Gambier sufficiently capacious for the occasion, and accordingly a large arbour was erected for temporary service. It was formed of a number of poles fixed in the earth, united at the top by cross pieces, and covered with a profusion of green boughs. The sides were protected in a similar manner, and thus a complete chapel was formed about sixty feet square. On a platform, at one extremity, was a pulpit and a communion table, and the rest of the area was occupied by benches. The convention assembled and was duly organized, after which morning service was performed, and Bishop Chase proceeded to read his episcopal address in the presence of a numerous congregation. In the course of this address, he animadverted severely on the conduct of the Rev. Mr. West, in respect to his agency in England in behalf of Kenyon College. Just as the condemnatory expressions were about to issue from his lips, a tall figure in black was seen gliding behind the boughs, and Mr. West himself, who was supposed to be at least a thousand miles distant, quietly entered the arbour, and unobserved by most of the assembly seated himself in front of the bishop. Bishop Chase not perceiving him continued his address, and at the conclusion was about to give out a hymn, when, to the surprise of all, Mr. West stood up, and requested that a copy should be furnished him of that part of the address relating to himself. The bishop complied with his request, and on the following day Mr. West was heard in his defence. It will be recollected that the same Mr. West afterwards asserted his Episcopal character on the ground of an alleged consecration by Bishop Chase, and made some ineffectual attempts, near Liverpool, to produce a schism in the Church of England. He has since been suspended from the performance of the clerical office.

Places of worship like those mentioned above are certainly very agreeable during the warm days of an American summer. But it is obvious, that, even in the most sequestered regions, all who have any relish for the regular service of the sanctuary will desire something more permanent and better adapted to the great varieties of weather. Accordingly the erection of a log-church is often one of the first efforts of the well-disposed settlers of the western forests. Such a church was that at Perry in the vicinity of Gambier. It was the work of a few Irish Episcopalians who had been educated in the established religion, and who in this distant land remained faithful to the Church of their fathers. Their pious undertaking was quickly accomplished. They sallied forth into the woods with their axes, and, having chosen a spot, felled the tall trees, hewed them square, cut them into regular lengths, and with their united efforts heaved up the great logs and constructed the walls of their sylvan temple. The floor was soon formed of planks and the roof was easily superadded. Benches supplied the place of pews, and the same stand answered for both the reading-desk and pulpit. In a building of this kind, of course, both tower and bell are out of the question, and nothing can be expected in the way of decoration.

The places of worship in the older villages are

H. Caswall inv.

Day & Haghe lith. to the Queen.

EPISCOPAL LOG-CHURCH (in the woods) near GAMBIER

Published by J. G. & F. Rivington, London, Jan.y 1839.

often very neat and commodious. The Methodist meeting-houses, however, are generally built in the same plain style which distinguishes them in England. Those also of the Baptists, and in many instances those of the Presbyterians, make few pretensions to architectural taste. Perhaps, the best specimens of country churches are to be seen in New England and the state of New York.

Throughout New England, the old Congregational meeting-houses resemble the village-churches in England. They have a tall square tower containing a bell, and usually occupy a central and conspicuous situation. Many of them are much more than a hundred years old, and the wood-work of which they are composed still remains sound. They are furnished with two rows of large square windows and with capacious galleries. A very elevated pulpit, large enough to contain half a dozen preachers, supplies the place of the smaller pulpit and the reading-desk of Episcopalians. Some of these edifices were designedly built north and south in opposition to the practice of the Church of England. They are generally kept perfectly clean, and are painted white both externally and internally.

The churches of Episcopalians in country villages are also frequently of wood, though churches of brick and stone are by no means rare. The prac-

1

tice of building them east and west has been
entirely abolished, excepting when circumstances
render such a position expedient. In New England,
and the state of New York especially, they are
finished with considerable taste, and kept in a beautiful state of neatness. They are to be distinguished from dissenting places of worship, not by
the steeple, for that is common to nearly all the
sects, but by a single row of pointed windows and
a few other appendages of Gothic architecture.
There are very few so small as not to contain
accommodations for four hundred persons.

Most of them are supplied with organs, which
are deemed almost essential to the proper performance of our public worship, and in a very few places
the seraphine has been lately introduced. The
organ is so great a favourite that even Presbyterians and Congregationalists have adopted it to
some extent.

The pulpit and reading-desk commonly stand at
one end of the church, but there is no desk for the
clerk, that functionary having no existence in
America. The communion-table seldom occupies
its appropriate place, but is often little more than a
narrow board placed in front of the reading-desk,
in the situation usually occupied by the clerk in the
Church of England. In front of the table are
the rails which divide what is called the chancel

from the body of the church, and include the pulpit, the desk, and the table. This arrangement was, doubtless, introduced in order to save room, but it is contrary to the usage of primitive times, and shows little respect to the altar so far as outward appearances are concerned. In some churches of recent erection the old plan has been again introduced with very good effect. The altar occupies a conspicuous and somewhat elevated position in a recess at the extremity of the building, opposite to the main entrance. Above it are suspended the Ten Commandments, the Creed, and the Lord's Prayer, and a railing separates it from the rest of the church. On the one side, without the rails, is a comparatively low and modest pulpit, and on the other side, also without the rails, is the reading-desk, a little elevated above the level of the pews.

The font is generally placed adjoining the rails, for the convenience of the minister, and never near the entrance, according to the ancient practice.

The pews are usually small, and diminish in value according to their distance from the pulpit. They are commonly sold in the first instance, to defray the expense of the building, and are afterwards subject to an annual tax, which is applied by the vestry, as I have already stated, to the support of the clergyman, and to other necessary expenses.

There are but few free-seats in Episcopal churches, and, in fact, there is not the same necessity for them as in England. Few persons are so poor as to be unable to pay for a seat, and still fewer would be willing to accept it as a gratuity. Still, for the benefit of strangers, and others who may be attracted by curiosity, a few places are always reserved. Negroes and other coloured persons have also the privilege of occupying free seats by themselves, distinct from the rest of the congregation.

The sign of the cross has lately made its appearance on many churches, agreeably with the early custom. Bishop Onderdonk, of New York, in a charge to his clergy, has commended the good taste displayed in this appropriate decoration; and has declared that only an *anti-protestant* feeling can consider the sign of the cross as symbolising the corruptions of Romanism.

Chimes of bells are very uncommon, and not more than five or six are to be found in the United States. There is, however, a strong disposition in their favour, and it is probable that before long many of the wealthier parishes will be provided with them. Nearly every church has one bell, but church-clocks are seldom seen in villages and country places.

At Christmas, the Episcopal churches are decorated with evergreens, tastefully hung in festoons.

The holly, the box, and the laurel cannot be obtained, and the boughs of the cedar, pine, and hemlock are employed in their stead. These decorations are commonly arranged by the young ladies of the congregation.

Many parishes have supplied themselves with parsonages, erected by voluntary contribution. A parsonage is always a great benefit to a parish, since it enables the congregation more easily to secure and to retain the services of a clergyman. Some few of these parsonages are quite in the English style. Lecture-rooms and Sunday-schools are also frequently erected in situations distinct from the place of worship. The burial-grounds are generally remote from the churches and are never consecrated.

In the large towns and cities the churches are similar to those described above, but on a larger and more costly scale. The following account of a new Episcopal church in one of the eastern cities is taken from a newspaper, and will serve to afford some idea of a class of buildings by no means uncommon.

"The Protestant Episcopal church of St. Peter is a finished specimen of Gothic architecture. The walls, which rise forty feet above the ground, are built of hammered bluestone trimmed with granite. The dimensions of the church are 65 feet in

breadth by 120 feet in length, including the tower
and vestry-room.   The tower, which is at the
north end, is 23 feet square and 138 feet high, supported by angular buttresses of four stages, and
finished at the top with eight pinnacles, each 30
feet high, crocketed and crowned with finials.
Buttresses are also attached to the walls of the
main building, the ends and sides of which, and of
the top of the tower, are crowned with embattled
parapets.   The roof is covered with metal; on each
side of the tower is an open screen of rich tracery-
work 30 feet high, supported by octagon towers,
surmounted by pinnacles, and crowned by finials.
There are five pointed windows on each side, and a
large oriel window in the south end; the large
window in front of the tower is 24 feet high and 12
feet wide.   The galleries in the church are supported by clustered columns and Tudor arches,
trimmed with projecting pendentives, filled between with rich tracery and ornamental carving.
The ceiling is composed of double-groined arches,
springing from massive pendants.   The pulpit and
reading-desk are in excellent keeping with the rest
of the work for beauty and richness of design.   On
each side of the pulpit, in the end wall, is a handsome niche, the design of which was taken from
Henry the Seventh's Chapel, at Westminster.
The ground-floor contains 138 pews, and the galleries 68.

" At the northern end of the building, in the gallery, stands the organ, a splendid instrument, built by Mr. Henry Erben, of New York; in height 31 feet, in breadth 21 feet, and in depth 13 feet. The case is a very rich specimen of the Gothic, and is furnished with three sets of keys (compass from GG to F alto), and pedals from GGG to an octave below the manuals to D, making the compass of the pedals one octave and a fifth. The number of draw-stops is 34, distributed as follows. In the *great organ*, 12 stops, namely, large open diapason, second open diapason, stopped diapason, clarabella, night horn, principal, twelfth, fifteenth, sesquialtra of three ranks, cornet of four ranks, trumpet, and clarion. In the *choir organ*, 7 stops, namely, open diapason, viol, de gamba, stopped diapason, flute, principal, and Cremona. In the *swell*, 9 stops, namely, open diapason, stopped diapason, dulciana, flute, principal, fifteenth, cornet of three ranks, trumpet, and hautboy. In the pedals, 3 stops, namely, double open diapason, open diapason, and principal; making in all 31 stops of pipes. The remaining three are coupling stops, one of which unites the great and choir organs; another, the choir organ and swell; and the third, the pedals, with the bass of the choir organ. The largest pedal pipes are 21 by 24 inches inside, and 22 feet long; the largest metal pipe is 10 inches in diameter, and about 12

feet long.   The cost of the organ was 5000 dollars
(1125*l*.)"

In the western country some very handsome
places of worship have been erected.   At Cincinnati, in Ohio, there are two new Episcopal churches
in the Gothic and Grecian styles of architecture,
respectively.   The former (Christ Church) cost
53,000 dollars (12,600*l*.), and the latter (St. Paul's)
24,000 dollars (5400*l*.).   Christ Church is modelled
after the new church at Stepney, near London, and
is 70 feet in width, by 110 in length.   The front
is composed of a lofty centre and two wings.   The
centre has a low entrance-door, with a flat pointed
arch, in a square moulded frame, above which is a
lofty transom-window, covered by a gable, and
flanked by two octangular towers, surmounted by
spires with ornamented finials.   The wings have
also low doors, with obtuse pointed arches, above
which are handsome canopied niches, and the walls
are surmounted with ornamented parapets.   At the
corners are oblique angular buttresses, relieved by
dwarf buttresses, and surmounted by crocketed
pinnacles.   The niches, parapets, pinnacles, casings,
&c., are of the light freestone of the country, and
the walls, which are of brick, are painted the same
colour.   There is an ascent of seven steps to the
terrace in front of the building, and five more steps
within the recesses of the doors lead to the floor of

the vestibule, in which are two flights of stairs to
the organ loft.

The organ was built by Messrs. Corrie and
Hubie, of Philadelphia, and does great credit to the
skill of the builders.

The basement of the building is divided into five
rooms, one of which is the vestry, two are school-
rooms, and two are used as lecture-rooms and for
Sunday-schools.   The interior of the church is
finished in a neat and appropriate style.   It has no
side-galleries, and contains 140 pews, all of which
are lined and cushioned in a uniform manner.   At
the north end of the church is the chancel, behind
which, on a raised platform, in a semicircular
recess, is the pulpit.   The railing of the chancel,
the pulpit, reading-desk, and six large candelabra,
standing on the platform, are wrought in light, open-
work Gothic tracery, bronzed, and lined with crim-
son silk velvet.   On each side of the pulpit is an
episcopal chair and reading-table, corresponding
with the pulpit; and above the arch of the recess
are inscribed the words " Glory to God in the highest; on earth peace, good will towards men."

In Louisville, more than a hundred miles west of
Cincinnati, are two Episcopal churches also known
as Christ Church and St. Paul's.   St. Paul's is unfinished; but will nearly or quite equal the church
at Cincinnati just described.   Christ Church is a

plain brick building, but contains a fine organ, which cost 4000 or 5000 dollars. I have mentioned in a former chapter the churches at Rochester, and also the beautiful Gothic building at Hartford, in Connecticut. Those which have been described are a few specimens out of perhaps nine hundred or a thousand.

Church architecture is rapidly improving, and a better taste is prevailing more and more. Cathedrals are still confined to the Roman Catholics; but a Protestant Episcopal cathedral was proposed some time since in New York. The Roman Catholic buildings of that description are often greatly inferior to Episcopal churches. The finest is that of Baltimore, which is an archiepiscopal see. It may be doubted whether a cathedral establishment would strictly comport with the American Episcopal system, in which the bishop derives his title not from any particular city, but from the territory over which his ecclesiastical jurisdiction extends.

On the whole, I think it may be said with truth, that in America the Episcopal churches greatly exceed those of all other denominations in elegance and finish. In many instances the expense of the internal decorations is even carried to the verge of extravagance, and beyond the limits of correct taste. There are churches which rather resemble splendid drawing-rooms than houses of worship, and in which the poor man could hardly feel himself at home. Handsome carpets cover every part of the floor; the pews are luxuriously cushioned in a manner calculated to invite repose; while splendidly-embroidered pulpit-hangings, superb services of communion-plate, and a profusion of silk and velvet, of gilding and of painting, excite the curiosity of the stranger more than his devotion.

I have already stated that churches are built by voluntary contribution, or by the sale of pews. The government, of course, never renders any assistance. An Episcopal Church-building Society was formed in New York a few years since; but it has produced little practical benefit, and is now almost, if not wholly, extinct. The good people of New York are in some measure excused for their neglect of this society by the repeated applications which they receive from infant parishes in every district of the country. The object of the institution was to raise a fund of 25,000 dollars (5625*l.*) to be paid in annual instalments, or otherwise, at the convenience of the donors. This fund was to be under the direction of a committee, and was to be loaned to rising congregations in the West, for the sole purpose of aiding them in the erection of churches. The loan was in no case to exceed 500

o

dollars (112*l*.), and was to be advanced on condition that the congregation should raise an equal sum, or as much more as would be sufficient to erect a small church. In all cases security would be exacted, and the whole amount was to be refunded to the society in a given time; the first instalment on the debt to be paid in two years from the time of the loan.

It is greatly to be desired that some association should be established on a more enlarged scale than the above. In the Western country such assistance is pre-eminently required. Most of the settlers in the new towns and villages are young persons, full of energy and industry, but destitute of the capital necessary to erect a decent place of worship. Could they be assisted with a liberal loan in the first instance, they would generally be enabled in a few years to repay it with interest. The wilderness and the solitary place would be made glad, and thousands would flock to the house of prayer in regions where but lately the white man feared to wander. Along with the Church, the comforts of Christian society, and the varied charities of civilized life, would be established upon an enduring basis. " The edifice of public worship, as it raises its sacred head, has its eloquence and its power. There is a moral attraction in its walls.

It speaks of the hallowed purposes for which it is reared.   It is itself a call to holiness, which will not quite be disregarded.   It shines forth a beacon and a monument, both of philanthropy and of prayer."

CHAPTER XVII.

CLERICAL DUTY AND COMPENSATION.

———

Definition of a Parish.—Institution of a Clergyman.—Clerical
Costume. — Sunday Services.— Performance of Worship.—
Character of Sermons.—Sunday Schools.—Baptisms.—Confirmations. — Marriages. — Churchings. — Funerals. — Regis-
ters.—Further Parochial Duties.—Pluralities.—Extra-paro-
chial Duties.—Examinations.—Ordinations.—Standing Committees. — Ecclesiastical Legislation.—Trials.—Church-poli-
tics.—Sources of Compensation.—Endowments.—Pew-rents.
—Voluntary Contributions.—Presents.—Money more plentiful
than men.—Remarks on the Voluntary System.

———

It has been already shown, that in the United
States the term " Parish" is very generally applied
to persons rather than to places. It is true that
for certain purposes a parish is defined by canon to
be every city, town, village, or township, in which
there is an Episcopal congregation. Within these
limits all Episcopal clergymen are forbidden to officiate except by invitation of the resident minister,
or, in his absence, of the vestry. With this exception,

however, there is no recognition of any geographical limits, and even in the city of New York, where the number of Episcopal Churches is more than twenty, no such division has yet been effected. Generally speaking, a parish may be said to consist of all the pew-holders attached to a particular congregation, with their families and dependents.

A clergyman is elected by the vestry of a parish, sometimes on a temporary, and sometimes on a permanent engagement. Should the engagement be of a permanent nature, he is often, though not always, inducted or instituted, according to the form prescribed in the American Prayer Book. This is done in the face of the assembled congregation, and is a solemn and imposing ceremony. The engagement thus ratified is considered indissoluble, except for some great and weighty reasons. Generally, however, and especially in the smaller parishes, no institution takes place; the minister and the people equally desiring liberty to dissolve the connexion when circumstances may render it expedient. A temporary engagement, in most cases, is not for a less term than one year, and often continues for a much longer period. Still it seldom happens, under the most favourable circumstances, that a clergyman remains for twenty years in the charge of the same parish. The appointment of a bishop to the care of a particular diocese is always for life, and translations, as such, are never permitted.

The ordinary clerical costume is much the same as in England, consisting of a suit of black, and a white neckcloth. The usual dress of a bishop is in no respect different from that of any other clergyman. In regard to the vestments used in divine service, it may be remarked that they are not designed to indicate collegiate distinctions. A bishop wears the usual full dress, with lawn sleeves, when performing acts peculiarly episcopal. At other times he appears in the vestments of an ordinary presbyter. The latter consist of a surplice, with a black silk scarf, a pair of bands, a gown of black silk, and sometimes a cassock and a sash. In the diocese of Kentucky, the bishop has made a distinction between the dress of presbyters and deacons, by restricting the use of bands to the former.

The regular Sunday services of a clergyman consist of morning and evening prayer and two sermons. These are always expected, and nothing more is absolutely necessary. Most of the clergy, however, in their zeal, go beyond these limits. Some personally superintend their Sunday-schools, and some add a third service at night. The Communion is generally administered once a month, and a weekly lecture is very frequent. During Lent, and in some of the city churches throughout the year, Wednesdays and Fridays are observed as days of worship. There is no place in America in which the service of the Church is performed daily, unless the General Theological Seminary at New York may be regarded as an exception.

As I have remarked in a former chapter, clergymen are more frequently tempted to exceed their strength than to become remiss. I have known a bishop request a clergyman to diminish his labours; but have never known a bishop stimulate to increased exertion.

In the performance of common prayer, the whole congregation join in the responses, and the psalms and hymns are given out by the clergyman. In the reading of the Creed a disagreeable confusion sometimes arises when a stranger officiates. In my own parish, on one occasion, a bishop performed the services in the morning, and two priests in the afternoon and evening. The bishop read the article on the descent into hell, as it stands in the English Prayer Book; the first presbyter read the substitute permitted in America, " He went into the place of departed spirits;" and the second omitted the article altogether. Very frequently the clergyman says one thing and the congregation another; and occasionally individuals, disapproving of their pastor's choice, repeat with marked emphasis the phrase which he rejects. The practice of turning to the east when the Creed is repeated has been entirely forgotten.

In the congregation there are few, if any, poor persons, so that it is often difficult to dispose of the communion-alms according to the regulations of the Rubric. The Episcopal congregations are generally composed of highly-intelligent and respectable people, many of whom have received an excellent education. Hence, intellectual sermons are held in great esteem, and elegant composition is duly appreciated. Common-place discourses are disregarded, and old or borrowed ones are never tolerated. Some oratorical genius is always necessary to clerical success in republican America. Yet it too frequently happens that ordinary sentiments are dressed in a florid and figurative style, approaching to the nature of bombast.

Sunday-schools are conducted on various plans. The American Sunday School Union has published books of instruction which are used by Baptists, Presbyterians, Congregationalists, and some Episcopalians. On the other hand, the Episcopal Sunday School Union designs in its publications to illustrate the peculiar principles of the Church, as well as the general doctrines of the Bible. It has issued a number of catechisms explanatory of the Church Catechism, of the Prayer Book, of the Life of Christ, of Episcopacy, of the Evidences of Christianity, &c. It has published also a course of Scriptural Study, Lessons on the Bible, Bishop Hobart's Liturgy for Sunday Schools, and various little religious books, adapted to a juvenile library. All classes of white children voluntarily attend the Sunday-schools, on terms of perfect equality. The instruction is almost wholly of a religious kind, reading and spelling being taught in the common or private schools. Still it too frequently happens that parents regard Sunday-schools as exonerating them from the pious instruction of their offspring, while the pastor devolves this important charge upon young and inexperienced teachers. These teachers also occasionally regard themselves as possessing independent powers, and forget that, although their labours are gratuitous, they act solely by the authority and with the permission of their pastor.

Baptisms are usually performed in the church in the presence of the congregation, and immediately after the second Lesson, as the Rubric requires. On account of the neglect into which infant baptism has fallen among other denominations, an Episcopal clergyman is frequently called upon to baptize adults. Both infants and adults are sometimes baptized by immersion, according to the Rubric. In one Episcopal church in Kentucky, the font is in the shape of a large bath, six or seven feet in

length.   Several persons in Philadelphia have been
baptized by Episcopal clergymen in the river
Schuylkill.   No fees are taken for baptism, nor,
indeed, generally, for any occasional service, except
matrimony.

In regard to confirmation, some satisfactory
evidences of serious feeling and religious character
are required by the pastor before a person is presented to the bishop.   Hence, the candidates are
usually of a riper age than in England; and the
rite is rendered solemn and impressive in the highest degree.   It is regarded as immediately intro-
ductory to the holy communion, and is performed
in the parish church to which the candidates
belong.

Marriages are generally performed by ministers
when the parties are respectable, and when a clergyman can be obtained.   They are sometimes
celebrated in private houses, and sometimes in
churches, although there is a growing preference
for the latter.   The laws of the different states, in
regard to marriage are various.   In some, the
banns must be published for three successive Sundays.   In others, licences are issued by the clerk
of the county court.   Young couples accordingly
often elope from one state to another in which the
laws are less severe.   Too great a facility is permitted in regard to the granting of divorces.   It

has been said that in Kentucky, upwards of two hundred divorces per annum are allowed by the legislature and the county courts. This, however, is an exaggeration, the average not exceeding fifty or sixty. Even in New England, a separation during the space of five years is sufficient to render a marriage void. The fee for matrimony varies from three dollars to a hundred, according to the wealth or liberality of the parties.

The service for the Churching of Women is seldom used, except in the case of English people, who desire to conform to the practice of their ancestors.

Funeral rites are generally performed at the residence of the deceased, as far as the termination of the lesson from 1 *Cor.* xv. The remainder of the services are read at the place of burial, which is either in a private garden or in a public unconsecrated grave-yard. The Methodist funeral-service is the same with that of the Church. The face of the deceased is generally left uncovered till it is committed to the ground, and the numerous spectators press forward to take a last look at the features. Great sympathy is usually manifested on these occasions, and no observer of a funeral would regard the Americans as a cold, unfeeling people.

Of the above occasional services, the minister is required by canon to keep a register, from which regular returns are made to the Diocesan, and thence to the General Convention.

Frequent and systematic visiting from house to house for religious conversation, is expected by the people, and is practised to a considerable extent. Bible classes, for the scriptural instruction of old and young, are also in general use, and extensively popular. In the slave states there is the further duty of attending to the spiritual wants of the negro population. Here the labours of a clergyman are restricted by the laws which limit the instruction of slaves to oral teaching. Still, much is done, even in this way, by our clergy, when the negroes have not previously come under the sway of other denominations.

In country places a clergyman often has the charge of two or three small parishes, which are sometimes twenty, thirty, or even forty miles distant from one another. In such cases the minister commonly resides in the most central station, and performs his journeys on horseback.

Besides parochial duties, there are many others which a clergyman is required to perform. He may, for instance, be called upon by his bishop to assist .in the *examination* of a candidate for orders. Candidates for deacon's orders must generally pass four different examinations in the presence of the bishop and two or more priests. The first examination comprises natural and moral philosophy, rhetoric, Hebrew, Greek, and Latin. The second is in reference to the various books of Scripture, their history, and interpretation. The third is on the evidences of Christianity, and systematic divinity. The last requires a knowledge of church history and polity, the Prayer Book, and the constitution and canons of the Church. The examination of candidates for the priesthood are of a similar character.

Presbyters may also be required to attend at the *ordination* of priests. On such occasions, they lay their hands on the candidates, together with the bishop, in token of their approbation.

They are likewise frequently required to discharge the responsible functions assigned to members of the *standing committee*, and described in the fifth chapter. As *trustees* of colleges, or of theological seminaries, they likewise perform many laborious duties.

Once a year, they attend the *Diocesan Convention* as ecclesiastical legislators, and may be appointed to perform a journey of perhaps a thousand miles or more as delegates to the General Convention at Philadelphia. Of course, they are not bound to act in such capacity unless they are able and willing.

When a *clerical trial* unhappily occurs, a clergyman may be called to the performance of painful and perplexing duties, requiring the closest attention and the most patient thought. These duties have been mentioned in the fifth chapter, in which the mode of conducting examinations of this nature has been described.

Clergymen of the Episcopal Church very seldom accept any office connected with the civil government. One of the few cases of this kind was that of Bishop Chase, who for some years was postmaster at Gambier. He thus obtained the privilege of *franking*, and was enabled to conduct an extensive correspondence in behalf of the college without charge. Many of the clergy do not even give themselves the trouble of voting at elections; and many consider it inexpedient to take any part in civil politics. Still there are *church politics*, which afford the clergy ample scope for conversation and action.

The compensation of the clergy is derived from landed or funded endowments, from pew-rents, from voluntary contributions, from the Board of Missions, from occasional presents, and from matrimonial fees. The endowments established for this purpose are considerable and increasing. So far from any general prejudice existing against them, it may be affirmed that endowments, both for churches and seminaries, are obtained as often as the people

can be induced to contribute them. The millions
of dollars possessed by Trinity Church, New York,
are derived from a small endowment made previous
to the revolution, the title to which has remained
unshaken by political disturbances and the lapse of
successive generations. From this source the clergy
of New York derive a considerable portion of their
subsistence, and the diocese of New York a large
share of its prosperity. The lands in Vermont,
originally granted to the Propagation Society, have
been recovered, as I have shown, by a legal process, and assist considerably in the support of the
bishop and clergy of that state. It is said that the
glebes in Virginia might be recovered on similar
principles, if the Church there deemed it expedient
to contend for her right. I have already mentioned
the endowment of more than a hundred thousand
dollars recently contributed in New York as a fund
for the support of the bishop. The same course
has been adopted in other dioceses with a good
prospect of ultimate success. A gentleman, once
rector of a parish in Connecticut, told me, that
having experienced some inconvenience from the
irregular payment of his salary, he stated his difficulty to his parishioners, who immediately raised
a fund of ten thousand dollars. The interest of
this fund, at 6 per cent., was sufficient for his
support.

It is probable that endowments may ultimately become a grand source of clerical compensation. At present, however, they are few compared with the number of parishes, and are principally confined to the older and wealthier portions of the United States. Accordingly, pew-rents are generally relied upon, and, when properly managed, afford a regular and permanent supply. Rents of this kind are collected with greater facility than voluntary contributions, and accord better with the mercantile habits of the people. The assessments are usually made by the vestry, and each person selects a cheap or an expensive pew, according to his inclination. Sometimes the pews are annually let at auction to the highest bidder, and in this case the clergyman may estimate his popularity by the prices which they bring. Should there be a considerable diminution in the amount of rent, he may regard it as a broad hint that he is expected to depart, and seek another parish.

Voluntary contributions are seldom depended on except in feeble and infant congregations. There is generally a disposition among the parishioners to pay the full amount of their subscriptions; but delay and thoughtlessness, on their part, sometimes embarrass the clergyman and involve him in difficulty. Yet, within the last few years, this evil has been greatly mitigated by the operation of the

Board of Missions. A parish which is unable to support its clergyman is usually made a missionary station, and the minister receives from the treasurer of the board a punctual quarterly payment, which is limited to 500 dollars (112*l.*) per annum, and is generally about half that amount. In this way, between voluntary contributions and a fixed income, a tolerably comfortable maintenance is secured. The missionary bishop is supported wholly by the Board of Missions, which voted him 2000 dollars a year (450*l.*), besides his travelling expenses. The foreign missionaries are of course sustained in the same way, and can expect no voluntary contributions from their flocks for an indefinite period.

Valuable presents are often made to a clergyman who possesses the affections of those under his charge. Not unfrequently he receives a waggon load of substantial comforts, such as two or three barrels of flour, ten or twelve bushels of apples, a barrel of cider, and a sack of potatoes. Sometimes he is agreeably surprised by the receipt of a complete suit of clerical apparel, a hat, a pair of boots, or a variety of articles for his wife and children. I am acquainted with a young clergyman who, within a few weeks, received two or three fees for marriage of a hundred dollars each (22*l.*) I have known fifty dollars (not a fee) to be presented to a clergyman on a baptismal occasion, and an equal amount at a funeral, though gifts of this description are not frequent. Medical men and lawyers seldom charge a clergyman for their services, and quite recently the missionary bishop was conveyed on board a steam-boat, without cost, from New Orleans to St. Louis, a voyage of more than a thousand miles. Other examples of this nature have been already mentioned in the seventh chapter.

It may be laid down as a general rule that no clergyman, possessed of agreeable temper and manners, with a moderate share of zeal and talents, will be suffered to want a competent support. Throughout the American Church money is more easily obtained than clergymen, and the Board of Missions is more urgent in its appeals for additional missionaries, than for increased pecuniary resources. The average stipend of an Episcopal clergyman, exclusive of presents, &c. is not far from 600 dollars. (135*l*.) It is seldom below 400, and in the large towns and cities varies from 1500 (337*l*.) to 3500. (787*l*.) The average may appear an inadequate compensation when the amount of labour is considered ; but on the other hand, it will be recollected, that in America living is, on the whole, cheaper than in England, while rates and taxes are almost too small to be mentioned. In the neighbourhood of Lexington, in Kentucky, where assessments of this kind are considered high, the entire amount paid by the owner of a house and farm worth 4000 dollars, is not more than seven dollars per annum, or less than one fifth of a dollar for every hundred.

In the eastern states, clergymen of economical habits are enabled to save enough for their support in old age, and to leave something for the benefit of their families. Clerical engagements are, however, generally unfavourable to health, and few ministers attain to their sixtieth year. There are several societies for the relief of the widows and children of deceased clergymen, but I have no reason to think that their funds are in great demand. A considerable number of the bishops and other clergy possess independent incomes, which they employ for the benefit of the Church.

Such is the voluntary system as it exists among American Episcopalians. It will at once be perceived that this system was not adopted from choice; but from absolute necessity. There is scarcely any such analogy between the circumstances of religion in America and in England, as would furnish an important argument in favour of, or against the English system. American Episcopalians are generally satisfied that to set up an establishment in America, would be the utmost folly, and that to break down the establishment in England, would be exceedingly unwise and injurious. That there are defects in the American system is freely admitted. It is, for instance, obvious, that clergymen are too dependent for their support on popular favour, and that although the present great demand for ministerial services counteracts the evil effects of this dependence, the time may arrive when a pastor will be too much under the control of his flock. At the same time, however, the increased operations of the Board of Missions suggest a method by which, whenever it becomes necessary, the clergy may be sustained by the Church collectively, and relieved from all dependence on individual congregations. A few years may effect great changes, and from the intelligence of the laity, and their deep interest in the real welfare of the Church, it can hardly be doubted that the system will finally prevail, which, on the whole, is best for clergy and people.

CHAPTER XVIII.

NON-EPISCOPALIANS AND ROMAN CATHOLICS.

———

Origin of the American Sects.—Their relative numbers.—Their
Unity of Doctrine.—Recapitulation of the Sects.—Revivals.
—Religious eccentricities.—True method of Christian Union.

———

HITHERTO the attention of the reader has been
chiefly confined to that body which, by distinction,
is denominated in England " the Church."   In
order to convey a correct idea of the relative importance of the American Church, it will be necessary to give a brief account of the numbers, character, and influence of those religious bodies which
are not comprehended within its pale.   I cannot
pretend to great minuteness in treating of a subject
so extensive and complicated. Yet such statements
as are given will be derived from credible testimony,
from official reports, and from personal observation.

The origin of many of the American sects has been briefly stated in the tenth chapter. The first Baptists, Roman Catholics, Congregationalists, Quakers, Swedenborgians, Methodists, and Presbyterians were emigrants from Great Britain. Holland sent forth the Dutch Reformed, and Germany, Sweden, and Finland, the Lutherans, Mennonites, Moravians, and German Reformed. The Jews emigrated from all the nations of Europe. The Shaker sect was founded by Ann Lee, an Englishwoman, the Campbellite Baptists by Alexander Campbell, a Scotchman, still living. The Dunkers were established by a German residing in Pennsylvania, and the Universalists and Unitarians derive their origin chiefly from English preachers of the last century. I am not aware that America has given birth to any entirely new sect, with the exception of the ridiculous Mormonites. Yet numerous subdivisions of sects have originated on the western side of the Atlantic. Among these may be reckoned a great variety of Baptists, the New School and Cumberland Presbyterians, the Protestant or Radical Methodists, the Hicksite Quakers, and others of less importance.

The great progress and numbers of many of the above sects, have also been accounted for in the tenth chapter. In the first place, it was remarked that the emigrants of the non-episcopal and Roman

1

Catholic denominations were originally more numerous than those of the English Church, and in
the second place, the British Government neglect-
ing to provide bishops for America, the number
and the influence of Episcopal clergymen was restrained within narrow limits. Estimating the
present number of Episcopalians at half a million,
it may be stated that the Baptists of all kinds are
about seven times as numerous as the Episcopalians, the Methodists of two kinds five-fold, the
Presbyterians of six kinds about four-fold, the Congregationalists between two and three-fold ; and
the Roman Catholics considerably more than equal.
The Universalists are about equal to the Episcopalians. The Lutherans about three-quarters of
their number ; the German Reformed one-half ;
the Dutch Reformed less than half ; the Unitarians
nearly a third, and the Quakers about a quarter.
With respect to the excellent Moravians, the Jews,
Mormonites, Shakers, Dunkers, Swedenborgians,
&c. their numbers are too small to admit of any
useful comparison, the whole together, probably,
not exceeding seventy thousand.

Of the above denominations, the greater part of
the Methodists, perhaps two millions of their number, the Roman Catholics, and the Moravians, recognise Episcopal jurisdiction equally with the
Protestant Episcopalians. The Moravians are

under bishops of their own, who trace their succession remotely to the Greek Church. The Methodist Episcopacy originated with Messrs. Asbury and Coke, two gentlemen appointed by John Wesley as superintendents of the connection in America. This episcopacy, notwithstanding its deficiency of Apostolic authority, exerts great power, and commands the obedience of preachers and people.

Precomposed forms of worship are used to a greater or less extent by the Roman Catholics, the Moravians, the Methodists, the Dutch Reformed, the Jews, the Unitarians, and the Swedenborgians.

In regard to doctrine, I have already remarked that the great majority of American religionists are orthodox. This is most emphatically the case ; and affords a strong evidence that the Bible alone is sufficient to impart a knowledge of all truth necessary to salvation. It is a fact, which even a high Churchman can contemplate with pleasure, that the Episcopalians, the Congregationalists, the Dutch Reformed, the German Reformed, the Lutherans, the Methodists, the Moravians, the Presbyterians, and most of the Baptists and Quakers, agree in maintaining nearly all the truths contained in the Apostles' Creed, the Nicene Creed, and the Thirty-nine Articles. Among these denominations is found almost the whole religious energy of the country, and from these the great philanthropic institutions of America derive their prosperity and vigour.

The Baptist sects, taken collectively, constitute the prevailing denomination. Yet their influence on society is little felt, on account of their divisions and their uneducated ministry. Altogether, they constitute a motley collection of religious bodies. Besides the old Calvinistic Baptists, who are the most numerous, there are the Free-will, the Seventh-day, and the Six-principle Baptists, who, I believe, are also found in England. The Christian Baptists deny the proper divinity of Christ. The Campbellite Baptists maintain that the Holy Spirit is promised only to those who have been immersed. Many of them do not wholly admit the doctrine of the Trinity, and hold the doctrine of Atonement in a modified sense. They profess to agree with Episcopalians in baptizing for the remission of sins, and quote many of our divines in support of their theory of baptismal regeneration. My own impression is, that the success of Alexander Campbell is greatly owing to a re-action in the public mind against the lax opinions on the subject of Baptism, the antinomianism, and the enthusiastic views of spiritual agency which commonly prevail in the west. The Campbellites have a new version of the New Testament, compiled by their founder from the versions of Macknight, Doddridge and others,

P

with some variations of his own. They are numerous in Kentucky, Tennessee, and Virginia.

A miserable sect of Seed Baptists, or Snake Baptists, is said to exist in the west, who carry the Calvinistic system to a tremendous length. They hold that all mankind are divided into two classes, the seed of the woman and the seed of the serpent. The seed of the woman are necessarily saved, and the seed of the serpent necessarily lost. This is one form of that fatalism which prevails to a great extent among the western and southern Baptists. It is quite common to meet with persons who consider that the religious education of children is a sacrilegious interference with the work of the Holy Spirit.

The Dunkers are principally German Baptists. They have a dress peculiar to themselves, consisting of a long coat reaching down to their heels, with a girdle round the waist, and a hood hanging from the shoulders like the dress of the Dominican Friars. The men do not shave the head or the beard. The men and women have separate dwellings, and do not meet even at their devotions. They live chiefly on roots and other vegetables, the use of flesh being generally prohibited. Each inhabits a distinct cell, with a bench for a bed, and a block of wood for a pillow. They consider penance and mortification necessary to salvation. They admit of works of supererogation, and deny the eternity of future punishment. Their number is less than thirty thousand.

The real strength of the Baptists lies in the eastern states. Here the ministers are orthodox and well-trained, and the people intelligent. They are making vigorous efforts to promote education and missions, and have the management of many respectable literary and theological institutions. The fatalism of the western and southern Baptists is a great obstacle to the growth of missionary and Bible societies among them, and, in short, of every thing which appears in the shape of *means*.

The Roman Catholics are principally Irish, or the immediate descendants of the Irish. In Maryland many of them are native Americans. In Louisiana the Roman Catholics are found chiefly among those speaking the French language. In the western states there are many of this denomination from Germany and Switzerland. The Roman Catholics increase rapidly, but almost entirely by emigration. Yet by means of their numerous and well-conducted schools and colleges, they are daily acquiring a more powerful hold upon the public mind; and not unfrequently their pupils become their proselytes. Their first bishop was consecrated in 1790, six years after the consecration of the Protestant Bishop Seabury. They have at present, fifteen dioceses, one archbishop, fourteen bishops, 547 congregations, 422 clergymen, 11 ecclesiastical seminaries, 148 clerical students, 15 colleges, 27 female religious institutions, 38 female academies, 39 charitable institutions, and 6 periodical publications devoted to their interests. They have, perhaps, gained strength by the rash and incautious manner in which they have been opposed by Presbyterians and others. The manifold subdivisions of the Protestant community afford them, likewise, a fruitful subject for specious argument in behalf of their own peculiarities.

The Methodists are numerous in all parts of the country. They have more than 3000 travelling preachers, who are under the superintendence of six bishops. These bishops have no dioceses, but are employed in travelling and visiting the different conferences. The Methodist laity have no voice in their ecclesiastical councils. The bishops and clergy preside over all, with no check from the popular ranks, and the congregations are seldom allowed any influence in the choice of a preacher. Hence the Methodist system is far from democratic, and possesses all the elements required for decisive and energetic action. The American Methodists are a useful people; but certainly are not without their faults. Their camp-meetings often present the most extraordinary spectacles of enthusiasm. Sermons and exhortations succeed each other in quick succession; the most lively hymns are sung, perhaps, for an hour together; and extempore prayers are offered with extreme force of language and energy of action. The people become powerfully excited; they shout " Glory" and " Amen ;" they scream, jump, roar, and clap their hands, and even fall into swoons, convulsions, and death-like trances. And all this is supposed by many to be the immediate work of the divine Spirit! Yet it is believed that the Methodists are changing for the better. They are making laudable efforts to promote education, and have seven colleges, twenty-one academies, and three periodical publications under their control. Their numbers are increasing, but not so rapidly as formerly.

A schism took place in this denomination in 1830. The separating party styled themselves Protestant Methodists, and differ from the main body chiefly in discarding the exclusive sway of the preachers in ecclesiastical government, and admitting the laity to a share. Their conferences are composed of an equal number of preachers and of elected lay-delegates. They do not, however, amount to a twelfth part of the Episcopal Methodists, and are not likely to increase.

The Presbyterians are a numerous, powerful, and intelligent denomination in the middle, southern,

and western states.   Until the present year they
have been divided into the following sects : Presbyterians of the General Assembly, Cumberland Presbyterians, the Associate, the Reformed, and the
Associate Reformed.   Of the last four subdivisions,
the Cumberland Presbyterians are the most numerous.   They resemble the Methodists in doctrine
and preaching.   They originated in 1810 in the
Presbytery of Cumberland, in Kentucky ; and are
found only in some of the western states.   They
have about 450 ministers, or not more than a sixth
part of those attached to the General Assembly.

The last-mentioned class resembles the Church
of Scotland.   They have just been afflicted with
another schism, the most extensive which they have
experienced.   In May 1838, the General Assembly
divided into two sects of almost equal strength,
containing about 1200 ministers respectively.   The
schism arose from the old controversy between the
adherents of the old and new schools, and there
are now two representative bodies, each of which
declares itself to be the General Assembly.   About
one third of the colleges in the United States are
under Presbyterian influence of some kind, besides
eight or nine theological seminaries.

The Congregationalists, as I have stated, are
principally descended from the Puritans, and are
chiefly found in New England.   They are an in-

telligent and powerful body, and possess seven colleges, four theological seminaries, and about 1200 ministers. They greatly resemble the Presbyterians in doctrine and worship, but differ from them radically in church organization. The Congregationalists possess no common creed; but the Presbyterians, at least those of the Old School, rigidly support and enforce the doctrines of the Westminster Confession. Mr. Colton, an American writer, who has been a minister in both of these denominations, asserts that in both systems the pastor is deprived of his essential influence by the interference of deacons in the former, and of elders in the latter. He who is appointed to supervise the flock, is himself supervised by members of the flock. If he does not quietly submit to their rule, his condition, according to Mr. Colton, will be uncomfortable. He may also expect visitations from women to instruct him in his duty; at least they will contrive to convey to him their opinions. A non-conformist minister, from England, is represented to have said, after a little experience on this side of the water, " I left England to get rid of my lords the Bishops; but here I find in their place my lords, the brethren and sisters; save me from the latter, and let me have the former."

The Dutch Reformed are found in New York,

New Jersey, and Pennsylvania. They have only 192 ministers and one college ; but are an orthodox, pious, and steady people. They greatly resemble the Old-school Presbyterians.

The Quakers are principally in Pennsylvania, and are a respectable denomination. One-third of their number have lately embraced the Unitarian doctrines of Elias Hicks ; and have in a great measure laid aside the quaint dress and language of their fathers. The Quakers of both kinds do not exceed 100,000 in number.

The German Reformed are also most numerous in Pennsylvania, where they have a college. They have about two hundred ministers, and differ but slightly from the Lutherans.

The Lutherans are numerous in Ohio and Pennsylvania. They have four theological seminaries and nearly 300 ministers. Their number is said to be nearly equal to that of the Episcopalians ; but this is very doubtful.

The Moravians or United Brethren live together in communities, and sustain a great number of missionaries in the most savage nations. In doctrine, discipline, and worship, they approximate to the American Episcopal Church, and are highly respectable in character and intelligence. They have only 33 clergymen, and a population of about

12,000. Their principal settlements are at Bethlehem, in Pennsylvania, and Salem, in North Carolina.

The Swedenborgians, or New Jerusalem sect, are the same with those of England, and are a body of mistaken, though perhaps, well-meaning visionaries. They have 33 preachers and a population of about 5000.

The Congregational Unitarians are found chiefly in Massachusetts. They have much wealth, refinement, and learning, and possess the control of Harvard University near Boston. Their ministers are 200 in number.

The Universalists claim a population of 600,000; but are generally a wild and irreligious class. Their doctrine of the eternal annihilation of the wicked is of course a pleasing one to those who do not love the restraints of Christianity.

The Shakers resemble the Dunkers, in living in communities and leading a single life. In their worship they have a regular, solemn, and uniform *dance*, to the music of a hymn which is sung by the elders. They assert that Ann Lee, their founder, is the woman mentioned in the 12th chapter of Revelations. They are industrious in cultivating the soil, and have all things in common. There are perhaps 6000 Shakers in various settlements.

The Jews are said to be 15,000 in number, and

are scattered throughout the States. Being placed on the same footing with all other classes, they are not so strongly attached to their faith and cere- monies as in Europe. Those who are wealthy enter into the best society, and often intermarry with nominal Christians. It is said that many of them have rejected all revealed religion, and sunk into Deism or Atheism. They have an amiable and talented rabbi in Philadelphia, who endeavours, with great fidelity, but little effect, to recall the American Israelites to the practice of their fore- fathers.

The Mormonites are the victims, and to a certain extent, the actors, of one of the grossest impostures ever palmed on the credulity of man. Their delusion seems to be founded upon a prevailing and plausible opinion, which derives the descent of the American Indians from the ten lost tribes of Israel. The Mormonites assert, that in the time of the Jewish kings, an Israelite embarked on the Persian Gulf, and, after many adventures, crossed the Pacific, and arrived on the American coast. To this indi- vidual various revelations were committed, which were written on golden plates, and hidden under a stone in that part of the country now known as the state of New York. In process of time, viz. in the year 1829, an angel appeared to a man residing in the vicinity, and directed his attention

to the spot where the precious deposit was concealed. He searched and found the golden plates ;
but the language inscribed upon them was unknown.
He was accordingly furnished with some talismanic
power, by which he translated the original, word
by word, and thus produced the " Book of Mormon."
This is a singular tissue of absurdities, not wholly
devoid of ingenuity. There are fifteen books,
which fill a duodecimo volume of 588 pages, first
published by Joseph Smith, of Ontario county,
New York. It is said to have been originally intended as a hoax, with the further object of deriving
profit from the sale of the book. It is needless,
perhaps, to say that the original golden plates have
never been produced. The Mormonites assert that
the Land of Promise is beyond the Mississippi.
They also declare that they possess the gift of
working miracles. They consider the study of the
Hebrew language to be a religious duty ; and at
one of their settlements, in Ohio, they recently
engaged the son of a Jewish rabbi, a distinguished
Hebrew teacher, to instruct the whole community.
They already amount to 12,000.

" Revivals of religion," as they are termed, are
frequent among the Methodists, Baptists, New-
school Presbyterians, Congregationalists, Campbellites, and some Unitarian sects. Sober divines
distinguish between genuine revivals and those

which are spurious. A genuine revival is a deep seriousness and a great tenderness of conscience, quickly extending over a congregation, a college, or an entire neighbourhood. It sometimes originates in no perceptible cause, but is more frequently the result of faithful, solemn, and direct preaching. Multitudes flock to the house of worship, and listen with the deepest silence, and often with tears, to the instructions of their minister. Many commence a religious life, and persevere in a steady and consistent course of action. Such revivals have occurred at Kenyon College, and in many Episcopal parishes; and much real benefit has been the result. The spurious revival has, however, of late almost supplanted the genuine revival. A number of preachers assemble, and continue their ministrations for many days in succession, with the avowed object of getting up an excitement. A fever is produced in the public mind, which is mistaken for religious fervour. Women pray and exhort in public, persons under excitement are called forward to the " *anxious benches*" to make confession, the ordinary business of life is suspended, and a vain, irreverent, showy religion is encouraged. The language of harsh denunciation is directed against all who disapprove of these irregularities; reason is outraged, common sense shocked, and the Holy Spirit blasphemed. Ultimately the evil recoils upon the preachers. Many sink under the labour which is necessary to continue the excitement, and suffer the penalty of their imprudence in disease and premature dissolution. Sometimes in endeavouring to make a convert, the unwise preacher makes a madman. Mr. Colton relates, that on one occasion in New York, a preacher having delivered a most exciting sermon, quitted the pulpit and came down among the congregation accompanied by a secretary furnished with a book and pen. Among other persons the preacher approached an interesting girl of fourteen, and having taken her name, asked the question : " Are you for God or the Devil?" Being overcome, her head depressed, and her eyes filled with tears, she made no reply. " Put her down then in the Devil's book", said the preacher to his secretary. From that moment the poor girl was a maniac. Such revivals as these, happily, have never existed among Episcopalians, who are consequently stigmatized as dull, cold, and formal.

American revivals, in general, are partly to be ascribed to the equality of the people, and their habit of acting and thinking in masses. Hence, an excitement of any kind is propagated with wonderful facility. It may be well to state, in connection with this, that religious mania is said to be the prevailing form of insanity in the United States.

The enormous eccentricities of some sects have tended greatly to bring religion into contempt, and to strengthen the hands of infidels.   Still there is much true piety pervading the heterogeneous multitude, and among the Methodists, Presbyterians, Congregationalists, and Baptists, are many shining examples of excellence.   Their Bible, missionary, and tract societies, with other institutions, afford an indubitable evidence of their activity and zeal. Yet it cannot be forgotten, that these divisions are a prodigious evil in practice ; while in principle they are utterly at variance with the Christian system. Many wise men are aware of this, and have proposed various plans for Christian Union.   But, after all, the most reasonable course for these sects would be to return to that pure Protestant Church from which they have generally seceded.   Here the clergyman is free from vexatious lay dictation, and the layman from arbitrary ecclesiastical control.   Here is a system under which the ministry is conformed to the primitive model, and the mode of government to the existing civil organization. Here is a form of worship, Scriptural in doctrine and orderly in arrangement, yet sufficiently diversified to meet that appetite for variety which is natural to man.   Here is a form of Church polity, which, with almost the strength of Romanism possesses none of its tyranny.   Here is a religious community which embraces the real piety of the Dissenters, while it rejects their eccentricities. Here is a Church which discourages enthusiasm, while it excites and cherishes heartfelt devotion : a Church which stands before the public under constitutional regulations, intelligible to all : a Church which is obviously calculated to secure popular rights, to remove just grounds of complaint, to inspire confidence, and to command respect.

CHAPTER XIX.

EXTRANEOUS INFLUENCES ON THE CHURCH.

Influence of the State.—Of the Church of England.—Of the Dissenters.—Disposition to compromise.—High and Low Church. —Effects of the Dissenting influence.—Irregularities.—Uniform front of the Church.

THE Church being composed of individuals, necessarily derives its character in a great measure from the circumstances in which those individuals are placed. Hence, in America, where circumstances in many respects are different from those in England, it cannot be expected that the daughter Church should resemble her mother in every feature and lineament. Mr. Reed, in his generally valuable work on the American Churches, among other mistakes on the subject of Episcopacy, has said that American Episcopalians are disposed " to sympathize with the mother Church so entirely, as that they must reflect all her features, whether they are in or out of a fair and lovely proportion." The facts recorded in the preceding chapters will be a sufficient refutation of this incautious assertion; and, indeed, a thoughtful mind will at once perceive its incorrectness.

One of the most powerful extraneous influences exerted upon the Church is that of the civil government. The American people are accustomed to republican modes of procedure, and, accordingly, it has been shown that the American Church is conducted almost entirely on the popular principle. But this is not all. While the benefits of a republican administration are secured to the Church, its evils are not wholly excluded. Hence the Conventions, both diocesan and general, have occasionally been the scenes of intrigue, while in the election of a bishop there is sometimes an exhibition of the same party spirit which always accompanies the election of a governor or a president. I am far from asserting that these evils prevail equally in the Church as in the State. On the contrary, Christian courtesy, gentlemanly feeling, and the absence of many conflicting interests, tend greatly to restrain the spirit of faction; I only state the fact, that such an influence is exerted, felt, and acknowledged.

A second important source of influence is the Church of England. The daughter sympathizes deeply with the mother, rejoices in her prosperity, and mourns in her adversity. She venerates her learning and piety, and desires to profit by her experience and wisdom. America, it will be recollected, has comparatively little native literature, and, accordingly, the books in common use are generally reprints of English publications. Hence, while the frivolous amuse themselves with the novels of Bulwer or Marryatt, the religious Episcopalian is edified by the writings of Southey, Hannah More, Bickersteth, or Horne. The books in Episcopal Sunday-school libraries are very generally the same which religious parents in England select for their children. The *Parish Library*, printed in New York, by the Episcopal press, contains the works of Leslie, West, Sherlock, Cudworth, Walton, Bishops Jewell, Gibson, Sumner, Jebb, Burnet, &c., with Chevallier's translation of Clement, Polycarp, Ignatius, and Justin Martyr. The Episcopal Theological Seminaries are supplied with the writings of the older and later divines of the English Church, which constitute in America, as in England, a necessary part of theological education. The private libraries of both clergymen and laymen are more or less furnished with the standard Anglican divinity. In addition to this, the *British Critic*, the *British Magazine*, the *Christian Observer*, and similar publications, are circulated to some extent, while copious extracts from their pages always enrich the Episcopal newspapers.

Hence, as it might be supposed, the views of Christian truth and ecclesiastical authority which exist in the English Church, are found also in the American Church in nearly all their variety. A great, and it is believed, an increasing number of the clergy, are strong in their assertion of the Apostolical succession, and decline ecclesiastical intercourse with dissenting bodies. Others recognise all who hold evangelical views as members of Christ's Church, connect themselves with some of their great societies, refuse to speak of them as living in a state of schism, and, in short, symbolize with them as far as the canons of the Church will allow.

Again, many of the Episcopal divines maintain unpopular views on the subjects of justification, baptism, regeneration, and the atonement. Some, on the contrary, are decidedly Calvinistic in their sentiments, and a few consider themselves warranted in describing the former class as " unsound," " destitute of vital piety," " semi-Pelagians," and " perverters of Gospel truth." Still, it must be admitted, to the credit of American Episcopalians, that none of them have countenanced such absurdities as have been exhibited in England by the followers of Edward Irving, and the new school of prophetical interpreters. They are also wholly free from the politico-religious controversies by which the mother Church has been agitated, and never for a moment anticipate the time when the secular arm will interfere with their privileges or deprive them of their endowments.

A third source of extraneous influence upon the Church is found in the multitude of persons who dissent from its principles. Episcopalians, it has been seen, still constitute a small minority of American religionists. In the ordinary intercourse of society they mingle with other denominations upon the most friendly terms, they intermarry with them, and form many agreeable intimacies among them. A vast proportion of Episcopalians have originally belonged to other denominations; and, although they have united with the Church from a sincere and intelligent preference, they naturally retain many of their former habits of thought and expression. They cannot forget who were their fathers, mothers, pastors, or teachers; and early associations are too strong to be easily laid aside. Nor is this influence confined to the laity alone. Probably more than one-half of the parochial clergy, and certainly almost half the bishops, have been originally Presbyterians, Congregationalists, Methodists, or Baptists. Hence, while a large and growing portion of the Church is rising up under the full influence of the Liturgy and Episcopacy; there is also a large portion which sympathizes with other denominations in a less or greater degree, until you come down to those who occupy a state of transition, and are Episcopalians in name rather than in principle. The latter class of persons easily coalesce with those who have already sided with the "evangelical" party in England, and greatly increase their numbers and strength.

The piety and real goodness which is often found among other denominations tends greatly to increase this disposition to approximate. Good people naturally love the society of the good, and it is often difficult to convince them that dangerous errors may co-exist with active benevolence and untiring zeal. In connexion with this it may also be stated, that the dissenting denominations generally extol the piety, the liberality, and the intelligence of those Episcopalians who are willing to merge their peculiarities, while they denounce those who adopt the opposite course, as Pharisees, formalists, and ungodly bigots.

The influence of other denominations is also exercised in another and a very different manner.

I have already remarked, that at a very early period the Churchmanship of Episcopalians in Connecticut had been rendered correct and well-defined by their frequent collisions with the dominant body of dissenters. The same effects are still produced throughout the Church by the same cause, and it may be doubted whether England itself contains an equal proportion of clergy and laity qualified to conduct a successful argument in behalf of Episcopal principles. Some, indeed, in their zeal have been carried to extremes, and, in defending the ancient bulwarks of the Church against modern innovations have almost forgotten themselves to be Protestants.

A few may be found who would prefer the ministrations of a Roman Catholic priest to those of a dissenter, and who consider prayers for the dead, invocations of the saints, a Latin liturgy, and an infallible pontiff, minor evils when compared with the camp-meeting fanaticism of Methodists, the fatalism of Baptists, the innumerable creeds of Congregationalists, and the divisions of all. Quite recently, the rector of a church in Mississippi, alarmed by the apparent readiness of some Episcopalians to amalgamate with other denominations, resigned his parish, repaired to Rome, reconciled himself to the Pope, and was appointed a professor in the college of the Propaganda.

The reader will not now be surprised when he is informed that American Episcopalians are distinguished as high Churchmen and low Churchmen. This distinction does not amount to a division, although it possibly might, but for the conservative influence of the Episcopate and the Liturgy. Under existing circumstances there is much good feeling between the two classes, and a mutual inclination to co-operate for the benefit of the Church. Yet it is not a distinction without a difference. The high Churchman submits to the Episcopate on the ground of its Apostolic authority; the low Churchman, because it is one of the "powers that be." The high Churchman supports the Church as the one Catholic society established by Christ; the low Churchman as the best Church out of many which are good. The one considers the ministerial office to be conveyed by the imposition of a bishop's hands; the other regards it as derived from an inward call of the Holy Spirit. The one scrupulously adheres to the laws of the Church as being ultimately the laws of God; the other is by no means so tenacious, but is inclined to place them upon the footing of expediency.

Many think that the terms of high and low Church should be entirely laid aside, as tending to excite animosity, and to produce a breach. But as long as the marked difference of opinion exists,

6

which these terms naturally indicate, so long these
terms, or similar ones, will of necessity be employed.
I mention the subject in this place, on account of
its close connexion with the influence of other
denominations.

This influence exhibits itself in many inferior
circumstances. Perhaps it produced that Rubric
of the American Prayer Book which permits a
clergyman to omit the sign of the Cross in baptism.
Perhaps, also, it led to that violent objection to the
article in the Creed on the descent into hell, which
has been already noticed. It is certain that some
clergymen, whose views of the Church are not very
high, consider it expedient to give way to the prejudices of the sects by which they are surrounded.
Some admit sectarians to their communion without
making confirmation a necessary condition, as the
Rubric requires. Some shorten the appointed
Sunday service, by omitting, on their own responsibility, the Ante-Communion, or even the Litany.
Some lengthen it by introducing an extempore
prayer at the close of the sermon. Some neglect
to wear the surplice, and a few reject both surplice,
gown, and bands.

Where Methodists are numerous, some clergymen allow the practice of singing various hymns as
the communicants approach the holy table or retire
from it. Occasionally, too, the cant phrases, the

loose style, and the violent gesticulation of sectarian preachers may be noticed in Episcopalian pulpits. In Baptist neighbourhoods there are Episcopal clergymen who greatly desire to see the old English Rubric restored, by which all persons were required to be immersed at baptism, except when they were sick and unable to bear it. I am acquainted with a small Episcopal congregation situated in the midst of Baptists, in which not a single infant has been presented for baptism during seven years, the parents being greatly influenced by the arguments of the sectarians.

Some clergymen, again, almost entirely neglect the observance of the feasts and fasts of the Church. I have known a few who have declined to celebrate Ash-Wednesday and Good-Friday, while they have united with other denominations in monthly meetings of prayer for missions, colleges, or other objects of interest.

The saints'-days, which occur during the week, are very frequently left unnoticed, while weekly lectures on the nights of Wednesday or Thursday are very general. The ancient practice of bowing at the name of Jesus is disused to a great extent; but some extenuation of this omission may be found in the circumstance that the custom is not enjoined by canon as it is in England. Once or twice I have known clergymen to omit on their own

Q

responsibility, the word " regenerate" in the baptismal office, and to show very little regard to the office of sponsors.   Instruction in the Catechism is sometimes almost wholly neglected, and the books of the American Sunday School Union, professedly common to all orthodox denominations, substituted in its stead.   The Matrimonial Service, though short, is sometimes made still shorter by the officiating clergyman, who occasionally takes the further liberty of dispensing with the use of the ring.

A learned and eminent American jurist mentioned to me a circumstance which appears in point. He had lived in a new part of the country, where few religious services were held, and, like many Americans, had grown up to manhood, and had become the father of a family without connecting himself with any religious denomination.   At length, he became convinced of his duty in this respect, and resolved to make as reasonable a choice as possible.

Under the influence of these feelings, he accidentally met with a Prayer Book in a country shop.   He purchased it from motives of curiosity, and commenced the study of it with the acuteness of a lawyer, and the devotion of a Christian.   While perusing the first pages, he was wonderfully pleased with the table of Lessons, and admired the system

1

which brings the whole of Scripture before the
people once in every year. The appointment of
regular days for fasting and abstinence appeared
reasonable and scriptural; and the Calendar afforded him equal satisfaction. The anniversaries of
the great events in our Saviour's life, together with
the commemorations of the early saints and martyrs
struck him forcibly, as powerful means of preserving
a knowledge of the fundamental principles of piety.
In the ten successive days appointed for religious
services at Easter, he perceived a plan comprising
all the benefits of the protracted meetings of the
Dissenters, with none of their defects. The devout
and scriptural character of the various forms of
worship deepened the impression which the first
few pages had produced, and he rose from the
perusal convinced that he had indeed discovered the
true Church. He subsequently removed with his
family to a town which contained an Episcopal
congregation, and here he connected himself with
the Church, which had alike commended itself to
his reason and his feelings. But, alas! he found
that the Church in practice greatly fell short of the
Church on paper, and that many of the excellencies
which he had been so happy to discover, were negli-
gently performed, lightly esteemed, and imperfectly
understood.

I have now mentioned, I hope with perfect candour, the divisions and irregularities which exist in the American Church. I have also traced them to what I believe to be their true source, namely, the combined influence of the Church of England and of the various dissenting denominations in America. Yet I would by no means assert that the irregularities referred to are exclusively confined to one class of persons in the Church. I would not be understood as saying that all, or even a majority of the low Church are transgressors of the ecclesiastical rules, nor that all of the high Church are wholly free from defects in this respect. It is a well-known fact, that in the older and more settled parts of the United States, the clergy of both classes are distinguished by their uniformity and their regularity; and that in these points of view they equal, or perhaps excel the English clergy in general.

The departures from order noticed above, are generally found in newly-settled districts, where society is imperfectly organized, where the clergy are young and inexperienced, and where the prejudices of the sects are strong and deeply rooted. Indeed, there is some reason to hope that the time will come when divisions and irregularities will almost wholly cease. Party spirit is by no means so strong as it has been; the high Church generally admitting that the low Church are growing more consistent, and the latter conceding that the former are becoming more " evangelical." Both classes have done much in the great work of extending religion ; the former by learned and dispassionate arguments for Apostolic truth and order ; and the latter by zealous personal efforts, united with direct and faithful addresses to the conscience. The former labour with energy in the promotion of missions within their own country ; and the latter with equal energy in the propagation of the Gospel abroad.

And, after all, the Church in its varied offices presents a uniform front, which both parties contribute to sustain. Some in their private opinions may regard the Church of Rome as wholly antichristian ; and may almost agree with the Presbyterian, who denies even the validity of its baptism. But in ecclesiastical practice, the Church of Rome is acknowledged, though corrupt, to be a true Church. Its members who renounce their errors must be admitted to membership by all Episcopal clergymen, without a second baptism, and its priests to the functions of their office by all Episcopal bishops, without a second ordination. In like manner, although some bishops may hold the opinion that an inward call of the Spirit conveys the clerical office, and that there are many true ministers who have only received Methodist or Presbyterian ordination; still they never can, and never do, admit a dissenting preacher to Episcopalian pulpits, until he has received the Apostolic laying on of hands. Some, perhaps, may be doubtful on the subject of an Apostolic succession; but the continued applications to England for an Episcopate, sufficiently evince the opinion of the American Church; while among the most sceptical, not one would submit to a bishop claiming his office on the ground of a mere election, and not having also received a valid consecration.

The time will probably arrive when the Church will be less sensible of extraneous influences, and will herself exert a powerful influence upon society at large. The moderation, the good feeling, and the courtesy displayed in her General and Diocesan Conventions, may afford an example which will be felt in the State Legislatures, and even in Congress itself. The regularity, the system, and the discipline of the American Church may re-act favourably upon the mother Church in Britain. Other denominations of American Christians, exhausted by continual schisms, may cast a friendly eye upon her unity and her constant improvement, and may ultimately seek a refuge in her bosom as in an ark of safety. Thus she may become what she ought to be, not merely the pillar and ground of the truth, but a grand centre of moral power, a main source of religious order, of civil obedience, and of general prosperity.

CHAPTER XX.

LETTER TO A CLERGYMAN PROPOSING TO EMIGRATE.

When a clergyman should not emigrate to the United States.—
Exclusion of American Clergymen from English Pulpits.—
Papers necessary to the emigrating Clergyman.—Books and
clothing.—Advice relative to the passage.—Methods of economy.—Advice on reaching New York.—Advice relative to
conduct in society and naturalization.—Remarks on slavery.
—Conclusion.

Rev. Sir,

In the preceding pages you have found a concise
account of America and the American Church.
I flatter myself that I have made you, in a considerable degree, conversant with the general
features of the country and of the national character. You understand the relation occupied by
the Church both to the civil government and the
people. You can form a correct idea of the history
and internal arrangements of the Church—of the
literary and theological institutions, and of the
standing, the duties, and the compensation of the

clergy. You are also acquainted with the efforts of the Church towards self-extension, of the style and appearance of the houses of worship, of the mode of conducting divine service, of the numbers and character of the dissenting denominations, and of the various extraneous influences exerted upon the Church. You are now enabled, in a measure, to judge how far your usefulness and comfort would be promoted by emigrating to America.

Yet before you take so momentous a step, permit me to make a few statements, and to give a few directions, the importance of which I have learnt by an experience of ten years, and a considerable acquaintance with English and American clergymen. I would not discourage your project; but |I would endeavour to guard against the possibility of a disappointment.

In the first place then, allow me to suggest, that if you are blessed with a moderate degree of success in England, you would, perhaps, find it the wiser course to remain in your native land. It would probably be the work of several years to acquire that familiarity with the habits and ideas prevalent in a new country, which is essential to a proper influence. Nor could you very soon feel perfectly at home among a people, who, however kind and hospitable, still differ from you in many points of sentiment and taste. This caution is peculiarly applicable to married clergymen. The difficulty of securing and retaining servants on this side of the Atlantic, is inconceivable by all but those who have experienced it. Not unfrequently a female delicately brought up is obliged, by stern necessity, even in the midst of wealth, to perform the lowest drudgery of sweeping, cooking, and washing. And apart from this, I have known many English ladies suffer exceedingly from the mere want of congeniality with those around them, and pine away under the cherished reminiscences of the mother country.

But if circumstances render it expedient for you to leave England, you should seriously consider whether you might not be more useful and happy in the British colonies, than in the United States. In Upper Canada, for instance, thousands and tens of thousands of your own countrymen are fearfully destitute of religious privileges. Although the Church of England has been established there by law, there is not one clergyman to six thousand souls. Even when the preachers of all denominations are included, there is not more than one to every two thousand, which is below the average of the western states in the American Union. The population is formed chiefly of emigrants from England, Ireland, and Scotland. Among these you can at once enter on your duties, not as an

alien and a foreigner, but as among your own kins-
men and fellow subjects.   It is true that Canada is
not England ; but, at the same time, it contains a
great amount of British feeling and character.
Many English clergymen, after a temporary residence in the United States, have removed to the
colonies, and have derived benefit from the change.

If however, on the one hand, you dread the
severe winter of Canada, and feel little satisfied
with its political situation, while on the other hand
you admire the prosperity of the United States,
and the flourishing condition of the Church within
their limits, you may be assured that, by divesting
yourself of prejudices, and by judiciously accommo-
dating yourself to circumstances, you may, in due
time, exercise your ministry with benefit to others,
and credit and happiness to yourself.   Many of the
American Episcopal clergy are Englishmen, and
are in no respect less acceptable to their flocks on
that account, than native ministers.   Among Episcopalians, at least, there is no prejudice whatever
against natives of England.   But, if you come to
this country, your primary object must be the promotion of religion, or you will experience certain
disappointment.   There is no room here for any
but the hard-working clergyman, who is ready to
devote his entire faculties to the fulfilment of the
grand duties attached to his commission.

And here let me remark, that it is highly desirable you should obtain full orders before leaving England.   By the Act of Parliament under which the first American bishops were consecrated, it is provided that no person deriving his ordination from that source shall thereby be enabled to officiate in any part of the British dominions.   If, therefore, you should receive ordination in America, and afterwards return to England, you would find yourself excluded from all the pulpits of the Establishment.   My own case may be stated as an example, and to some extent, may be regarded as a warning to others.   I was ordained a deacon by Bishop Chase, whose consecration was derived from the Archbishop of Canterbury through Bishop White.   My ordination as a deacon was consequently equally valid with your own, or that of any other English clergyman.   After some time it appeared probable that circumstances might hereafter require my return to England.   Accordingly, I applied to my great uncle, the late Dr. Burgess, Bishop of Salisbury, for admission to the priesthood.   My venerable relative, who had always treated me with the utmost kindness, was strongly disposed to grant my request ; but being anxious to proceed according to law, considered it his duty to state the case to the Archbishop of Canterbury.   The Archbishop referred him to Dr. Lushington, who gave a direct negative to my application. I was, therefore, admitted to the priesthood by Dr. Kemper, the missionary bishop, and ecclesiastically speaking, am bound for life to the Episcopal Church of America. Were I to visit England, and were I there to be invited by my own father to occupy for an hour his desk, or his pulpit, I should be compelled to decline. At the same time, Methodist, Baptist, and Congregational preachers visiting England are freely admitted to the pulpits of their brethren, and a mutual interchange adds strength to their respective denominations on both sides of the Atlantic. Certain it is, that, in this country, the want of a visible intercourse between the Episcopal Churches of America and England, has given force to an erroneous but extensive and injurious notion that our ordination is not recognized in England. It is not, however, my object to find fault with the Act of Parliament, which has been defended by very plausible arguments. I merely state the facts of the case, in order that you may not, by an American ordination to the priesthood, deprive yourself for ever of the privileges of an English clergyman.

In the next place, do not forget to bring with you the papers which certify to your ordination. The American Bishops are, very properly, strict in this respect, on account of the numerous impositions which have been attempted by persons from

England. Yet I have known worthy clergymen, who have been so negligent, that when their letters of orders have been demanded, they have not been able to produce them. Something more, however, is absolutely necessary. You must bring a letter, from your bishop as a testimonial to your good character and standing in the diocese from which you have removed. This letter should be addressed to any American bishop, and should state the reasons which have led to your change of residence. It is also highly important and desirable that you should obtain private letters of recommendation from clergymen and laymen in England to their friends in America. Many of the American bishops and other clergy have visited Great Britain, and are personally known to the leading characters in the religious world. By furnishing yourself abundantly with such papers as I have described, you would be immediately admitted to confidence, and after your canonical probation of one year had expired, you would be placed on the same footing with the American clergy, and allowed to assume the charge of any parish to which you might be elected.

Before leaving England it would also be expedient to furnish yourself liberally with books and clothing. Every emigrant is allowed to import the tools of his trade duty free; and books being regarded as a clergyman's *tools*, are admitted without

expense. In regard to clothing, the difference of
cost in favour of England is such that, by providing
yourself beforehand with six good suits of black
broad-cloth, you would save the entire expense of
your voyage. There are other methods of economy
with which experienced travellers are conversant.
Quite recently, a gentleman of London, having
occasion to visit Cincinnati, in Ohio, found himself
richer at the termination of his journey than at the
commencement of it. He accomplished this desirable result by purchasing New York paper in London at a discount of ten or twelve per cent. Arriv-
ing in the former city, he laid out his New York
money in the purchase of Ohio paper at a discount
of five per cent. This gain of fifteen per cent. on
three or four hundred pounds not only paid his expenses, but left a considerable surplus. A change
in the money market would enable the same individual to return to London with a very trifling
loss.

If practicable, you should by all means engage
your passage on board a packet-vessel instead of a
merchant-ship. You will thus not only be more
comfortable, but will have an opportunity of cultivating an acquaintance with the respectable Americans whom you will find among the passengers. If
they form a good opinion of you, as a gentleman
and a clergyman, you will probably derive benefit

from them in more instances than you would expect. A bishop or parish-minister returning from abroad may be your companion, and may render you the most valuable assistance in deciding on your plans for the future.   At the same time, it may be well to remark in this place, that the slightest laxity of conduct while on the passage is always noticed, and often turned to the disadvantage of the imprudent clergyman.   A person in holy orders, who should suffer himself to be tempted to play at cards or to drink much wine during his voyage, would soon find reason to repent his unhappy indiscretion in the injury of his character and the destruction of his prospects.

Having arrived in New York you should call upon the bishop as soon as convenient, and request him to give you directions in regard to your future course.   State your plans to him with candour, and exhibit to him your most important documents. But, unless you should have an immediate offer of employment, it would not be expedient to remain long in New York.   That metropolis presents comparatively few advantages for the study of the American character.   Living is also very expensive there ; and most clerical situations are pre-occupied. By removing some distance into the country you would not only sustain yourself during your probation, at a comparatively small cost, but would have many opportunities for learning the peculiarities of the people. If you should desire it, you could likewise, in all probability, obtain an immediate support by teaching.

It is highly important that the people should regard you, to a considerable extent, as one of themselves. You should therefore lay aside the Englishman as much as possible, consistently with a good conscience. You should not talk much about England, nor institute invidious comparisons between the old country and the new. Above all, you should be guarded in your expressions in regard to monarchy and the union of Church and State. The mass of the people have strong feelings on these subjects, and although topics like those which I have mentioned may be freely discussed in highly refined circles, you must be cautious as to the persons with whom you discuss them.

On the same principle, you should avoid spending too much time in the society of natives of Great Britain. Englishmen, when they meet in a foreign land, naturally converse on subjects connected with England; they compare the relative advantages of the two countries; they cherish discontented feelings in their own bosoms, and, perhaps, terminate their conference by rendering themselves dissatisfied in the midst of plenty. You should rather endeavour to make yourself happy and at home in

America, by studying the good features of the people and the country, by giving due praise to all that is praiseworthy, and by seeking the friendship of those numerous individuals whom you will find deserving of your esteem.

Some English clergymen in America have gone the length of renouncing their allegiance to Great Britain, and enrolling themselves as citizens of the republic.   But I would not recommend you to take a step which, however justifiable, and even proper, must be, I am sure, exceedingly grating to your feelings.   I do not think that the sacrifice is followed by any adequate compensation.   An Englishman who conducts himself with discretion, and with due respect to the constituted authorities, is not the less esteemed on account of his theoretical subjection to the sovereign of England.   The chief benefits attached to naturalization are, some advantages in the tenure of real estate, eligibility to office under government, and the privilege of voting at elections. As a clergyman you would not desire the two latter benefits, and the practical utility of the first is not considerable.   For my own part, I can testify that, having received ordination in America, having bought and sold landed property to some extent, and having resided in the country for ten years, I have seldom, if ever, been asked the question as to my British allegiance, or American citizenship.

There are certain subjects of a semi-political and semi-religious nature, in regard to which I would rather state facts than offer advice. Such is the subject of slavery, upon which you are probably aware, that a violent controversy at present exists in the United States. Many in the free states have gone the length of asserting that Christianity cannot dwell in the soul of a slaveholder; while, on the other hand, the slaveholders and their friends in the free states, accuse the abolitionists of aiming at a dissolution of the American union. The subject is involved in difficulties unknown in England, because American slavery exists in the very heart of the country, while in the British dominions it has been confined to remote and comparatively inconsiderable colonies. The ministers of the various denominations in this country maintain very different sentiments on this point. Some assert the lawfulness of slavery, others remain neutral, while an increasing number strenuously advocate immediate emancipation. Great opposition has been excited against the last-mentioned class; they have been insulted, stoned, and beaten; the houses in which they have met for discussion have been consumed and levelled with the ground; their printing-presses have been overthrown and broken; and recently, in a free state, one of their number has been murdered, while obstinately defending his senti-

ments. Some English clergymen in America have
heartily joined the abolitionists, and in consequence
have found it necessary to resign their parishes and
return to British soil. It is said also, that their
zeal in behalf of the slave has retarded emancipation
by calling national prejudices into action. I mention these facts in order that you may count the
cost before you undertake a crusade against
American slavery, or even give utterance to an
opinion favourable to abolition.

The work which I have proposed is now completed. I have given you and my readers in general some information upon a new and curious subject, which I hope has proved interesting as well as
instructive. The American Church is probably
destined to become one of the most important and
serviceable churches in Christendom. While it is
unquestionably growing in piety, in resources, and
in unity of action, so also it is increasing in numbers
more rapidly than any other Protestant denomination in America. It has even gained on the fast-
extending population of the United States, so that
it has quadrupled itself during the last twenty-four
years, while the population of the Union has little
more than doubled. Should it continue to increase
in the same ratio, it will out-number the Church of
England before fifty years have elapsed; and before
the end of a century, it will embrace a majority of

the population of the States. That it possesses the proper elements for a healthy increase is proved by the fact, that among the clergy and laity there exists a growing disposition to return as closely as possible to the primitive model, in doctrine, in discipline, and in worship. From the surrounding sects it has nothing to fear, but everything to hope. The more severely it is scrutinized, the brighter it will shine; and the more clearly its principles are developed, the more powerfully it will commend itself to public estimation.

Let the clergy of the American Church then be faithful to their professed principles; faithful to truth and charity; faithful in following the example of their Master; and it will be impossible to predict the extent and usefulness which await the body to which they belong. And while the politician contemplates the future importance of the western progeny of Britain, let the Christian behold with interest the daughter of the Church of England, and adopt the feelings so beautifully expressed by the Psalmist:—" Pray for the peace of Jerusalem, they shall prosper that love thee. For my brethren and companions' sake, I will now say, Peace be within thee."

APPENDIX.

INDIAN TRIBES IN 1836.

(*From Official Returns.*)

I. INDIAN TRIBES EAST OF THE MISSISSIPPI.

1st, *Under Stipulations to remove to the West of the Mississippi.*

Ottawas of Ohio	230
Potawatamies of Indiana	3000
Chippewas, Ottawas, and Potawatamies	6288
Winnebagoes	4500
Cherokees	16000
Creeks	4000
Chickasaws	5400
Seminoles	2600
Appalachicolas	400
Ottawas and Chippewas in Michigan	6500
Total under Stipulation	**48918**

2nd, *Not under Stipulations to remove.*

New York Indians	4176
Wyandots	575
Miamies	1100
Ottawas and Chippewas of the Lakes	2564
Total not under Stipulations	**8415**

II. Indians who have emigrated to the west of the Mississippi.

Chippewas, Ottawas, and Potawatamies..............	1712
Choctaws	15000
Quapaws......................................	476
Creeks	17894
Seminoles.....................................	407
Appalachicolas	265
Cherokees	6072
Peorias and Kaskaskias	132
Kickapoos......................................	588
Delawares	826
Shawnees	1272
Ottawas	200
Weas	222
Piankeshaws....................................	162
Senecas	251
Senecas and Shawnees	211

Total number who have emigrated   **45,690**

III. Indigenous tribes near the western frontier.

The total number of these is about **150,341**

Recapitulation.—Indians East of the Mississippi, 57,433.—Emigrant Indians, 45,690.—Indigenous Tribes, 150,341. Total, 253,464.

NUMBER OF EMIGRANTS LANDED AT NEW YORK AND QUEBEC IN EIGHT YEARS.

(From the " New York Times.").

	at Quebec.	at New York.
1829	13,356	15,064
1830	24,391	30,224
1831	49,250	31,739
1832	51,422	48,509
1833	22,062	41,702
1834	30,217	48,110
1835	11,580	35,303
1836	27,515	60,541

POPULATION OF THE UNITED STATES,

ACCORDING TO FIVE ENUMERATIONS, FROM THE OFFICIAL
RETURNS.

State.	1790.	1800.	1810.	1820.	1830.
Maine	96,540	151,719	228,705	298,335	399,955
New Hampshire	141,899	183,762	214,360	244,161	269,328
Vermont	85,416	154,465	217,713	235,764	280,652
Massachusetts..	378,717	423,245	472,040	523,287	610,408
Rhode Island ..	69,110	69,122	77,031	83,059	97,199
Connecticut	238,141	251,002	262,042	275,202	297,665
New York	340,120	586,756	959,949	1,372,812	1,918,608
New Jersey....	184,139	211,949	249,555	277,575	320,823
Pennsylvania ..	434,373	602,365	810,091	1,049,458	1,348,233
Delaware......	59,098	64,273	72,674	72,749	76,748
Maryland......	319,728	341,548	380,546	407,350	447,040
Virginia	748,308	880,200	974,622	1,065,379	1,211,405
N. Carolina....	393,751	478,103	555,500	638,829	737,987
S. Carolina.....	249,073	345,591	415,115	502,741	581,185
Georgia	82,548	162,101	252,433	340,987	516,823
Alabama	..	..	20,845	127,901	309,527
Mississippi	..	8,850	40,352	75,448	136,621
Louisiana	..	..	76,556	153,407	215,739
Tennessee	35,791	105,602	261,727	422,813	681,904
Kentucky	73,077	220,955	406,511	564,317	687,917
Ohio	..	45,365	230,760	581,434	937,903
Indiana	..	4,875	24,520	147,178	343,031
Illinois........	..	..	12,282	55,211	157,455
Missouri	..	..	20,845	66,586	140,445
Michigan......	..	..	4,762	8,896	31,639
Arkansas......	..	..	..	14,273	30,388
District of Columbia	..	14,093	24,023	33,039	39,834
Florida	..	..	..	..	34,730
Total..	3,929,827	5,305,925	7,239,814	9,638,131	12,866,920

SLAVES IN THE UNITED STATES,

ACCORDING TO FIVE ENUMERATIONS, FROM OFFICIAL RETURNS.

	1790.	1800.	1810.	1820.	1830.
Maine	..	..	..	..	..
New Hampshire	158	8	..	..	..
Vermont	17	..	..	..	..
Massachusetts ..	..	..	..	..	..
Rhode Island ..	952	381	103	48	17
Connecticut	2,759	951	310	97	25
New York......	21,324	20,343	15,017	10,088	75
New Jersey	11,423	12,422	10,851	7,657	2,254
Pennsylvania ...	3,737	1,706	795	211	403
Delaware	8,887	6,153	4,177	4,509	3,292
Maryland	103,036	105,635	111,502	107,398	102,294
Virginia.........	203,427	345,796	392,518	425,153	469,757
North Carolina..	100,572	133,296	168,824	205,017	245,601
South Carolina..	107,094	146,151	196,365	258,475	315,401
Georgia	29,264	59,404	105,218	149,656	217,531
Alabama.,......	..	..	..	41,879	117,549
Mississippi	..	3,489	17,088	38,814	65,659
Louisiana.......	..	..	34,660	69,064	109,588
Tennessee......	3,417	13,584	44,535	80,107	141,603
Kentucky	11,830	40,343	80,561	126,732	165,213
Ohio	..	..	..	..	..
Indiana	..	135	237	190	..
Illinois	..	..	168	917	747
Missouri	..	..	3,011	10,222	25,081
District of Columbia	..	3,244	5,395	6,377	6,119
Florida	..	..	..	..	15,501
Michigan	..	..	24	..	32
Arkansas	..	..	..	1,617	4,576
Total	697,897	893,041	1,191,364	1,538,064	2,009,031

COLLEGES, &c., IN THE UNITED STATES, IN 1837.

(From the " American Almanack.")

Whole number of Colleges 95
Teachers in the same 730
Students in ditto 9240
Volumes in College Libraries 280,930

LAW SCHOOLS, 1837.

Whole number of Law Schools 8
Professors 12
Students 227

MEDICAL SCHOOLS, 1837.

Whole number of Medical Schools 26
Professors 141
Students 2489

THEOLOGICAL SEMINARIES, 1837.

Whole number of Theological Seminaries 35
Professors 83
Students 1057
Volumes in Libraries............................. 72,550

SCHOOLS IN MASSACHUSETTS, 1836.

(From the "American Almanack.")

School Districts in the State 2517
Children between the ages of 4 and 16 166,912
Male children attending school (from 4 to 16)........ 75,552
Female children attending school (from 4 to 16) 70,987
Instructors (Male, 2154; Female, 2816) 4,970
Scholars at Academies and private Schools 28,752
                                                               Dollars.
Amount raised by tax to pay Teachers of Common Schools 356,694
Amount raised by voluntary contribution for Common
    Schools 47,593
Amount paid for tuition in Academies and private Schools 326,642

COMMON SCHOOLS IN THE STATE OF NEW YORK, 1836.

(From the "American Almanack.")

Amount of the Common School Fund, September 30, 1836,
    1,917,494 dollars.
Number of School districts that made returns in 1836.. 9696
Number of Children taught in these districts* 532,167
Number of Children between 5 and 15 or 16 in these
    districts 538,396

---

* Many of these children attend School only during two or
three months in the year.

	Dollars.
Public Money distributed for Schools in 1836..........	313,376
Amount paid for Teachers' wages besides public money.	425,643
Interest on 2,183,200 dollars invested in School-houses.	130,992
Annual expense for books (532,167 scholars)	266,083
Fund for 9916 School-houses (10 dollars each)...........	99,160

Total expense for Common Schools, in 1836 1,235,254

METEOROLOGICAL TABLE FOR MARIETTA,

IN OHIO, 1836.

(From the "American Almanack.")

Months.	Mean Temperature.	Maximum Temperature.	Minimum Temperature.	Range of the Thermometer.	Fair Days.	Cloudy Days.	Rain and Snow water.	Prevailing Winds.
Jan. ..	31.30	63	—10	73	17	14	2.55	W. and N.W.
Feb...	27.23	56	—18	74	14	15	1.80	W. NW. S. & SE.
March	36.23	62	3	59	17	14	2.80	W. SW. E. & SE.
April..	44.24	89	22	67	18	12	3.87	S. SE. and E.
May ..	65.76	90	38	52	20	11	6.63	S. SE. and E.
June ..	69.66	88	48	40	20	10	2.04	SE. E. and SW.
July ..	75.20	86	56	30	22	9	3.92	S. SW. and N.
Aug...	69.80	85	48	37	20	11	3.16	E. SE. and N.
Sept. .	68.08	88	38	50	20	10	3.16	S. SE. and SW.
Oct. ..	45.32	76	22	54	16	15	2.08	W. NW. and SE.
Nov. .	36.90	75	12	63	17	13	2.50	N. NW. & WSW.
Dec. .	30.70	54	6	48	18	13	2.25	W. SW. and NW.

PROGRESSIVE INCREASE OF THE EPISCOPAL CLERGY SINCE 1792.

(From the Records of the General Convention.)

	Clergy in 1792.	Clergy in 1801.	Clergy in 1811.	Clergy in 1820.	Clergy in 1829.	Clergy in 1832.	Clergy in 1835.
Maine	..	..	..	2	4	5	5
N. Hampshire ..	no list	3	5	4	8	7	6
Massachusetts ..	no list	9	8	12	33	36	41
Rhode Island ..	2	5	3	7	7	9	20
Vermont	..	..	2	5	9	15	18
Connecticut	22	29	31	39	57	57	80
New York	19	23	47	75	129	163	192
New Jersey	9	7	8	15	20	19	32
Pennsylvania ...	14	16	21	28	63	60	79
Delaware	3	4	no list	4	7	6	5
Maryland	33	38	35	48	49	54	63
Virginia.	61	58	no list	29	42	56	68
N. Carolina	..	..	..	7	13	16	22
S. Carolina	15	no list	16	27	35	34	44
Georgia........	..	..	1	no list	3	3	6
Ohio	..	..	..	7	14	19	31
Kentucky......	..	..	..	..	3	9	16
Tennessee	..	..	..	..	3	7	13
Alabama	..	..	..	..	1	3	4
Illinois	..	..	..	..	..	..	7
Michigan	..	..	..	..	2	6	8
Missouri and Indiana	..	..	..	..	..	..	2

N. B. Between 1801 and 1832 the dioceses of Connecticut and S. Carolina increased *two-fold;* the dioceses of Massachusetts and Pennsylvania *four-fold;* and the diocese of New York *seven-fold.* —*Churchman's Almanack.*

In 1801 there were 200 Episcopal clergymen in the United States. Since that time they have increased *five-fold,* being now (July 1838) about 1000.

EPISCOPAL INSTITUTIONS IN THE DIOCESE OF NEW YORK.

(From the " Churchman's Almanack.")

Society for the Promotion of Religion and Learning in the State of New York.
Corporation for the Relief of Widows and Children of Clergymen in the State of New York.
Auxiliary New York Bible and Common Prayer Book Society.
Protestant Episcopal Tract Society.
Education and Missionary Society of the diocese of New York.
New York Episcopal City Mission Society.
New York Episcopal Sunday School Society.
Young Men's Education and Missionary Society.
New York Episcopal Public School.
New York Episcopal Press.

STATISTICS OF CINCINNATI.

(Rev. Mr. Brooke, Rector of Christ Church.)

Population of Cincinnati in 1827	16,230
Population of do. in May 1838	39,000
Common School Buildings do. do	9
Teachers in ditto, male and female	52
Scholars in regular attendance	2,800
Literary Colleges	3
Medical Colleges	2
Theological Seminary	1
Students in the College and Private Seminaries	900
Newspapers (7 daily—6 weekly—2 monthly magazines —1 quarterly.)	16

(Of the weekly newspapers, 1 is Baptist, 1 Roman Catholic, and 1 New School Presbyterian.)

Literary and Scientific societies	10
Places of Worship	29
Number of Communicants in Christ Church (Episcopal).	125
Number of Families in do	100
Number of Worshippers	600
Number of Sunday Scholars	150
Contributions per annum to religious objects	$1200
Salary of Rector	$2000
Contributions towards the Bishop's support	$550
Cost of Church	$53,000
Number of Communicants in St. Paul's (Episcopal)	60
Number of Sunday Scholars in do	60
Rector's Salary	$1,500
Cost of Church	$24,000

RECEIPTS OF THE PRINCIPAL BENEVOLENT SOCIETIES,

In 1836 or 1837.—(From the " American Almanack.")

	Dollars.
American Board of Foreign Missions (Congregational)	176,232
——— Tract Society	130,991
——— Bible Society	90,578
——— Home Missionary Society	86,803
——— Sunday School Union	72,524
——— Education Society	65,574
Methodist Missionary Society	61,337
Baptist ditto	60,000
American Colonization Society	51,662
Episcopal Board of Missions (Foreign)	48,977
Ditto ditto ditto (Domestic)	32,740
American Anti-Slavery Society	36,567

EXPENSE OF LIVING, &c., AT MADISON, INDIANA, 1838.

	Dols.		£.	s.	d.	
Board and Lodging, per week,	3½	or	0	15	9	
Beer, per keg	1¼	..	0	5	7½	
Bread (20 small loaves)	1	..	0	4	6	
Butter (4 to 6 lbs.)	1	..	0	4	6	
Candles (Sperm), per 2 lbs.	1	..	0	2	3	per lb.
Ditto (Tallow), per 10 lbs.	1	..	0	0	5½	———
Cheese, per 6 lbs.	1	..	0	0	9	———
Coals, per 8 bushels	1	..	0	4	6	
Coffee, per 6 lbs.	1	..	0	0	9	per lb.
Eggs (4 to 6 dozen)	1	..	0	4	6	
Fish (salt) per 10 lbs.	1	..	0	0	5½	per lb.
Flour, per barrel	7¼	..	0	6	6¼	per bushel.
Fruit, apples, 3 bushels	1	..	0	1	6	———
——— oranges, per dozen	1	..	0	4	6	
Ginger, per 4 lbs.	1	..	0	1	1½	per lb.
Honey, per 3 lbs.	1	..	0	0	6¾	———
Lard, per 12 lbs.	1	..	0	4	6	
Meat, beef, per 12 lbs.	½	..	0	0	4½	per lb.
——— veal, ditto	1	..	0	0	4½	
——— sausages, ditto	1	..	0	0	4½	———
——— pork, per 15 lbs.	1	..	0	0	3¾	———
——— fowls, 2 couple	1	..	0	4	6	
——— ham, per 12 lbs.	1	..	0	0	5	per lb.

	Dols.		£.	s.	d.	
Milk, per 16 quarts	1	..	0	0	3¼	per quart.
Molasses, 1 gallon and 1-3rd ..	1	..	0	3	6	per gallon.
Rice, per 10 lbs..............	1	..	0	0	5½	per lb.
Salt, per 12 lbs..............	0¼	..	0	0	1⅛	———
Sugar, per 10 lbs. (brown)	1	..	0	0	5½	———
——— per 5 lbs. (loaf)........	1	..	0	0	10¾	———
Tea, per lb...................	0¾	..	0	3	6	
Vegetables, potatoes, 2 bushels..	1	..	0	2	3	per bushel.
——— beans, per 6 pecks..	1	..	0	0	9	per peck.
——— cabbages, per dozen	1	..	0	4	6	
——— turnips, per 3 bushel	1	..	0	1	6	per bushel.
Water, per 8 barrels	1	..	0	0	6¾	per barrel.
Clothes, suit of black cloth......	48	..	10	16	0	
——— calico, per yard........	1	..	0	4	6	
——— 1 pair of boots	5	..	1	2	6	
——— silk, per yard	1	..	0	4	6	
——— hat...................	5½	..	1	4	9	
Medicine, calomel, per lb........	1½	..	0	6	9	
——— salts, per lb.	1	..	0	4	6	
Tuition, per quarter	4 to 8	..	0	18	0	to 36s.
Rent, (brick house with 5 rooms)	200	..	45	0	0	
——— brick house, with 8 rooms and garden............	250	..	56	5	0	
Taxes, city-tax, per annum.....	½	..	0	2	6	
Wages, labouring-man, per day	1¼	..	0	5	7½	
——— female-servant, per week	1½	..	0	6	9	
Washing, per dozen	0¾	..	0	3	4½	
Wine, Port, per bottle	1	..	0	4	6	
——— Madeira, per bottle	0½	..	0	2	3	
——— Claret, per bottle	0¾	..	0	3	4½	
Wood (for fuel), per load	1½	..	0	6	9	
——— (for sawing and splitting)	0½	..	0	2	3	
Hire of horse, per day	1	..	0	4	6	
——— horse and gig, per hour..	1	..	0	4	6	
Travelling (steam-boat, 50 miles)	2	..	0	9	0	
——— (stage-coach, ditto)..	4	..	0	18	0	
Writing-paper, per quire	0¼	..	0	1	1½	

THE END.

GILBERT & RIVINGTON, Printers, St. John's Square, London.